DAVID A. HORNER

MIND YOUR FAITH

A STUDENT'S GUIDE TO
THINKING & LIVING WELL

IVP Academic
An imprint of InterVarsity Press
Downers Grove, Illinois

InterVarsity Press
P.O. Box 1400, Downers Grove, IL 60515-1426
World Wide Web: www.ivpress.com
E-mail: email@ivpress.com

InterVarsity Press® is the book-publishing division of InterVarsity Christian Fellowship/USA®, a movement of students and faculty active on campus at hundreds of universities, colleges and schools of nursing in the United States of America, and a member movement of the International Fellowship of Evangelical Students. For information about local and regional activities, write Public Relations Dept., InterVarsity Christian Fellowship/USA, 6400 Schroeder Rd., P.O. Box 7895, Madison, WI 53707-7895, or visit the IVCF website at <www.intervarsity.org>.

All Scripture quotations, unless otherwise indicated, are taken from the Holy Bible, New International Version®, NIV® Copyright © 1973, 1978, 1984, 2011 by Biblica, Inc.™ Used by permission. All rights reserved worldwide.

While all stories in this book are true, some names and identifying information in this book have been changed to protect the privacy of the individuals involved.

Cover design: Cindy Kiple
Interior design: Beth Hagenberg

ISBN 978-0-8308-3932-2

Printed in the United States of America ∞

Library of Congress Cataloging-in-Publication Data

Horner, David A., 1956–
 Mind your faith: a student's guide to thinking and living well /
David A. Horner.
   p. cm.
 Includes bibliographical references and index.
 ISBN 978-0-8308-3932-2 (pbk.: alk. paper)
 1. Thought and thinking—Religious aspects—Christianity. 2.
Apologetics. 3. Universities and colleges—Religion. 4.
Students—Religious life. I. Title.
 BV4598.4.H67 2011
 248.8'34—dc22

                                                                    2011013670

P	20	19	18	17	16	15	14	13	12	11	10	9	8	7	6	5	4	3	2	1
Y	28	27	26	25	24	23	22	21	20	19	18	17	16	15	14	13	12	11

"The opportunities for a reflective Christian student in the university are nearly endless. *Mind Your Faith* is a captivating resource that will help prospective and current students engage more carefully both with their faith and with the world of the university. Horner's analysis and applications are crystal clear and are born out of decades of experience in the academy. Every Christian student and parent ought to reflect carefully on this book."

Gregory E. Ganssle, Rivendell Institute at Yale

"Medieval cartographers, mapping the college years, might well have warned, 'Here be dragons!' David Horner knows the territory—and how to tame the dragons—and has offered us a wonderful guidebook. Based on his extensive experience as a minister to college students and as a college professor, Horner understands the challenges Christian students face as they enter college. But what sets his guidebook apart from many others is his unifying vision of what makes for genuine human flourishing. Mind, faith and character stand or fall together. Any student who follows Horner through these pages will have the tools to flourish in college and emerge with mind, faith and character greatly strengthened. I plan to give this book to several high schoolers I know, and I recommend you do the same."

Garrett J. DeWeese, author of *Philosophy Made Slightly Less Difficult* and *Doing Philosophy as a Christian*

"Secular universities have not only forfeited the mission of building students' wisdom, faith and character, they often work in ways contrary to these goals. David Horner offers sage advice, drawn from personal and professional experience, about how Christian students can recognize and counter these challenges and emerge from the college experience as wise Christ-followers. Parents of university-bound students should buy two copies: one for their student and one for themselves."

Steve Wilkens, professor of philosophy, Azusa Pacific University, and author of *Hidden Worldviews*

"*Mind Your Faith* is a feast of insights about thinking, believing and living well. Page after page one finds warm, personable, intelligent reflections about how to flourish well in the contemporary milieu. Horner provides a unique combination of spiritual formation and Christian thought, and I know of no other book that does this so well. It should be read not only by college students but also by pastors and laypersons who want to flourish with a confident faith for our times."

J. P. Moreland, Distinguished Professor of Philosophy, Biola University, and author of *The God Question*

"How can the development of a faithful mind and a mindful faith lead to a virtuous character? This is not the first question Christian students are likely to ask their university to answer. But it should be. David Horner helps students—young and old—seek an answer that is based on sound reasoning and deep, faithful personal commitment to Christ. May this book live long and prosper, leading believers to thoughtful, faithful and virtuous lives."

James W. Sire, author of *The Universe Next Door*

"Dr. Horner brings a wealth of experience to this wise and winsome operating manual for godly Christian engagement on the college campus. Colleges and universities shape culture more than any other contemporary institution, and souls are saved or lost there on a daily basis. This clear, incisive and enjoyable book will equip students to develop a Christian orientation to this challenging arena that will serve them not only as they pursue their degrees but also for a lifetime of discipleship unto the Lord Jesus Christ."

Douglas Groothuis, professor, Denver Seminary, and author of *Christian Apologetics*

"Many Christians heading off to college are simply unprepared for the intellectual, spiritual and moral challenges that await them. Confronted with new ideas, strong desires and relational pressures, it's not surprising that so many drift away from their childhood faith. But it doesn't have to be this way! In this timely book, David Horner offers students a compelling vision of what it means to follow Jesus Christ with a mature faith during the college years and beyond. High school graduates need to read this book!"

Jonathan Morrow, author of *Welcome to College* and founder of www.thinkchristianly.org

"There are many excellent books on the subject of preparing students for college, but few written with the same passion, clarity and genuine concern for the life of the mind of a college student. David Horner's *Mind Your Faith* helps us understand the delicate relationship between faith and reason: that behavior follows belief and doctrine informs duty. Parents, this is the best high school graduation gift you can give to your student. Student, this is a must-read because there's simply too much at risk. Lose faith, lose your mind, and vice versa. Neither of which is good."

Harry Edwards, founder and director of Apologetics.com, Inc.

"More than just enabling you to sidestep the many pitfalls awaiting young Christians who enter academia, *Mind Your Faith* will equip you to flourish at the university in your mind, faith and character. The clarity with which David Horner envisions a thoughtful Christian presence in the university's marketplace of ideas is what will make this an essential read for my four children before leaving high school."

Brent Cunningham, teaching pastor, Timberline Church, Fort Collins, Colorado

GOD IS NO FONDER of intellectual slackers than of any other slackers. If you are thinking of becoming a Christian, I warn you, you are embarking on something which is going to take the whole of you, brains and all. But, fortunately, it works the other way round. Anyone who is honestly trying to be a Christian will soon find his intelligence being sharpened: one of the reasons why it needs no special education to be a Christian is that Christianity is an education itself.

C. S. Lewis

For Judi
Ad Memoriam

CONTENTS

PREFACE

Mind Your Faith is the result of some fourteen years as a student in undergraduate and graduate university education, and thirty years of nearly continuous university ministry in the United States and Europe—as a campus ministry worker, pastor, and now as a scholar and professor. No, I'm not *that* old. Several of these were going on simultaneously, as I cobbled together graduate school, teaching, ministry and trying to put food on the table.

While I'm glad that I'm no longer doing all of these things, I'm deeply grateful for the rich experiences they afforded, for the questions I've had to face and the things I've come to learn—typically the hard way, by making mistakes (no surprise to those who know me well). Along the way, by the grace of God, I've been able to help others navigate their own university experience. This book reflects much of what I have learned and have sought to pass along to others.

In this journey I have benefited greatly from the freedom and opportunities to pursue such a calling, and also from the insights and models of many friends—colleagues, teachers and students. They have shaped the content of these pages and, more importantly, my own life. Most of what is worth remembering here should have their names attached to it, not mine.

Among my many influences, a few individuals stand out for special mention. My brother, Bob Horner, has devoted his entire adult life to engaging students in secular universities with the person of Jesus Christ in creative, winsome and compelling ways. Growing up in his shadow, long before I was a college student myself, I developed a love of the university and a desire to influence it. Bob has been a constant mentor, encourager and fly-fishing companion through these years. He has shaped my perspective on just about everything.

Jimmy Williams and Jon Buell first exposed me to an intellectually robust vision of the Christian faith within a university context, and gave me the initial tools to pursue this vision myself. Tom Trento and the late Dan Davis were instrumental in helping me connect the intellectual life with practical, street-level skills in thinking and apologetics, and their influence is evident here, as is that of my long-time mentor, Gordon Lewis. J. P. Moreland's example of thinking and living well, and especially his faithful friendship and consistent encouragement, have inspired and shaped much of this book. Rick Howe has been a dear friend and colleague for many years in the quest to cultivate robust Christian intellectual community within the secular university. Because of Rick's visionary, creative and generous leadership I have had many of the opportunities that made this book possible, and while serving with Rick the idea for it was born. Special thanks to my colleague Garry DeWeese, who shared this vision from the beginning. I also thank my other colleagues at Biola University, too many to list, for their sharpening and encouragement, and for making teaching there such a joy. Two deserve special mention, however. Doug Geivett has influenced much of my thinking on truth, belief and knowledge, and Jason Oakes has helped me bring these thoughts together by generously trying out earlier versions on his students and providing me valuable feedback and encouragement.

Many thanks as well to the supporters of the Illuminatio Project for enabling me to set aside the time to write; to Jac, Larry and Paul, my band of brothers, who consistently encouraged and challenged me along the way; to Greg Ganssle, a friend who has walked this path with me for a long time and who gave me extensive and very wise feedback on a previous draft; to Kathy Randol, for writing at just the right time; and to the many students, teaching assistants and various audiences in the United States and Europe on whom I've tried out these ideas over the years, who asked good questions and gave helpful feedback. Special thanks also to Marj Harmon for her amazing facility and generosity in tracking sources, to Richard Park and Kurtis Olson for their help in matters too numerous to recount, and to Joe Verardo for his creative assistance.

It's been a great pleasure to work with Al Hsu, a patient, wise and encouraging editor. Special thanks to him and three other readers who asked hard questions and made excellent suggestions. This book is far better for their thoughtful feedback. Responsibility for inadequacies that remain is my own.

I'm grateful beyond words to Debbie, who is, besides the Lord, my primary encourager and my chief source and model of wisdom. *Te amo ex toto corde meo.* And also to my precious daughters, Stephanee and Jessica, who have thought and lived well as university students and beyond, and who continue to give me hope for the future. I'm very proud to be their dad.

As I wrote this book, my dear sister Judi's courageous struggle with cancer came to an end and she went home to be with her Savior and Friend. Judi was a gracious, effervescent, consistent example of godliness and unselfish care for others, and a constant encouragement and advocate in prayer. I dedicate this to her memory.

1

SANITY IN THE UNIVERSITY

GETTING STARTED

The fear of the LORD is the beginning of wisdom,
and knowledge of the Holy One is understanding.

PROVERBS 9:10

The beginning is the most important part of any work.

PLATO, *Republic*

College can drive you crazy.

I learned this as I stepped on campus as a freshman at a secular state university. Beyond the standard challenges—navigating the trail of alcohol-induced vomit in the dormitory halls, trying to sleep amid the smells of marijuana and the sounds of sexual adventures in neighboring rooms—I had three experiences within my first year that largely motivate this book. First, my former high school locker partner, overwhelmed by the drug scene at our university, took his own life. Second, another friend from high school, an impressionable young Christian, was drawn into an anti-intellectual religious cult active on our campus. She dropped out of school, married someone in the group and disappeared. The next time I saw her, twenty years later, she had just escaped (with her children) from the cult—bitter at religion, wanting nothing to do with God and faced with going back to finish college as a single parent.

And, third, I almost lost my faith.

As a freshman I was far better prepared than most for college life. I was raised in a loving, devout Christian home. Our church was a vibrant community of Christ followers, where I heard the Scriptures taught faithfully and intelligently, and saw them lived out in practice. When I committed my life fully to Jesus in high school, during the 1970s Jesus movement, it was not a superficial or merely emotional matter, or just a phase: I was confident that Jesus was real and the gospel was true, and I knew that I needed to be forgiven and changed. I became heavily involved in church youth group leadership, and I was outspoken about my faith at school.

Because of my older brother's involvement in campus ministry, I had been exposed to college students who were intelligent, vibrant and joyful believers. I arrived at the university already familiar with several of the campus-ministry organizations and their staff. Before my first class started, I was plugged into Christian community and sharing my faith with others on campus.

Despite these resources, during my first semester at the university I experienced a crisis of faith. In the classroom I was confronted with intellectual objections to belief in God I was not prepared to answer. I took these questions seriously and became plagued with doubts. Because of what I had already experienced in my own life and seen in the lives of others, I think I still believed, deep down, that the Christian faith must be true. But I did not know *how* it was true—how it *could* be true.

So I stepped back. Providentially, as I came to see later, I remained in community with Christian students. But I backed off from sharing my faith with others and publicly identifying as a follower of Christ. I sought answers to my questions and grounds for my faith, but didn't find others who could address them adequately. I became discouraged and disheartened.

Later that year a group of Christian intellectuals came to my campus for a week of lectures—similar to what the Veritas Forum now does at secular universities. During the week they spoke in some ninety classrooms, dormitories and Greek houses, providing thoughtful Christian perspectives on various academic disciplines and a broad array of issues and questions.

That week was dramatically life changing for me. In the speakers I saw individuals who loved Jesus and loved people, whose lives were committed to following Jesus and making a difference in the world, and who had fun and loved life. But they also took the life of the mind seriously as an expression of their commitment to Jesus

The Veritas Forum

Founded at Harvard University in 1992, Veritas sponsors public forums at secular universities to "engage students and faculty in discussions about life's hardest questions and the relevance of Jesus Christ to all of life" (www .veritas.org).

and his call on their lives. They knew what they believed and why they believed it. They had thought through hard questions and objections to the faith, and were committed to a lifelong pursuit of understanding all of life and intellectual endeavor from a Christian perspective.

Obviously, this could not have come at a better time for me. Beyond merely getting many of my questions answered, a great thing in itself, I caught a vision of what my life could become. It was my first glimpse of what is possible for Christian thinking and life within a university context. Even at that point I knew that *this is the way it's supposed to be*— and it's what I want to devote my life to.

At the end of the week the speakers held an apologetics conference.

Apologetics—Based on a Greek word found in 1 Peter 3:15, *apologia*, which means "rational defense." Christian apologetics is the art and science of explaining and defending the truth claims of the Christian worldview (see chap. 11).

There I was introduced to some tools—books, concepts, perspectives and skills—that helped me begin to understand and engage the ideas and perspectives that make up the university experience. Some of those tools, subsequently hammered out on the anvil of years of experience and refined and combined with other insights,

have made their way onto these pages. My hope is that *Mind Your Faith* plays a similar role in your story.

GOING TO COLLEGE

Although my siblings and I all went to college, as have our children, neither of our parents completed a university education. My mother did not attend college (it wasn't something many women did in those days), and my father had to drop out during the Great Depression in order to work in the family business. Historically the pattern of our family is pretty typical of Americans.

Going to college is far more common than it used to be. With the rise of wealth and opportunity in recent decades, some Americans view a university education as a right they are entitled to—or an experience they are destined to endure, like it or not. Still, going to college remains out of reach for many Americans, especially in stressful economic times. And from a global perspective it's clearly the opportunity of a blessed few. A university education is a significant privilege.

In 2010, 6.7 percent of the world's population held college degrees—up from 5.9 percent in 2000. As of 2007, 40.4 percent of American adults aged 25 to 34 held an associate degree or higher, putting the United States in eleventh place, globally, in post-secondary education. (Canada is first, at 55.8 percent.)[1]

It also represents an important accomplishment. Your college degree shows employers and others that you have a measure of initiative, discipline and intelligence that bodes well for your future progress and productivity. It opens doors for vocational paths, increases your earning potential and boosts your confidence and self-esteem.

Going to college also shapes who you are and how you view the world. It opens up a new world of learning and life in ways that are unique and transformational. College is a time for broadening your horizons, choosing your career path, (often) finding a spouse—and for deciding what you, and not just your parents, believe about the most important issues of life. There may well be no period in your life that is more influential and life defining. The stakes are high. So it makes sense to approach the time you spend in college as intelligently as possible.

COLLEGE PREPARATION

College is not for everyone. But I assume you're reading this book because it is, or may be, for you. You and your parents have probably been thinking about your college education, about where to go and how to get in, for years. If you're not yet a university student, chances are you're actively preparing to be one.

The college preparation industry is big business these days, far more than in the past. Yet in the most important areas of the university experience, few students are adequately prepared. As a result, their college experience is often difficult at best, and sometimes it's disastrous. This may or may not be reflected in academic struggles, because the issues go far deeper. Even those students who excel in their academic performance frequently find college a disaster in terms of *life*—spiritually, morally and intellectually.

The spiritual struggles that university students encounter are well documented. Despite the presence of vital campus ministries at secular universities, Christian students often struggle with their faith in college. Many end up abandoning it altogether. Some adopt atheism or agnosticism, while others embrace alternative religions or join one of the cult groups that proliferate on campus.

Secular universities can be moral minefields. Away from the constraints of their parents for the first extended period in their lives, students are confronted with what is often a no-holds-barred party scene, with drugs, binge drinking and casual sex as the norm. In the classroom as well as the university ethos more generally, traditional moral beliefs, values and practices are frequently called into question, critiqued, even ridiculed.[3] At the same time, academic cheating, plagiarism and other forms of fraud are widely practiced and often seen as

> "More than 52 percent of incoming freshmen who identify themselves as born-again upon entering a public university will either no longer identify themselves as born-again four years later or, even if they do still claim that identification, will not have attended any religious service in over a year."
>
> STEVE HENDERSON[2]

necessary to academic success. The moral fallout from many students'
university years—sexually, psychologically, physically, relationally—
can be devastating.

These spiritual and moral struggles are related, of course. Moral "experimentation" in college is often prompted by spiritual doubts. And
acting against your conscience and moral principles can't help but erode
your spiritual convictions. In the face of moral temptation and pressure,
battered and weakened beliefs about what is morally and spiritually real
are not much protection.

A further connection, between these spiritual and moral struggles
and the intellectual dimension of a student's life, extends far beyond
academic matters. Our mind, our faith and our character are essentially
bound together. Because of the role thinking plays in every area of life,
the mind is particularly crucial. Ideas have consequences: what we believe will determine how we behave, and ultimately who we become.[4] It
is no surprise that the spiritual struggles and moral confusion students
encounter in college are often fueled by the intellectual challenges to faith and morality they encounter.

Worldview—A worldview is the set of beliefs, attitudes and values that shapes the way we see the world and live our life (see chap. 7).

Your spiritual and moral well-being in the university and be-
yond, then, depends crucially upon *how you think*—especially how you think about what is real, about
what is important and valuable, about how to live and why. That is:
how you think about the most important things. Your beliefs about
these things make up your worldview, your fundamental orientation
toward the world. And they are the very beliefs that are most at stake
in your university experience.

A MARKETPLACE OF IDEAS

College, if nothing else, is about ideas. Ideally, a university is a "marketplace of ideas": an arena in which different perspectives in areas such
as science, philosophy, history, art and politics are honestly and freely
considered and rationally evaluated. The beauty and power of a univer-

sity education largely consist in the opportunities you have to be exposed to the greatest and most influential ideas, and to develop the skills and discernment needed to reflect well upon them and trace their implications for all of life. In reality, of course, universities seldom represent a completely *free* market, where all perspectives are allowed to stand or fall on their own merits. In particular, in many university contexts more traditional religious and moral views are ignored or subjected to a special level of criticism.[5]

This has led some to charge secular universities with engaging in a "secular humanist" conspiracy of discrimination against religious believers. My own experience in secular academia suggests that while this is true in some cases, the bigger picture is not so tidy. Most nonreligious faculty members in secular universities are fair-minded people who seek to represent diverse perspectives in a balanced way. When their class discussions lack a fair representation of an intelligent Christian perspective, the important question is why this is the case.

Typically secular academics ignore or dismiss Christian ideas because they are unaware of them. They've simply never been exposed to a thoughtful Christian perspective on these matters—largely because over the past century so many Christians, particularly American evangelicals, abandoned the university.[6] This exodus was often prompted by good motives, out of a desire to preserve and protect the church from liberal theology or bad ideas in general. But the tragic result is that, to a great extent, Christians have simply not been *in* the university's marketplace of ideas to represent Jesus and his view of the world in a credible way. We can hardly blame secular folks for ignoring perspectives we were not there to provide them.

Our absence from the university disengages a thoughtful Christian presence from the give-and-take of the university's marketplace of ideas, limiting the perspectives to which students and faculty are exposed and the possible impact that biblical truth can have on them. It also deprives the church of the regular challenges and intellectual sharpening that come from engaging the university. As a consequence believers have lost intellectual rigor and become increasingly comfortable with faulty, anti-intellectual views and values related to mind, faith and character. These perspectives further perpetuate the problem because they are inadequate to prepare the next generation of students and scholars to encounter the university effectively. Not only is this tragic, but it's alien to the Christian worldview itself.

Thankfully, things are beginning to change. There is a growing movement of Jesus' followers who are committed to thinking well, to engaging the marketplace of ideas intelligently and to contributing to the life of the university as representatives of the kingdom of God. My hope is that this book, by providing some very specific training in this area, will add fuel to that fire.

THINKING WELL

With or without an intelligent Christian presence, the university remains a marketplace of ideas. Whether or not you experience a truly free and open exchange of ideas in your college classroom, you will certainly experience *ideas*—indeed, a veritable cascade of conflicting, challenging, important, trivial, compelling, captivating and sometimes absurd ideas. Ideas are not created equal; not all have earth-shattering consequences. But all have consequences of some sort. And some are far-reaching and deeply significant for all life and thought—for you, your family, your community, the church and the world. Encountering and engaging these ideas in all of their complexity is good; it's what a university experience is all about. But to navigate these waters sanely, both in the university and beyond, you need to think well.

Few students are adequately prepared to do so. As a university professor I can attest that shrinking numbers of students can think and write adequately at the levels required for basic academic work in the university. Fewer still are prepared to think well at a yet more comprehensive level, both in their academic disciplines and beyond. To flourish intellectually in the fullest sense, we need to be able to understand and engage ideas within their thought contexts, analyze and evaluate them in insightful ways, and integrate them with the rest of life—to connect them to the bigger worldview commitments that inform how we live, how we spend our time, whom we marry, how we vote and how we worship.

None of this happens automatically. It takes hard work. And it also requires some training. However well you may be prepared in other areas, unless you are prepared and equipped intellectually, spiritually and morally, college can truly drive you crazy.

THE FOCUS

Excellent resources are available to guide your journey into higher education, providing advice from how to pay for college and choose your major to basic training in dating, sharing your faith and leading Bible studies. Many of these resources are listed in the appendix.[7] *Mind Your Faith* has a different focus.

A seasoned teacher and mentor of college students, Steven Garber sought to identify the crucial factors that distinguished those individuals who began well as Christians in college but in subsequent years and decades came to "disconnect what they said they believed from how they lived" from others who followed Jesus with integrity and coherence throughout their lives.[9] Garber conducted a series of interviews with those in the latter category (call them "sustainers") and concluded that they share three essential characteristics. First, beginning in college, sustainers developed a worldview that was sufficient to meet the many "questions and crises" of the subsequent years, including engaging competing worldviews. Second, each sustainer found a mentor who practiced and modeled this way of seeing the world, and who apprenticed them in living it as well. And third, sustainers chose to live in community with peers who shared their vision of life, meeting regularly to encourage and hold each other accountable to keep living consistently with it.[10]

Garber's research confirms what I have seen in my own life and in

> "What is it that happens when a person, moving from student years into adulthood, continues to construct a coherent life? How does a worldview become a way of life? How do students learn to connect presuppositions with practice—belief *about* the world with life *in* the world—in the most personal areas and the most public arenas?"
> STEVEN GARBER[8]

the experience of students I've known. Sustainers keep their sanity—
their mind, faith and character—in college and for the long haul. This
is the vision I invite you to embrace for yourself.

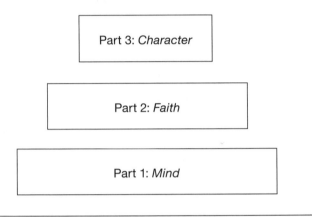

Figure 1.1. The mind-faith-character order of *Mind Your Faith*

My approach here is unique in its focus on mind, faith and character, dealing with each in detail and bringing them together into an
integrated vision of flourishing as a college student and beyond. The
mind-faith-character order is intentional and cumulative: it builds a
structure in which the earlier parts establish the foundations for what
follows (see fig. 1.1). Because of the importance of thinking well, the
longest section is part one, focused on mind. Parts two and three, on
faith and character, are progressively shorter, not because they are less
important, but because each chapter builds on the ones that precede
it. Much is left to say about each subject, of course. My objective is
simply to help you get started, by focusing on how to think about
these things.

Because philosophy is the academic discipline that focuses on thinking, I draw upon it quite a bit throughout, especially in part one. But
this is not a philosophy text. Nor is it a book of theology or a handbook
of apologetics, although we engage with theological and apologetic
topics, especially in part two. It's not an ethics text or a manual of
spiritual formation either, although we touch on those subjects as well,

particularly in part three. We are interested in each of these things because they are crucial to flourishing as a follower of Jesus in the university. Our approach is to pull them together into a coherent vision.

THE TARGET

Mind Your Faith is written primarily for those who are (1) university students or college-bound high school students, (2) followers of Jesus who aspire to grow and flourish as his followers while in college, and (3) attend a secular university. Those who fit this profile are at the center of my target. But I hope that at least two other kinds of readers will also find this book helpful.

First, I welcome readers who do not consider themselves followers of Jesus at this point, yet desire further insight into a Christian perspective of intellectual, spiritual and moral life. If you are a seeker (someone who is checking out what it means to follow Jesus) or a doubter (one who used to follow Jesus but has now rejected that path or is contemplating doing so—particularly because of objections and challenges that are typical of the university experience), I especially invite you to read further. I can relate. Over the years I have discovered that many struggles people (myself included) have with the Christian faith are rooted in distortions and misunderstandings of what a Christian understanding of thinking, believing and living actually is—and in related misconceptions about science, reason, truth, belief, faith and doubt. What we often need most are not apologetic arguments or evidences for the truth of the Christian faith, but a clear, accurate picture of *how to think* about these things.

Second, Christian students who attend a Christian university should also find much here to help them negotiate their college experience. My years in secular and Christian university contexts have convinced me that both can drive you crazy, and in some of the same ways. If you're a student at a Christian institution you (typically) do not face overt hostility for your basic Christian beliefs. But if your university is worth its salt, you also do not study within an entirely insulated bubble that seals out contrary views or challenges. Although an excellent Christian university uniquely provides its students with substantial biblical and theological training, it is still a university, a marketplace of ideas, and as such it will engage the most important and influential ideas and literature. If you attend such a school, simply by virtue of being a college student and engaging honestly with various academic subjects and views—not to mention listening to music, watching TV and films, surfing the Net, working part time and hopefully being involved in some kind of ministry—you face most of the same questions, struggles and needs as your counterparts at secular schools. What you need are the same sorts of perspectives and skills that they need.[11]

> Should you attend a Christian or a secular university? It depends on a number of factors, including what you seek from your college experience and what opportunities are available to you. See Jonathan Morrow's *Welcome to College: A Christ-Follower's Guide to the Journey*, particularly appendix B.

THE VISION—FLOURISHING

The aim of *Mind Your Faith* is to help you keep your sanity: to go to college without losing your mind, your faith or your character. But this is much more than a "survivor's guide" to the university. The English word *sanity* derives from the Latin *sanitas*, which means "health," "wholeness," "soundness" or "well-being." It's a condition of functioning properly and fully, where things are the way they are supposed to be, doing what they were made to do. Sanity is *flourishing*, not merely surviving. The vision that animates this book is positive rather than negative. The goal is not merely to endure college but to thrive within it: to enjoy the many gifts and opportunities that college brings, and to grow and develop intellectually, spiritually and morally as you do so —to think and live well.

Unfortunately, Christianity has come to be thought of, by many believers as well as nonbelievers, in largely negative terms: don't do this, stop doing that. The aim is to avoid what is evil rather than to pursue what is good. This especially characterizes how Christians often think about university education, particularly in a secular setting. For many students (and their parents) the goal of college education is merely to "make it through" the experience without suffering too much damage. Their primary motivation is fear. As a result they never really enjoy their time in college. They live on the periphery, attending classes, taking notes, writing papers and taking exams, without truly engaging the subject matter; not really learning, unless it is in a purely technical field, where much of the content does not explicitly threaten their faith. Or if they do learn—if they pay attention and imbibe the broader academic culture—they often end up experiencing a crisis of faith between (what appear to be) new, liberating, exciting mind- and life-expanding ideas on the one hand, and the fearful, stifling, suspicion they associate with Christianity on the other. Understandably, many opt for the former. I don't blame them.

But this is a false choice. The Christian church is actually very much at home in the world of ideas. Many of the leading philosophers, scientists and artists of the Western intellectual tradition—Augustine, Aquinas, Johannes Kepler and Jonathan Edwards, to name a few—have been devout followers of Jesus. (Christianity is often designated "Western" not because it is a Western religion—its origins are in the Near East—but because Christian thought and practice has so distinctively and decisively shaped the thought and institutions of Europe and North America.) Indeed, it is difficult to overestimate the intellectual and educational influence of Christianity on the world. More than any other single institution in history, the Christian church has promoted universal literacy and education, started schools, and put languages into writing.

In fact, the university as we know it is largely an invention of the medieval Christian church.[12] My graduate studies were at the University of Oxford, which is one of the first universities, established around A.D. 1200. Like other medieval universities, Oxford was founded with the explicit aim of forming a community of Christian scholars to pursue knowledge in all areas of thought, informed by the light of Christian understanding. Oxford's vision is captured in its Latin motto, *Dominus Illuminatio Mea*: "The Lord is my light," the first words of Psalm 27:1.

Similar sentiments are reflected in the founding visions of other universities in Europe and North America. Prior to the nineteenth century, all but two colleges founded in the United States, including schools such as Harvard, Yale, Princeton, Columbia and Dartmouth, were established by faithful Christians for the purpose of seeking knowledge in light of God's revelation in Word (Scripture, theology) and world (science, arts), in order to train ministers and scholars within a deeply Christian perspective.[13] The mottos and mission statements of many of these colleges are as explicitly Christian as Oxford's.

Let every Student be plainly instructed, and earnestly pressed to consider well, the maine end of his life and studies is, to know God and Jesus Christ which is eternal life (John 17:3) and therefore to lay Christ in the bottome, as the only foundation of all sound knowledge and Learning. And seeing the Lord only giveth wisedome, Let every one seriously set himself by prayer in secret to seeke it of him (Prov. 2:3).

RULE OF HARVARD COLLEGE (1646)

In reality, the work of the university—serious thinking, rigorous discovery, passionate creativity, courageous exploration—is not only compatible with an historic Christian perspective, it is a noble pursuit that finds much of its historic origin and intellectual basis in that perspective. For a follower of Jesus the pursuit of a university education should be seen as a positive, exciting endeavor, not something simply to be endured or escaped. It is to be loved rather than feared.

Yes, the university can be a challenging place to be a follower of Jesus, where it is possible to lose your mind, your faith and your character. It is understandable that some would seek to be "punch the clock" students who aim merely to emerge from their university experience wholly unchanged. But going to college is far too valuable, not to mention expensive, for that. A university education is a uniquely valuable experience, not just for career preparation but even more for the opportunities to grow—in exactly those areas that make it such a challenge: learning to think well about conflicting ideas, dealing with doubt and questions, owning your own faith, and learning to live with integrity as an adult.

THE MODEL—DANIEL

In the Old Testament book of Daniel we can find a model for doing college well, one we will return to throughout these pages, especially in parts two and three. Its story begins with Daniel as a college-age man, who, with several friends, exhibits biblical thinking, faith and character within a religiously alien, sometimes hostile intellectual and cultural environment.

In 605 B.C. the nation of Babylon began its conquest of Judah, and ultimately destroyed Jerusalem. Daniel and some other Jewish young men, followers of the God of Israel, were taken from Jerusalem, their own, traditional religious context, and placed in the "university" of Babylon for the purpose of being educated and trained for leadership in that culture.

> In the third year of the reign of Jehoiakim king of Judah, Nebuchadnez-zar king of Babylon came to Jerusalem and besieged it. . . . [And he] ordered Ashpenaz, chief of his court officials, to bring into the king's service some of the Israelites from the royal family and the nobility— young men without any physical defect, handsome, showing aptitude for every kind of learning, well informed, quick to understand, and qualified to serve in the king's palace. He was to teach them the lan-guage and literature of the Babylonians. (Dan 1:1, 3-4)

These men represented the Israelite "honors" or "gifted and talented" class. They were selected for their potential to rise to high levels of cultural leadership. And rise they did, especially Daniel, who became a high political and administrative leader over the nation of Babylon (Dan 2:48). How did that occur?

Daniel succeeded in the "University of Babylon" and in his subse-quent public service not by merely doing what was expected of him but by excelling—by out-thinking and out-living his peers. Wisely and faithfully, in the company of like-minded friends, Daniel flourished within Babylon's intellectual and cultural arena as an insider who brought biblical truth and values to bear on it in credible ways. He earned, fairly and honestly, the true respect of those around him.

"Daniels" within the university context today have the same effect. They not only keep their sanity as followers of Jesus within that context, but they are a blessing to those around them and to the university itself. Daniels do more than anything else to reverse the lost awareness of credible Christianity in the university.

As an undergraduate student at a secular state university, my friend Michael caught a vision for the Daniel model of following Jesus in that environment. He made it his aim as a philosophy major to become the best student in the department, one who would represent Jesus with academic excellence and a gracious and winsome spirit. He also worked to multiply his impact over time by mentoring younger Christian philosophy majors who could take his place after he graduated. As a result of Michael's influence the philosophy department came to trust and respect the Christian ministries on campus and even cosponsored public events such as the Veritas Forum. Other students followed Michael's example and carried on the work after he left. Michael eventually became one of my graduate students, as did one of the students he had mentored, and I can tell you that these are two of the most gifted philosophers, as well as godly, wise men, that I have had the privilege to teach. And their influence at that university continues. As a result of Michael's work, a Christian study center has been established that is the hub of an ongoing Christian intellectual community within the broader university, providing resources to help students and faculty engage thoughtfully with a Christian worldview.

WORSHIP AND WISDOM

Central to the vision of flourishing as a college student and to the Daniel model that exemplifies it are two themes that thread their way throughout these pages: worship and wisdom. For followers of Jesus, worship is more than a style of music or a kind of activity. It's the ultimate reason we do all that we do. Drawing upon Old Testament worship imagery, Paul writes, "Therefore I urge you, brothers and sisters, in view of God's mercies, to offer your bodies as a sacrifice—alive, holy and pleasing to God—which is your reasonable expression of worship" (Rom 12:1, my translation). In gratitude for all that God has done for us, Paul reasons, we offer *ourselves* as a worship sacrifice—to worship God in how we live our life, in everything we do. From a biblical perspective, worship is everything and everything is worship. Worship is everything: it's what life is about. We were created to worship. If not God, we will worship something or someone else, a false god. It is only "in view of God's mercies" that we are liberated from our idolatry to worship the *true* God, in whom is found true flourishing. And everything is worship: it involves all of life. Every area of life is an arena in which we can and should seek to bring God honor, to live in a way that says thank you.

This means, ironically, that we can truly flourish in college only if flourishing in college is *not* our ultimate aim in life. That's reserved for loving and honoring our Creator and Redeemer. As in all of life, we need to keep first things first. The beginning is all-important.

Such an orientation is obvious in the model of Daniel and his friends. So also is the second theme: wisdom. If worship reflects the "why" of all of life, including going to college, wisdom represents the "how"— *especially* for going to college. Wisdom, from a biblical understanding, is not merely the accumulation of information, although that is (often) important. A wise person understands the meaning and significance of that information, sees how it fits together and applies to the whole of life, and has the cultivated character and developed skills to live it out consistently. Wisdom integrates mind, faith and character; a life of wisdom is a sane, flourishing life in each of these respects.

Proverbs 9:10 connects the "why" and the "how" of life explicitly. Like this chapter, it is about beginnings: "The fear of the LORD is the beginning of wisdom, / and knowledge of the Holy One is understanding." In biblical language, fearing the Lord represents worship. It's an orientation to life in which we understand that he is God and we are not, and living accordingly. Fearing God is seeing everything in relation to him.

So wisdom begins with getting our perspective straight—how we think—and living it out faithfully and skillfully in all of life. I can't think of a better summary of what it means to "mind your faith."

Part One: *Mind*

*To these four young men God gave knowledge and understanding
of all kinds of literature and learning. And Daniel could understand
visions and dreams of all kinds.*

*At the end of the time set by the king to bring them into his
service, the chief official presented them to Nebuchadnezzar.
The king talked with them, and he found none equal to Daniel,
Hananiah [Shadrach], Mishael [Meshach] and Azariah [Abednego];
so they entered the king's service. In every matter of wisdom
and understanding about which the king questioned them, he
found them ten times better than all the magicians and enchanters
in his whole kingdom.*

DANIEL 1:17-20

*Daniel . . . was found to have a keen mind and knowledge
and understanding.*

DANIEL 5:12

Part one is about the life of the mind. It's important that we begin here because it is foundational to everything that follows. Our thinking undergirds everything else that we do, including our believing and acting. Yet the mind is usually the least understood and developed aspect of all, which has devastating consequences for our faith and character. We "lose our mind," and the rest follows.

Because it is focused on the mind, part one is the most philosophical and technically difficult section of the book. This is especially true of chapters three and four, where I examine the important concepts of truth, belief and knowledge. In chapters five through seven we explore essential thinking skills: thinking contextually, logically and world-viewishly.

LOVING GOD WITH YOUR MIND

Brothers and sisters, stop thinking like children.
In regard to evil be infants, but in your thinking be adults.

1 CORINTHIANS 14:20

"Do you remember the last book you read?"
"Do magazines count?"

JAY LENO'S on-the-street interview "Jaywalking"

In southern Poland lies a small farming village called Oswiȩcim. Like countless other small towns dotting the globe, it would hardly register a blip on the radar screen of important places—except that during World War II Nazi forces built a concentration camp there, to which they gave the German name: *Auschwitz*. In Auschwitz the Nazis murdered perhaps as many as four million innocent people.

Back in the late 1970s and early 1980s I led university mission projects in Poland and had the opportunity to visit Auschwitz several times. These were, to put it mildly, deeply disturbing experiences. Various rooms in the prison compound are now open to view, with one wall in each room replaced by glass in order to display different aspects of the horrors experienced by the innocent victims. One room is filled with human hair, shaved from the prisoners' heads (to be sent to Germany as material to make blankets and clothing). Other rooms contain further items taken from the victims, such as combs and eyeglasses. One is filled with human teeth, pulled from the victims' mouths to extract the gold fillings in order to help fund the Nazi war effort. And then there are the shower rooms, where prisoners were stripped and promised that they would finally be able to clean themselves. But instead of water, the rooms were flooded with poisonous gas, and the prisoners were asphyxiated. Finally, are the rooms containing the notorious ovens specially designed for the mass destruction and removal of the remains of the dead bodies.

The room that most moved me is the room full of *suitcases* of varying sizes piled from floor to ceiling. They were carried to Auschwitz by individuals—mothers and fathers, grandparents and children, aunts and uncles, neighbors, lovers, friends—and they contained all of the earthly goods these poor people still possessed. When prisoners entered Auschwitz, they handed their suitcase to a soldier who painted their name (and birth date and prisoner number) on it and assured them that it would be returned when their time in the camp had been completed. So each of the hundreds of suitcases in that room bears the name of an individual human being, a life, someone with a story. The victims of Auschwitz were not merely an abstract mass of humanity; they were persons, individuals—created by God.

The second time I visited Auschwitz, this time with the woman I was dating (now my wife), something occurred to make the impact for me deeper still. As we stood in silence, looking into the suitcase room, Debbie nudged me and pointed to something I had not seen: a particular suitcase sitting in the center of the pile of cases bearing the name Eva Horner. Auschwitz immediately became infinitely more personal to me.

I don't yet know whether I'm directly related to Eva. At this point I know little about her. Besides her name, and how she likely died, I am confident of only one thing: Eva Horner was the victim of an *idea*.

Some regard horrors like those of the Nazi death camps and the Holocaust as mysteries. How could the most highly educated and culturally advanced nation on earth, as Germany was at that time, be capable of committing such incredible atrocities? It is inexplicable: an absurdity, a mystery. It is more accurate, however, to understand Auschwitz as a monument to an idea: *lebensunwertes Leben*, "life unworthy of life," the notion that some lives are unworthy to be lived, and so should be ended.[1] The idea did not originate in Auschwitz.[2] Decades earlier, in the 1920s and 1930s, it was an intellectually fashionable perspective that captured the minds of leading German intellectuals—scholars, judges, legislators and medical doctors. Nor did its application to the killing of innocents begin with Jews in Auschwitz. It was originally practiced in German society with the killing of ethnic Germans, particularly children with disabilities.[3] Hundreds of thousands of Germans were taken from hospitals, nursing homes and psychiatric institutions and put to death because others determined they were not worthy of life—including deaf-mutes and those who had lost limbs in the previous war.[4]

To understand the nature of the Holocaust we must see that it did not begin at Auschwitz or other death camps. The Holocaust began in books and classrooms and courtrooms and cafés—the marketplaces of ideas. Its origin lay not in the activities of Nazi thugs but of bookish intellectuals and their students. Auschwitz is a monument to an idea. And Eva Horner is one of over six million victims of that idea.

Ideas have consequences: what we believe will determine how we behave, and ultimately who we become. This is true for individuals, for families, for institutions, for nations and for cultures. We see these consequences in the grand, sweeping stories of the movements of political forces and nations. But also, and most importantly, we see them played out in the lives of individual women, men, boys and girls. Like Eva Horner. Like you and me and those we love.

If we care about our families and loved ones—indeed, if we care about ourselves—we had better care deeply about ideas. If we want to follow Jesus as colaborers in his kingdom project in the world, loving people and seeking to be agents of his goodness in their lives, we had better care deeply about ideas. And if you hope to stay sane in college, you need to care deeply about ideas, for in the university the debate about the most important ideas takes center stage. Followers of Jesus need to be participants in that debate, minding our faith.

LOSING OUR MIND

Among American Christians there is great suspicion about thinking and the life of the mind. This is not limited to Christians, of course; it's reflected in American culture more generally. In both cases it's lethal. Head wounds are deadly: they cause brain damage, paralysis and ultimately death.

> "We live in what may be the most anti-intellectual period in the history of Western civilization."
>
> R. C. SPROUL[5]

Nothing is gained and everything is lost by trying to avoid thinking. It is, in any case, an impossible goal, because we *always* think—the question is whether we think well or badly. And if we think badly, the consequences we reap will be bad ones. Ironically, the attempt to avoid thinking is itself motivated by thinking, by accepting a certain idea: that thinking is bad and should be avoided.

Over the past one hundred years or so, strongly anti-intellectual sentiments have become unquestioned values in many churches. Here are a few:

- There is a divide between head and heart, and the latter is the more important.

- The biblical ideal is to have "simple, childlike faith," rather than faith that is complicated by scholarly or rigorous thinking.

- Science and philosophy are particularly suspicious and questionable endeavors: science, because of the influence of evolutionary theory, philosophy because it deals with the big questions of life while seriously engaging answers that are opposed to Scripture.

- *All* arenas of thought and lines of reasoning that are not explicitly or directly drawn from Scripture are suspicious, and if possible, best avoided.

Such sentiments render the entire university enterprise questionable, and they contribute to the insanity of those who find themselves there. But however well intentioned, they fall seriously short of a fully biblical understanding of truth and the role of the mind in the Christian life. They are *mis*conceptions—bad ideas that have had some very bad consequences for both the university and the church.

Those who embrace such assumptions naturally become unengaged intellectually—not intellectually curious but overly accepting of simplistic and superficial analyses of complex issues, even in the areas of theology and biblical interpretation. They are ambivalent at best about matters of serious thought, particularly regarding science, philosophy and the life of the university. If they *are* involved in these arenas, they tend to handle them by splitting their intellectual lives into two spheres: *faith*, on the one hand, where they place their relationship to God, fellowship with believers and reading the Bible, and *reason* (the world of ideas, science, politics, and education) on the other—with little or no relation between them.

This arrangement works as long as everything stays rigorously segregated. But reality does not ultimately cooperate. These elements of life and thought inevitably bleed into each other. A strict separation between them is not only unbiblical, it is impossible to live out in any coherent way. Not only has two-spheres thinking contributed to Christians abandoning the university, it produces deeply incoherent lives, as believers attempt to lead twin, schizophrenic existences. We lose our sanity, because we have lost our mind.

The biblical picture is far different, as we see in the example of Jesus.

THE MOST IMPORTANT THING IN LIFE

Jesus was not a scholar in the modern, professional sense of the term. Yet besides being a skilled carpenter, he was a learned rabbi and teacher. His arguments were logically sound, he winsomely out-thought those who opposed him, and he graciously led his followers into penetrating truth about all of life. Mark records that after Jesus engaged a series of hard questions and challenges by both of the major scholarly religious factions, the Pharisees and the Sadducees, a specialist in biblical law steps up to test him with a question: "Of all the commandments, which is the most important?" (Mk 12:28). The Greek term translated "most important" here means literally "first" or "primary" (*prōtos*). In Matthew's account of a similar conversation (Mt 22:36), Jesus is asked which commandment is the "greatest" (*megas*). The idea is the same:

"Jesus reasoned with his intellectual opponents. He did not simply declare propositions, threaten punishments to those who disagreed, or attack his adversaries as unspiritual. He highly valued argument and evidence."
DOUGLAS GROOTHUIS[6]

Which is the first, primary, most important—greatest—of all the commandments in the Bible?

There are many commandments in the law writings of the Old Testament. The rabbinical tradition identified 613: the Ten Commandments were most basic, plus 603 other commandments that flow from them.[7] Even for specialists, keeping track of all the regulations would be extremely difficult, not to mention impractical. Moreover, the commandments are not equally stringent. Some are more fundamental than others. Because of this, legal scholars organized the different commandments in terms of stringency and importance. Some commands were seen as greater or weightier, others as lesser or lighter. In light of this background, we can see that Jesus is being asked a technical, legal question: Which commandment, of all of them, is most weighty, stringent and fundamental? That is, which is the most important—the one we should strive our utmost to fulfill, if we can do nothing else?

This is not just a technical question for specialists, of course.

"Hear, O Israel: The LORD our God, the LORD is one. Love the LORD your God with all your heart and with all your soul and with all your strength."
THE *SHEMA* (DEUT 6:4-5)

It's the central question of life, because it's about what is most important. What should shape my life above all else? *What is the most important thing for me to do?*

Jesus' famous answer appeals to the basic Jewish creed, recited by observant Jews twice a day: the *Shema* (Hebrew "hear"): "The most important [commandment]," answered Jesus, "is this: 'Hear, O Israel, the Lord our God, the Lord is one. Love the Lord your God with all your heart and with all your soul and with all your mind and with all your strength.'"

Jesus follows this command with a close second, also drawn from the law (Lev 19:18): "The second is this: 'Love your neighbor as yourself.' There is no commandment greater than these" (Mk 12:31).

It couldn't be clearer: love God and love others. These two priorities should shape everything about our lives. Our focus is on the first: to love God. Jesus doesn't tell us here exactly *how* to love God, although it's unpacked throughout the rest of the Bible (e.g., Jn 14:21; 1 Jn 4:20-21). But what he does say and what underlies these statements in their original Old Testament context help us see how the life of the mind fits into following Jesus. Note three aspects of Jesus' answer.

First, as is evident in the original context of the *Shema* in Deuteronomy 6, when the Scriptures speak of loving God, they refer most essentially to worship: our response to God (who he is

> "This simple phrase embraces the human whole: the corporeal heart, the mind as the higher intellectual and mental nature, and the soul as their mediator."
> GREGORY OF NYSSA
> (c. A.D. 335-c. 394)[8]

and what he has done) by honoring him, praising him, and serving him. To worship God is to love him above all else, to see him as our greatest good and highest value, as the chief object of our affection—and, thus, as the highest priority of our lives. In biblical terms, what we love most is what we worship.

Second, according to Jesus and the *Shema*, loving God involves all of life: all of our heart, all of our soul, all of our mind, all of our strength—everything. Because all that we are and have and do comes from God and ultimately belongs to God, it is only right for us to take what we have been given and in gratitude offer it back to our Creator and Savior in worship. Worship is everything, the most important thing in life. And everything is worship: every area of life is an arena in which we can and ought to love God and seek to bring honor to him.

Finally, notice that loving God, according to Jesus, specifically includes our mind. Loving God with our mind is not all there is to loving God, but it is a part. And it is a particularly important part, especially for those who seek to love him in college.

HEAD VERSUS HEART

Most of us have little difficulty understanding the first item in Jesus' list: loving God with our heart. But loving God with our mind is another matter. These days, not only do many believers emphasize the former over the latter, they tend to pit the two against each other. If there is a conflict, there is no question as to which takes priority: what's *really* important is the heart, not the head. There may be some value in studying theology, possibly even apologetics, according to many Christians, but even these are inferior to Christian activities related to the heart. It's better to have a "warm heart for God" than a "cold head for doctrine," we might say. But such sentiments are never found in Scripture. This draws a division between things that God never separates.

Like most confusions, it is based on a true insight: there is much more to responding to God and living the Christian life than just thinking and knowledge. A person may give intellectual assent to the gospel, yet never commit him- or herself to Jesus. It is possible to spend a great deal of time studying or even teaching the Bible without knowing or serving the Person it is about (an important fact to keep in mind when leading Bible studies on campus). It is common for believers to address this danger by distinguishing between head and heart, and stressing the limitations of mere "head knowledge." As long as we're clear about what we mean (and don't mean) by the distinction, it can be useful. But putting things this way is easily misleading, if we invest it with the kind of dichotomy that I have been describing—when we separate thought from devotion.

Yes, it is possible to have knowledge of true doctrine without personal commitment. But it is also possible to be passionately committed to what is false, to be devoted to a destructive fantasy. And that is at least as much a danger for us in our day.

What we believe matters. Our beliefs (what we hold to be true) are the rails our lives run on. They determine how we act, what we do. The reason you plug your computer cord into the wall socket is that you have beliefs about what happens when you do so. Without those beliefs you would not act as you do. You may have minimal understanding of the physics involved. Still, you believe things like: My computer runs on electricity and can't run without it, and I have access to electricity by plugging into the wall. So that's what you do.

But not all beliefs are true; they do not all match up to reality. If what we believe is false, then our actions on the basis of that belief will ultimately fail. In some cases the truth or falsity of our beliefs is a matter of life and death. Paul Little tells of a nurse who thought she was putting silver nitrate into a newborn baby's eyes, but it was actually acid. She sincerely believed it to be silver nitrate, and she sincerely sought to help the baby. But her belief was factually false. Tragically, Little notes, her sincerity did not save the baby from blindness.[9]

Sincerity and passion in our beliefs are not enough. What matters even more crucially is whether what we believe is *true*. Earnestness and emotional conviction are good things in service to the truth, but they are not enough to get us *to* truth. For that, God has given us minds. Trying to separate the head and the heart is a fool's errand, and it is unbiblical. No wonder that, according to Jesus, we are to love God with all of our mind, as well as our heart.

WHAT IS THE HEART?

Part of our confusion comes from misunderstanding what it is to love God with our heart. Are we not supposed to love God passionately and emotionally? Of course! There are many aspects to how God made us—emotional, rational, social, moral, imaginative, physical, relational, artistic—and we should love God with all of them, responding to him and his worth in all the ways appropriate to the nature he has given us. This includes, importantly, our emotions.

But it is a mistake to think that this is all, or even chiefly, what is meant by loving God with all our heart. Biblically, it is a confusion to think of the heart simply as emotions. Hebrew is the language in which the Old Testament was written, the original language of the *Shema* passage that Jesus cites. The Hebrew term (*lēb*) translated "heart" refers to the emotional aspect of our lives but also to much more. Our *lēb* is the center of our life—the seat of our personality, the source of our motivations and desires, the core of our attitudes, values and thoughts.[10] Biblically, your heart is the real you. That's why it is so important. As

Proverbs 4:23 says, "Above all else guard your heart, / for everything you do flows from it." Dallas Willard renders this verse, "Put everything you have into the care of your heart, for it determines what your life amounts to."[11]

From a fully biblical perspective *heart* refers to the whole package, the whole inner you, not simply your emotions. It includes each of the three elements commonly distinguished in one's personality: intellect, emotions and will. *Lēb* appears in the Old Testament some 850 times. Typically it refers simply to the self in general, including all three elements. In some contexts, however, there is a specific focus on one of the elements: intellect, emotions *or* will. Which of these do you suppose is in view most of the time? The answer is surprising (to us): according to one scholarly analysis, *lēb* refers specifically to emotional states and desires 166 times, to will, purpose and volition 195 times, and to intellect 204 times.[12] In the Bible, then, *heart* actually refers to thinking more often than it does to feeling. In fact, it refers to feeling least of all!

To put it mildly, in the Bible there is no divide between the head and the heart. That is a prejudice we bring to our understanding of Scripture, not a conclusion we rightly draw from it. Yes, we are more than thinking or reasoning creatures—we feel, choose, desire and love, and each is a crucial aspect of being made in the image of God. But we are also not less than thinking or reasoning creatures. Thinking is central to who we are. As classical thinkers put it, humans are "rational animals": thinking and rationality are bound up in everything that we do.

WHERE IS THE MIND?

In the *Shema* passage Jesus cites, the ideas of thinking and the mind were already included in the idea of loving God "with all your heart." So why does the Bible go further and specifically state that we are to love God with all our *mind*? You may have noticed something even more curious: the *Shema* itself does not actually say "mind." But Jesus does. In fact, he does so every time he refers to the *Shema*. Why does Jesus add to the original text?

The answer is in what we've already seen. The original Hebrew text of Deuteronomy 6 does not include the word *mind*. It didn't need to, since the concept of intellect or thinking was already included in the Hebrew understanding of the heart. In the centuries after this Old Testament passage was written, however, Greek became the dominant written language of the Hellenistic world, including Middle Eastern countries like Israel. It is the language of the New Testament, including the Gospel records of Jesus' words. But the Greek term for "heart" (*kardia*) is not as rich as the Hebrew concept. It doesn't carry the same connotations of thinking and intellect. To clarify and preserve the original meaning of the text, apparently, Jesus (as well as some earlier Greek translations of the Old Testament) added a Greek term for "mind," *dianoia*, when referring to the *Shema*.

The Septuagint—Several hundred years before the time of Jesus, in order to bring the Old Testament to a wider audience, a group of scholars translated the Hebrew text into Greek. This translation is called the Septuagint (abbreviated LXX). It was the Bible known and used by the majority of people in Jesus' day, and it is the one Jesus and the apostles typically cite when they refer to the Old Testament. Like Jesus, some versions of the Septuagint include *dianoia* (mind) in the text of Deuteronomy 6:5.

Even if he had not used the word *mind* in citing the *Shema*, however, we can be sure that Jesus would have seen thinking as part of the greatest commandment—because it was already there, included in the original biblical idea of loving God with our heart.

LOVING GOD WITH OUR MIND

What is it to love God with our mind? Minimally, of course, it's *not* denigrating thinking as unimportant. We should not think that the Creator of our mind is glorified when we treat his gift in this way. As Augustine said, "God forbid that he should hate in us that faculty [reason] by which he created us superior to other living things."[13]

But what *does* it mean to love God with our mind? Is it to be careful what we think about—to run from pornography, depictions of violence and other unhealthy and sinful thinking? Yes, of course. That is obvious from biblical teaching as a whole (Phil 4:8), and it is clearly a part of loving God with our mind. But there is much more to it than that.

Does it mean we should read only "Christian" books? No. Nothing in Scripture indicates anything of the kind. Christian thinkers throughout the ages affirm that "all truth is God's truth." Because God is the creator of all things apart from himself, anything that is actually true—whether or not it is articulated by a follower of Jesus or discovered in the Bible—comes ultimately from God. This is the theological foundation for our entering with excitement and wonder into the intellectual arena of the university, into all of its subjects and disciplines. We have nothing to fear, as Christ followers, from knowing what is true. On the contrary, truth is something we should seek passionately as a way of loving God. But this requires that we develop skills in thinking, to discern between what is true and what is false. *That* will be part of loving God with our minds.

> "It is a noble thing to do one's kindnesses toward the whole of the human race. But it is ever more seemly that you should give to God the most precious thing you have, that is, your mind, for you have nothing better than that."
>
> AMBROSE OF MILAN (A.D. 339-397)[14]

Does loving God with our minds mean memorizing and meditating on Scripture? Yes, of course (Ps 1). It is a singularly life-transforming spiritual discipline that each of us should practice regularly—especially in college. I regularly draw upon passages I memorized as a student, when my memory was much better than it is now. But loving God with our mind goes beyond even this. Here is one important reason: you could in fact memorize the entire Bible, and yet be wholly unchanged by it. Suppose you memorized it in a language that you do not understand—as many Muslims memorize the Qur'an in Arabic, although they speak no Arabic. Would it change your life? No. The Bible only affects our lives and changes them, as we understand it—as we think, and think well, about it, so that we can apply it properly.

I think the best way to understand what it means to love God with our mind is to consider what our minds are—what they do, what they are for. And what is that? Our minds are for *thinking*, in all of its many aspects: knowing, reasoning, analyzing, understanding, choosing, creating, imagining, inferring. We use our minds for distinguishing between truth and falsity, learning, evaluating, memorizing, communicating, planning, inventing and deciding. In fact, we use our minds in doing everything else that we do. Loving God with our mind, then, is doing *all* of those things—the best we can, for the glory of God, as an expression of gratitude, love and worship of him.

STUDENTS AND SCHOLARS

Although every follower of Jesus is called to love God with all of his or her mind, not all are called to be scholars, to inhabit the university's marketplace of ideas for a lifetime. Each of us is given different gifts and tasks; we are called to love God through the unique exercise of our own gifts and the unique expression of our own personality.[15] But all are called to be thinkers: to be wise, to do the best job we can with what we have been given.

What about you? You may not be wired to be a professional scholar. But the fact that you are accepted into a university indicates that you possess a relatively high level of intellectual ability. And you will be held accountable for how you use that ability. When God places you in a university environment, he expects you to engage in the intellectual life of that arena in a way that honors him. Since few in the world have that opportunity, you will be held to a high level of responsibility, indeed.

During World War II, while a professor at Oxford University, C. S. Lewis preached a sermon in the university church. He addressed the question of how Christians could justify devoting themselves to education and the life of the mind while England was at war with Hitler's forces and fighting for its very life. Lewis pointed out that as important as it is during times of war to take up arms to defend freedom and innocent lives, people do not cease to think, simply because it is war time. Their lives and institutions are still, and will be in the future, shaped by ideas. At a level deeper than the physical conflicts of war, there is an ongoing battle of ideas that is even more important in the long run. For those Christians who are given the privilege and responsibility of study, it is crucial that they do so, to the best of their ability. Building on the war analogy, Lewis challenged his audience:

> To be ignorant and simple now, would be to throw down our weapons and betray our uneducated brethren who have no other defense, but us, against the intellectual attacks of the heathen. Good philosophy must exist, if for no other reason, because bad philosophy must be answered.[16]

Do you see how important it is to love God with your mind in the university? Going to college is a stewardship from God, an opportunity he has entrusted to you. It should be taken seriously, especially in its intellectual dimension—because ideas have consequences and as a college student (and later) you have a particularly important role to play in the marketplace of ideas.

BACK TO WISDOM

Loving God with your mind will be at the heart of your flourishing in the university. You can't do better than follow the example of Daniel and his friends, who excelled in "every matter of wisdom and understanding" (Dan 1:20). Although wisdom encompasses more than thinking, it does involve hard intellectual effort, as we see in the Bible's textbook on wisdom, Proverbs. Notice the verbs (which I have emphasized) in Proverbs 2:1-5:

> My son, if you *accept* my words
>   and *store up* my commands within you,
> *turning* your ear to wisdom
>   and *applying* your heart to understanding—
> indeed, if you *call out* for insight
>   and *cry aloud* for understanding,
> and if you *look* for it as for silver
>   and *search* for it as for hidden treasure,
> then you will *understand* the fear of the LORD
>   and *find* the knowledge of God.

It's a picture of passionate, diligent seeking for understanding. Thinking is hard work. It takes discipline and self-control, two character virtues that Proverbs also emphasizes as parts of wisdom. There is no better place to cultivate these than in college. Of course, there is more to life than study, and it is important for life in college to include fun, exercise, relaxation and other extracurricular activities. But it's easy for such things to take over, for "study breaks" to become occasional breaks *for* study. Truly loving God with your mind means being intentional about your intellectual life, learning to think well. Here, as in most areas, community is essential. Find some like-minded friends to study with, those who will hold you accountable to pursue the life of the mind. Ask God to give you a mentor, perhaps a professor, graduate student, campus minister or pastor who particularly exemplifies loving God with his or her mind, and ask this person to apprentice you into this way of living.

Earlier generations of Christ followers considered study to be a spiritual discipline: a practice that, when offered to God in worship, is used by the Holy Spirit to help shape us to become like Jesus. As I have, you may find the words of this "Scholar's Prayer," by Anglican bishop and Cambridge University scholar H. C. G. Moule (1841-1920), to be a helpful way to begin your times of study:

> Lord and Saviour, true and kind,
> be the master of my mind;
> Bless and guide and strengthen still
> all my powers of thought and will.
>
> While I ply the scholar's task,
> Jesus Christ be near, I ask;
> Help the memory, clear the brain,
> Knowledge still to seek and gain.
>
> Here I train for life's swift race;
> let me do it in Thy grace;
> Here I arm me for life's fight;
> let me do it in Thy might.

Thou hast made me mind and soul;
I for Thee would use the whole:
Thou hast died that I might live;
all my powers to Thee I give.

Striving, thinking, learning still,
let me follow thus Thy will,
Till my whole glad nature be,
trained for duty and for Thee.

3

THE TRUTH ABOUT TRUTH

*I am the way and the truth and the life. No one comes to the
Father except through me.*

JOHN 14:6

1. *truthiness (noun)*
   "truth that comes from the gut, not books" (Stephen Colbert,
   The Colbert Report)
   *"the quality of preferring concepts or facts one wishes to be
   true, rather than concepts or facts known to be true"* (American
   Dialect Society)

MERRIAM-WEBSTER'S #1 WORD OF THE YEAR FOR 2006

Standing before an audience, I hold up a book with the forbidding title (it was first published in 1724): *Logic: Or the Right Use of Reason in the Inquiry After Truth with a Variety of Rules to Guard Against Error in the Affairs of Religion and Human Life, as well as in the Sciences.* I spend a minute or two reading rapidly through some of the many chapter and section titles (e.g., Of the Various Kinds of Propositions: "Of universal, particular, indefinite, and singular propositions"; "Of affirmative and negative propositions"; "Of the opposition and conversion of propositions"; "Of pure modal propositions"). I explain that this book was the most influential logic text of its time, the standard one used at Oxford, Cambridge, Harvard and Yale universities. And its influence continued for many decades, printed in some twenty editions.

I then invite my audience to describe the author: What do you suppose he was like? What was his vocation?

Typical answers include: he was very smart; he was very analytical; he was boring (usually some suggestions have a negative edge). And he was, obviously, a philosopher, a logician. No one has suggested that the author was likely a pastor, a theologian or a devotional writer. Or a writer of hymns. Yet the author of *Logic* was all of those. His name is Isaac Watts—known to the musical world as "the father of the English hymn," composer of such beloved works as "Joy to the World," "When I Survey the Wondrous Cross" and seven hundred more. He was also a pastor in active ministry and a significant theological and devotional writer. And the most influential logician of his time.

Isaac Watts (1674-1748)—Pastor of Marks Lane Church, London. He wrote many scholarly and popular philosophical and theological works, as well as poetry and hymns. Seeking to improve the poor quality of musical worship in his day, Watts composed expanded English hymns based on the Psalms. He also wrote hymns to accompany his sermons and hymns for the instruction of children.

Those were days when Christians did not simply assume that one must choose between a sharp mind and a passionate heart. But times have changed. Contrast Watts with the men's conference speaker I heard criticize someone's perspective by complaining: "He was thinking logically, but he should have been thinking theologically." It's a cute statement—but deeply unbiblical and terribly destructive. It turns on the assumption that logic and theology are incompatible. But why think that? In fact, why think that there is a difference between thinking logically and thinking theologically?

Isaac Watts recognized no such division. "Logic," he writes, "is the art of using Reason well in our inquiries after truth, and the communication of it to others. Reason is the glory of human nature . . . the common gift of God to all men."[1]

> Now the design of Logic is to teach us the right use of our reason, or intellectual powers, and the improvement of them in ourselves and oth-

ers. This is not only necessary in order to attain any competent knowledge in the sciences, or the affairs of learning, but to govern both the greater and meaner [lesser] actions of life. It is the cultivation of our reason by which we are better enabled to distinguish good from evil, as well as truth from falsehood; and both these are matters of the highest importance, whether we regard this life, or the life to come.[2]

Since by discovering truth we "discover our duty to God and our fellow-creatures" and "learn to confirm our faith in divine revelation, as well as to understand what is revealed," good thinking is also necessary for the development of our spiritual lives.[3]

Theology is thinking about God and about all of reality in relation to God and his purposes, as revealed in the Scriptures. If it is to be good thinking about God and reality, based on a sound understanding of the Scriptures, it will be logical thinking—thinking that employs the right use of our intellectual powers. Good theology is good, logical thinking about God and all of reality in relation to God.

Watts, not the men's speaker, is on the side of the Bible and the history of the Christian church. All truth, including the laws of logic, is God's truth. Since all truth comes from God and points ultimately back to him, followers of Jesus have every reason to be confident that if "thinking logically" ever runs into conflict with "thinking theologically," something has gone fundamentally wrong. We are misapplying logic, misunderstanding theology or both. But we are not thinking too logically. We are not thinking logically *enough*.

> Theology is "reasoning or discourse concerning the Deity."
> AUGUSTINE (A.D. 354-430)[4]

Logic is not all there is to thinking, of course. In the strict sense, logic concerns the internal structure of thought: it is to the whole of thought as the frame is to a house. Although there is more to a house than its supporting structure, without the structure there would be only a pile of materials. Similarly, there is much more to thinking well than its logical structure. But without logic there can be no coherent thought at all.

Whether or not one studies it formally, logic is inescapable, as it underlies all that we study and think. We will touch upon various aspects of logic in subsequent chapters, but we are chiefly interested in it in this chapter because of its relation to truth. As Watts puts it, "The pursuit and acquisition of truth is of infinite concernment to mankind. . . . Our wisdom, prudence, and piety, our present conduct and our future hope, are all influenced by the use of our rational powers in the search for truth."[5]

HOW WOULD JESUS THINK?

The most common epigraph over entrances to American university libraries is a statement by Jesus: "The truth shall set you free" (Jn 8:31). It also serves (in Latin) as the motto of Johns Hopkins University: *Veritas Vos Liberavit.*

Jesus constantly spoke about truth. When I lecture in secular university contexts, I often challenge students to check this out: to consult a concordance (a book listing all the words of the Bible and where they appear) and look up the terms *truth*, *true* and *truly* to see how often Jesus uses them. The Gospel of John is particularly remarkable in this respect, as these terms appear on almost every page and regularly more than once on a single page.

Truth is the focus of one of the best-known incidents in Jesus' life and ministry. Standing on trial before Pilate, the Roman governor, Jesus spoke of his "kingdom."

> "You are a king, then!" said Pilate.
>
> Jesus answered, "You say that I am a king. In fact, the reason I was born and came into the world is to testify to the truth. Everyone on the side of truth listens to me."
>
> "What is truth?" retorted Pilate. With this he went out again to the Jews gathered there and said, "I find no basis for a charge against him." (Jn 18:37-38)

In this statement Jesus not only affirms the importance of truth to his mission on earth, he indicates two important aspects of truth that we will explore. First, truth is something to "testify" to—to speak of or point to. This is the *propositional* aspect of truth, that which is captured in statements or descriptions (propositions). Second, Jesus says that those who are "on the side of truth" listen to him. This points to what we will call the *personal* aspect of truth. Truth rightly engages our loyalties and affections as persons. In fact, properly orienting our character to truth is necessary for at least some knowledge of what is true. Blaise Pascal (1623-1662), the French physicist and philosopher, a Christian, noted, "Truth is so obscured nowadays and lies so well established that unless we love the truth we shall never recognize it."[6] Truth is not merely a matter of knowledge or information, but of wisdom.

WHAT IS TRUTH?

At the conclusion of this exchange with Jesus, Pilate asks the question that has become associated with his name: "What is truth?" It is not clear what Pilate hoped to gain by asking this question. Francis Bacon observed, "'What is truth?' said jesting Pilate; and would not stay for an answer."[7] In any case, Pilate's question remains one of the most important we can ask. Unsurprisingly, there is significant disagreement in our time about what truth is and whether it may be known. We won't attempt to examine all the significant issues related to the nature of truth here, but we'll consider some of the most fundamental. As we work toward an answer to Pilate's question, we will follow Isaac Watts and appeal directly (but briefly) to logic—specifically, to the pioneering logical system developed by Aristotle.

The three primary elements in Aristotelian logic are terms, propositions and arguments. Consider two statements:

(A) It is raining.
(B) Barack Obama is president of the United States.

(We will return often to [A], as an example. To be clear, let's stipulate that we agree on all the variables: when stated, [A] refers to raining outside, here and now, and we agree on what "raining" means.)

Notice the three elements of logic imbedded within these statements. Terms are words, like *president* and *rain*, that refer to concepts. Putting terms together in certain ways, we form sentences like (A) and (B).

Propositions assert something about what reality is like, about what is the case. Both (A) and (B) are sentences that express propositions, as they describe facts about the weather conditions outside and about the identity of the president of the United States. Speaking somewhat loosely (I'll qualify this later), we may simply refer to (A) and (B) as propositions.

Aristotle (384-322 B.C.)—Greek philosopher, student of Plato, tutor to Alexander the Great, one of the greatest thinkers of all time. He did ground-breaking work in logic, metaphysics and science. Other than the Bible, the most influential book of ethics in the Western tradition is Aristotle's *Nicomachean Ethics.* His views had a significant influence on medieval Christian thinkers like Thomas Aquinas.

We put propositions together in certain ways to form arguments. An argument is a sequence of premises and a conclusion, organized in such a way that the conclusion follows logically from the premises.

Here is a simple argument that uses (A) as a premise:

1. If it is raining, the streets are wet.
2. It is raining.
3. Therefore, the streets are wet.

Assume that premises 1 and 2 are true. When presented this argument, do you need to go outside to check and see whether the streets are wet—that is, to see whether the conclusion (3) is true? No; if the premises are true, the conclusion must be true—its truth follows logically from the truth of the premises. This is the case with any (deductive) argument that is logically valid.[8] Logic analyzes the relationships between terms and propositions, and between premises and conclusions.

We'll return to these three elements of logic in subsequent chapters. Here let's focus on the second, because, in an important, philosophical sense, truth is a property of propositions.

THE NATURE OF TRUTH

Consider a third sentence:

(C) Shut the door!

Compare (C) to our previous sentences:

(A) It is raining.
(B) Barack Obama is president of the United States.

Unlike (A) and (B), (C) is a command, an imperative; it does not assert anything. It plays a different role. The aim of imperatives is not to describe reality but to effect a change, to bring something about.[9]

Is (C) true? No? Then is it false?

> Did Aristotle "invent" logic? (Is it merely a matter of convention—relative to person, culture, time or place?) No more than Isaac Newton "invented" gravity. Just as Newton developed new, fruitful ways to understand features of the physical world that were already there, so Aristotle clarified and made evident still deeper, universal aspects of thought and reality that were already true.

You may be wondering if I've lost my own sanity in asking these questions. Why? Because (C) is neither. It is not something that *could* be true or false, because it does not describe reality. Propositions, by contrast, can be true or false, and each proposition *is* either true or false.

Propositions are sometimes called "truth claims," because they claim to express what is true about reality. Not all propositions are actually true, of course, although they are claims to the truth. For example, "Barack Obama is president of the United States" is a truth claim about the identity of the president of the United States: that it is Barack Obama. When I began writing this book in the fall of 2008, (B) was false, because the president of the United States at that time was George W. Bush. A different proposition was true at that time:

(D) George W. Bush is president of the United States.

But now, as I edit this chapter, (D) is false and (B) is true, because Barack Obama has succeeded George W. Bush as president.[10] Both (B) and (D) are claims to the truth, but only one of them is in fact true.

Earlier I said that, speaking loosely, we may refer to (A) and (B) as

propositions, but I would qualify this. Consider the following statements:

(A) It is raining.
(E) Es Regnet.
(F) Pluit.
(G) Está lloviendo.

How many propositions are listed here? It might appear that there
are four propositions, because four assertions are made about the way
things are. However, these sentences all mean the same thing, expressed in different languages (English, German, Latin, Spanish).
They have the same content or meaning—what philosophers call
"propositional content"—but that content is expressed in different
words in the different sentences. Although four different sentences
are listed, representing four different languages, there is actually only
one proposition expressed in those sentences. And that proposition,
properly speaking, is what is true or false. (Suppose it is raining outside, so each of the four sentences is now true. While there are four
true sentences, they do not represent four different truths, but only
one—the truth of the proposition that is expressed in each of the
sentences. And it would remain true even if it were not expressed in
any sentence; if, for example, I simply had the thought that it is raining.) Speaking loosely, we may refer to sentences like (A) and (B) as
propositions, but keep in mind that a proposition is actually the
thought that is expressed in a declarative sentence, and that thought
is what is true or false.

THE CLASSICAL DEFINITION OF TRUTH

If all propositions are claims to the truth, what makes one actually
true? Consider proposition (A): *It is raining.* It should be clear (recall
the stipulations we made earlier) that (A) is either true or false. Suppose (A) is true. What makes it true? Or suppose it is false. What
makes it so?

In neither case is it our going outside and checking to see whether it's
raining. Doing that would help us to know whether (A) is true or false,

but it would not make it so. If (A) is true, it is true whether or not you or I or any other human being knows it to be true. (Suppose we are locked in a room and have no way to check the weather outside. If it's raining outside, [A] is true—even if none of us knows it.)

There is a crucial difference between what makes something true and how we know it is true. In philosophical terms the first is a "metaphysical" question (about what reality is like) and the second is an "epistemological" question (about our knowledge—what we know and how we know it). These are often confused, which in turn leads to further confusions.

At this point we're interested in what makes a proposition true (or false). So what makes (A) true, if it is true? The answer should not be surprising: the fact that it's raining outside. What would make it false? That it's not raining outside. In other words, what makes a proposition true or false is reality: the way things actually are. Propositions are assertions about what reality is like, so if a proposition or thought fits or matches up to reality, it is true. If it does not, it's false.

To be a bit more specific, truth is a relation between a proposition and reality—a relation of fit or correspondence. Relations hold between two or more things (called *relata*)—like the relations "in between" and "taller than." To say that Fred is taller than George is to say that Fred stands in the relation *taller than* to George.

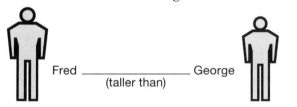
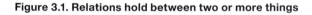

Figure 3.1. Relations hold between two or more things

Similarly, truth is a relation that holds between a proposition (a thought), which is about reality, and reality itself. The relation is one of correspondence.

If, as in figure 3.2, it is actually raining, the proposition *It is raining* is true: it corresponds to reality. If it is not actually raining, the proposition is false. The same idea applies to other propositions that are familiar to college students: *They're serving "mystery meat" in the cafeteria tonight*, or *I'm going on a date this weekend*. These statements are true if they correspond to reality.

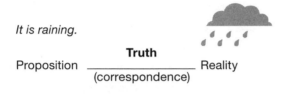

Figure 3.2. Truth: A relation that holds between a proposition and reality

This picture of truth as correspondence to reality represents the "classical definition of truth," the standard philosophical view held by the vast majority of thinkers from ancient times to this day. It is also the commonsense understanding by which we operate in everyday life. If you are crossing the street and someone says, "Watch out, there's a truck coming!" you will look to see if there really is a truck coming—to see whether the statement corresponds to reality. Even skeptics about truth as correspondence live according to it whenever they cross a street, read a newspaper, converse with their spouse or write a check.

> "To say of what is that it is not, or of what is not that it is, is false, while to say of what is that it is, and of what is not that it is not, is true."
>
> ARISTOTLE[11]

In fact, they live according to it even as they argue against it, for their argument has no point unless we assume they think the position they are arguing for is an accurate account of the way things are and they expect their hearers to interpret their propositions as corresponding to reality. All of these activities and many more (I would say all intentional activities) presuppose or assume the correspondence view of truth.

TRUTH IN DIFFERENT AREAS

This may seem obvious—just basic common sense. I agree. That is only right, for surely things have gone awry if something as basic as truth is defined in a way that's at odds with how virtually everyone understands it. Good philosophy usually clarifies and refines our most basic intuitions rather than subverts them.

On the other hand, it may not seem so obvious when we're not talking about things like the weather or dorm food, but about morality or the existence of God. Does truth mean something different once we move into the arena of ultimate questions? Many people assume that it does. But this is a mistake.

There are different kinds of propositions—propositions about different kinds of things—and it is important to keep those differences in mind as we consider whether they are true. Propositions about weather (*It is raining*) are quite different from propositions about mathematics (*5 + 7 = 12*), history (*Abraham Lincoln was shot*), science (*At sea level, water boils at 212° F*), geography (*Australia is a continent*), morality (*It is wrong to torture children for fun*), philosophy (*Truth is correspondence to reality*), or religion (*God exists*).

Because of their differences in subject matter, what constitutes relevant evidence for the truth of each proposition will differ widely. (A common mistake is to think, for example, that all evidence is or must be "scientific" evidence.) But this does not mean that truth is a different kind of thing in these different cases. What makes the proposition true or false is the same in each: whether it corresponds to reality. For example, the proposition *Abraham Lincoln was shot* is true if Abraham Lincoln was actually shot—if it corresponds to reality. If he was stabbed, instead, or died of old age, the proposition is false. Because it is a claim about history, the evidence for this proposition will be historical, not meteorological: we can't step outside and check the weather in order to confirm whether or not it's true. But its truth is still determined by whether it corresponds to reality, whether it fits what actually happened.

Similarly, the proposition *God exists* is true if it corresponds to reality—if there actually is a God. If not, then the proposition is false. The sort of evidence appropriate for determining whether this proposition is true is different from both meteorological and historical truth claims. But the question of God's existence is still a factual one; it's a claim about what reality is like.

Some have attempted to "save" religion and religious belief by removing them from normal standards of truth and rationality, appealing to a different kind of truth: "spiritual truth." In this view, propositions about God and religious matters are not true in the normal (historical, geographical, scientific, etc.) senses of the term, but are nonetheless "spiritually true": they help to make life meaningful, orient people around larger goals and concerns, comfort the grieving, help people behave better and so on. But they are not "factual" claims about reality that can be evaluated by normal, rational standards.

But appealing to "spiritual truth" is a dead end—whether or not there is a God.

First, suppose there is no God. Nothing substantial is gained by pretending that God exists. (That's exactly what it is: pretending.) Suppose I believe that I am Napoleon. That would certainly change the way I view myself and how I behave. It would give me larger goals (conquering the world, for example), and by having such goals I may behave in a more disciplined way than I did before and perhaps improve my life. But it is factually false. At best, I pretend that it is true.

A tragic consequence—Author Douglas Adams rejected Christianity after encountering believers who held "the view that you couldn't apply the logic of physics to religion, that they were dealing with different types of 'truth.'"[12]

And that means I'm not engaging with reality. Suppose I really were deluded in this way. Would it actually help me if someone were to redefine truth and declare that, well, actually Horner's claim to be Napoleon is true; not as normal, historical truth, of course, but as "Napoleonic truth"—since it gives Horner a higher goal to live by? Not at all. Being out of touch with reality is not a good thing, even if it improves certain aspects of my life. And ultimately, of course, it won't improve my life, because at some point I will run into reality. Ideas have consequences. Being systematically disengaged from reality is a kind of mental illness. It does not help the mentally ill for us to define mental illness out of existence, any more than it helps those suffering with AIDS if we define AIDS as a fully healthy condition. As C. S. Lewis put it,

Christianity claims to give an account of *facts*—to tell you what the real universe is like. Its account of the universe may be true, or it may not, and once the question is really before you, then your natural inquisitiveness must make you want to know the answer. If Christianity is untrue, then no honest man will want to believe it, however helpful it might be: if it is true, every honest man will want to believe it, even if it gives him no help at all.[13]

In any case, there is no need to "save" belief in God in this or any other way, because there are strong rational grounds for believing that God exists. Those who appeal to "spiritual truth" typically do so because they have an inadequate view of reason and evidence. They often assume, for example, that only "scientific" proof counts. But that is false, as we will continue to see.

The spiritual truth approach also conflicts with a biblical perspective. In 1 Corinthians 15:15-19 the apostle Paul flatly asserts that if Jesus did not actually rise from the dead, those who believe in his resurrection are most to be pitied: their faith is in vain! Believing that Jesus rose from the dead is a revolutionary, life-changing belief, but only because it corresponds to reality. It is important, that is, because it is true—in the normal sense of the term. It actually happened.

Suppose, on the other hand, that God does exist. Appealing to spiritual truth in this case is equally a dead end. Relegating God's existence to spiritual truth robs it of any of its real power and makes it indistinguishable from self-denial and fantasy. This is certainly not how the early Christians thought. Jesus' disciples were willing to suffer and die rather than stop proclaiming Jesus as the resurrected Messiah, because they were convinced that the resurrection actually happened. They understood it to be factual, just as much a part of reality as the law of gravity. Only such a conviction explains their behavior and that of thousands who followed them. If they had tried to save Christianity by appealing to spiritual truth, there would be no Christianity today.

Truth is correspondence to reality, not just for propositions in certain areas but in every area.

KINDS OF TRUTH

We speak of truth in other ways as well, however. We refer, for example, to "True North," "true friends," "true Christians" and "true hearts" (as Elvis Presley sang, "Don't be cruel to a heart that's true"). Wedding ceremonies include a pledge to be "true" to one another. Truth in these cases refers to relations like genuineness, authenticity, stability, faithfulness or correspondence to a correct standard (as when we "true up" a line or a wall in construction). The Bible's rich understanding of truth includes all of these shades of meaning.[14]

The primary Hebrew term for truth in the Bible is *'ĕmet*. Its most basic or original meaning is the idea of stability, strength or solidity—like a rock that is fixed, dependable and solid. Over time *'ĕmet* came to refer to "truth," both in the sense of being factual or accurate when speaking of statements, and in the sense of being faithful, dependable and genuine when speaking of persons or objects. Here are a few examples of how *'ĕmet* (rendered by the English term in italics) is used in these different ways: Yahweh is the *true* God (2 Chron 15:3), the *faithful* God (Ps 31:5). His decrees are firm (Ps 19:9), and his word is *true* (Ps 119:160).

> Love and faithfulness meet together;
> righteousness and peace kiss each other.
> Faithfulness springs forth from the earth,
> and righteousness looks down from heaven. (Ps 85:10-11)

A prayer that I memorized as a college student and prayed almost daily since, is

> Lead me in Thy truth [*'ĕmet*] and teach me,
> for You are the God of my salvation;
> for You I wait all the day. (Ps 25:5 NASB)

As these passages suggest, *'ĕmet* is typically translated into English as either "truth" or "faithfulness," depending on the context.[15] It is important to remember, however, that *'ĕmet* means both—and we should keep both in mind as we read the Bible. The biblical understanding of truth includes factuality or the correspondence of statements to reality, but it also includes faithfulness, genuineness and authenticity. The two aspects are related, and both are essential. Jesus' understanding of truth reflects this richness. Not only does he emphasize speaking and telling the truth, as opposed to lies—truth as propositional (Jn 8:14, 16, 17, 40)—he also emphasizes being true and living truthfully (Jn 3:19-21; 7:18; 8:26). I noted earlier that in his exchange with Pilate Jesus spoke of testifying to the truth (propositional), but he also referred to those who are "on the side of truth." The latter relates to persons rather than propositions.[16]

Understanding truth as personal as well as propositional enables us to respond to a further challenge to propositional truth. Some disparage propositional truth as unimportant or even nonexistent, in favor of things like "authenticity" and "integrity." It should be clear how this is mistaken. Authenticity and integrity are not alternatives to truth, even to propositional truth. Rather, they are expressions of truth, in its personal aspect. Both aspects are necessary. Although truth is more than propositional, as I have been arguing, it is not less. Indeed, propositional truth is necessary for authenticity and integrity: trustworthy and authentic persons are those who can be trusted to tell the truth—to assert propositions that correspond to reality, even when it may not pay them to do so. That is not all there is to being authentic and having integrity, but it is a necessary condition.

Propositional truth is fundamental to any coherent thought and life. In fact, it is inescapable. Even to articulate the position, for example, that "there is no propositional truth," is to assert a proposition that is itself either true or false. In this case it must be false, because it refutes itself: it amounts to the proposition that there are no true propositions. But if that proposition is true, then no proposition is true—including that one! If it is true, in other words, it must be false.[18]

> "God has given me a mind to put nothing before the discovery of truth, to wish for nothing else, to think of nothing else, to love nothing else."
>
> AUGUSTINE[17]

Truth is both propositional and personal. I'll explore the personal aspect of truth further in part three. Because our concern here is with truth as it relates to the fundamentals of thinking, our focus is on the propositional side. Even here, however, we must not forget that, from a biblical perspective, truth is ultimately personal. The final ground of truth is not a proposition but a Person—who is true, solid, *'ĕmet*. This is why Jesus could make the astonishing claim that "I am the way and the truth and the life" (Jn 14:6), and Paul could affirm that "in him all things hold together" (Col 1:17). In my experience Christian believers tend to have greater confidence in the existence and knowability of truth. And for good reason—it's rooted in the conviction that ultimate reality is One who is true and tells the truth. Indeed, we who follow him should regard seeking truth as nothing less than a joyful, holy calling.

"The pursuit and acquisition of truth is of infinite concern to mankind," as Isaac Watts asserted,[19] because we always act according to what we believe to be true. If what we believe *is* true, it will work. If it's not true, on the other hand, the result will be painful: instead of corresponding to reality, we'll run into it. But how does this work? How exactly does belief relate to truth? And how do belief and truth relate to knowledge? These are the questions we explore in chapter four.

4

THE TRUTH ABOUT
BELIEF AND KNOWLEDGE

My people are destroyed from lack of knowledge.

HOSEA 4:6

People perish for lack of knowledge, because only knowledge
permits assured access to reality; and reality does not adjust
itself to accommodate our false beliefs, errors, or hesitations in
action. Life demands a steady hand for good, and only knowledge
supplies this. This is as true in the spiritual life as elsewhere.

DALLAS WILLARD, *Knowing Christ Today*

I once appeared as a guest on a television talk show, in dialogue with Bill, the state president of American Atheists. At one point in our discussion, Bill remarked, "I have no beliefs; I have only scientific knowledge."

Similar sentiments are expressed regularly, often in the university. *Belief* and *knowledge* are commonly seen as mutually exclusive: if you believe something, you don't know it; if you know something, you clearly don't believe it. Being rational is rejecting belief in favor of knowledge. And the best kind of knowledge—perhaps the only *true* knowledge—is "scientific" knowledge, what is established by science.

Religious believers often feel threatened in the face of such statements. As believers they obviously have beliefs, and some of those concern matters—such as the existence of God—that are not strictly susceptible to scientific proof. Does that make believers irrational? Is there something inferior, at best, about religious beliefs? Is Bill right?

No. Even apart from religious considerations, Bill's position has deep difficulties. On standard philosophical understandings of belief and knowledge (including scientific knowledge), Bill's statement is not only false but incoherent. We will return to this example several times, as we assemble the conceptual structure of belief and knowledge that enables us to understand and respond.

BELIEF

You've probably heard people say, "That's true for you, but it's not true for me."

There are at least two ways to interpret this statement. Understood in its most obvious sense, it is confused.

I often catch flights out of Los Angeles International airport (LAX). Suppose I'm heading to my home state of Colorado and I have the following conversation with an airline representative. "Do I have the correct information, that flight 1462 to Denver leaves at 7:05 from gate B7?" He answers, "Well, that's true for me, but it may not be true for you."

"What are you talking about?"

"Well, you see," he explains, "we're tolerant here at LAX. We don't want to be narrow-minded or impose our notions of time, space, geography or flight plans on other people. We leave the 'truth' of these matters up to each individual."

My response?

"Look, I don't *want* the air traffic controllers to be tolerant about where the airplanes are, or the engineers who build the aircraft to be tolerant about the laws of physics and the tensile strength of the materials. Do me a favor: be narrow-minded about the truth of these things— because my life is at stake!"

This (entirely fictitious) conversation illustrates something about truth that is inescapable: *truth is objective*—it depends upon reality, the way things are. It's not up to you or me and what we prefer or think about it. This follows from the nature of truth as correspondence to reality.

That seems clear enough. But things get more complicated when we take into account that people have very different views about reality. Here clarifying the distinction between truth and belief becomes crucial.

OBJECTIVE AND SUBJECTIVE

What does it mean to say that truth is objective? We have seen that (propositional) truth is a relation between a proposition and reality. What a proposition is about is called the *object* of the proposition. In proposition (A), *It is raining*, the object of the proposition is the weather conditions outside. This proposition characterizes those conditions by the fact that it is raining.

To say that (A) is objectively true (or objectively false) is to say that the truth (or falsity) of (A) depends solely upon the object of the proposition—upon whether or not it is in fact raining outside. Period. It is an objective matter.

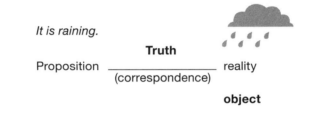

Figure 4.1. The object of a proposition

Suppose, however, that we introduce a person, Fred, into this scenario. Suppose Fred asserts (A): he claims that it is raining. Does that affect the truth or falsity of (A)? That is, does the truth of (A) depend in any way upon Fred? No. If it is not raining outside, Fred's asserting (A) does not make it true. Nor would Fred's denying (A) make it false. The truth of (A) depends entirely on the weather and not at all on Fred. In this example, Fred is the *subject*. A "subject" is a person who asserts or believes a proposition.

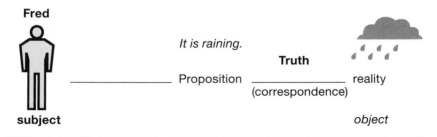

Figure 4.2. The subject of a proposition

Are some truths subjective—as in matters of taste? There are importantly subjective elements in matters of taste, but even there truth is objective. The sense in which the proposition *I like chocolate ice cream* is subjective is different from what we're discussing. The proposition's object (what it's about) is my preference in ice cream. This, unlike the weather conditions outside, is internal to my consciousness—it can't be accessed or known apart from my experience *as a subject* (my "subjective" experience). But the proposition is objective in the relevant sense: it's true if it corresponds to reality (if I do like chocolate) and false if it doesn't (if I don't like chocolate). Its truth does not depend on whether or not a subject (Fred, for example) believes or asserts it.[1]

Saying that something is subjective means that it is about or depends upon the subject. As figure 4.2 makes clear, truth is not subjective; it depends solely on the object. That is not to say that subjects are unimportant. It is only to say that *truth* is strictly objective.

It should now be clear why the statement "That's true for you, but it's not true for me," understood in the way we have been considering, involves a confusion about what truth *is*. The truth of a proposition does not change from person to person.

Sometimes, however, when someone says, "That's true for you, but it's not true for me," what the speaker *means* is something different: "You believe that's true, but I don't believe it's true."

This, of course, is not incoherent at all. Whereas, the first proposition is about *truth*, the second concerns *beliefs*. They are not the same. Different people (subjects) from different backgrounds with different assumptions and access to differing kinds and degrees of evidence have different beliefs—for example, about the shape of the earth. But these do not represent different truths. There is only one truth about the shape of the earth, grounded in how the earth is actually shaped. Even if, in the distant past, most or all people on the planet believed the earth to be flat, that would not in any way change the truth about the shape of the earth. The proposition *The earth is (roughly) round* was and is true whether or not anyone on earth believed it. Truth is objective.

When belief enters the equation, however, a partially subjective element is added—in this sense: subjects have beliefs. Although the truth of those beliefs depends entirely on their correspondence to reality, the existence and nature of the beliefs depends in various ways on the subjects who have them.

WHAT IS BELIEF?

What does it mean to believe something? As with truth, we'll follow the classical philosophical understanding here. (The branch of philosophy devoted to the analysis of belief

Is "objective truth" the same as "absolute truth"? Although the terms are similar in meaning, *absolute* carries further, negative connotations for many people: arrogance ("I know more than you"), dogmatism ("I cannot be mistaken") and intolerance ("I impose my views on you"). Logically, none of these connotations actually follows from understanding truth as absolute (or objective). In fact, just the opposite: if truth is just "whatever I believe," as subjectivism implies, then I can *never* be mistaken, by definition—not a position that suggests humility or tolerance. Still, since *absolute* has these unfortunate connotations, it's best to avoid the term and simply focus on truth as *objective*.

and knowledge is called "epistemology." Ironically, in my television discussion with Bill, the skeptical talk-show host referred approvingly to Bill—for no other reason than the fact that Bill is not a religious believer—as an "epistemologist." But if Bill had been familiar with epistemology, he would not have made the claim he did.) On this understanding, belief is construed in terms of *propositional belief:* to believe something is to stand in a certain relation to a proposition, namely, to hold it to be true. What does this mean? Here are some examples of belief statements:

- I believe that it is raining.
- I believe that God exists.

- I believe that the earth is (roughly) round.
- I believe that Barack Obama is president of the United States.
- I believe that 5 + 7 = 12.
- I believe that torturing children for fun is wrong.
- I believe that my car is in the Sam's Club parking lot.

Note that while these statements differ widely from each other, in one respect they are similar. They have the same form: I believe that _____. What differs is what fills the blank. But in each case it is the same *kind* of thing: a proposition. In *I believe that it is raining*, the proposition that fills the blank in my belief statement is *It is raining*. And so on. Belief is propositional.

Just as truth is a relation between a proposition and reality, belief is a relation between a person (a believing subject) and a proposition—in this case the relation is: *holding to be true*. When Fred believes that it is raining, Fred holds the proposition *It is raining* to be true (to correspond to reality).

We can now complete the figure we have been constructing, filling out the left side in terms of belief (see fig. 4.3).

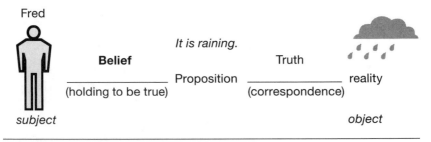

Figure 4.3. The relation of belief to truth

Why say that believing a proposition amounts to holding it to be true? Suppose I tell you, "I believe that my car is in the Sam's Club parking lot," but I go on to remark, "Of course I know that my car is not in the Sam's Club parking lot, because I left it at home. I walked to Sam's Club." You would rightly say, "That makes no sense! You obviously *don't* believe that your car is in the Sam's Club parking lot—

you believe it's at home." Intuitively you recognize that to believe a proposition is to hold it to be true.

DOES BILL HAVE BELIEFS?

Knowing the nature of belief enables us to uncover some initial difficulties in Bill's statement. For simplicity, let's call Bill's claim (H).

Belief and faith—Many scholars understand these terms to refer to different concepts. *Belief* is propositional: holding a proposition to be true. *Faith*, as in religious faith, is something different. Disagreement arises over what the difference amounts to. (We explore this question in part two.)

(H) I have no beliefs; I have only scientific knowledge.[2]

Understood on the standard philosophical account of "belief," (H) is false for at least two reasons. First, to have a belief is to hold a proposition to be true, and at the moment he made this statement, Bill held any number of propositions to be true. He believed, no doubt, that he existed, that I was talking to him, that he was sitting in the studio, that he had had breakfast, that 2 + 2 = 4, that there is no God—and many other propositions he held to be true. One cannot be alive and conscious, as a rational being, and have no beliefs at all.

Second, (H) expresses a proposition: the proposition (as asserted by Bill) that he has no beliefs but only scientific knowledge. As a proposition, then, (H) is either true or false. It's false, as we've just seen. But Bill thinks it's true, which is just what he claims when he asserts it. But this means that Bill holds (H) to be true—that Bill *believes* (H). Do you see the problem? In the very act of asserting (H), Bill expresses a belief: the belief that he has no beliefs! Bill's belief undermines itself (it is "self-refuting"). Not only is (H) false, it is incoherent.

True belief. So far we have spoken only of propositions being true or false. But we also think of beliefs as true or false. A belief is true when the proposition one holds to be true is, in fact, true. If Fred believes that it is raining—he holds the proposition *It is raining* to be true—and it *is* raining (the proposition corresponds to reality), Fred has a true belief.

People have beliefs about all kinds of things, and not all of those beliefs are true. Only those that correspond to reality are true beliefs. The truth of beliefs, then, is just as objective as the truth of propositions. Beliefs are about propositions, so their truth is grounded in the same thing: reality. Again, this applies just as much to religious beliefs as to beliefs about the weather. The belief that Jesus rose from the dead is a true belief if (and only if) Jesus rose from the dead.

Things become more complicated, however, as we pay more attention to the *subject*, the one who is doing the believing. For not only do we speak of having true beliefs, we also speak of "reasonable" or "rational" beliefs.[3]

From a biblical perspective we are fallible (we can go wrong) in our reasoning not only because we are finite but also because we are fallen or sinful. Our alienation from God has damaged and corrupted our relationships to each other, our environment and ourselves. We are inclined to distort even what we do know, to suit our own purposes—especially the most important truths about God. The effects of sin remain to some extent even for those who have been restored to a relationship with God through Jesus.

Rational belief. Rational beliefs are those we have good reason to think are true. Let's call reasons to believe a proposition is true *evidence*. Evidence does not make a proposition true (only reality can do that), and it does not guarantee its truth for thinkers like us. That's because we're finite (spatially, temporally and cognitively limited): we don't know everything, we don't have access to all the evidence there is, and we imperfectly evaluate the evidence we do have. Still, evidence for a proposition generally points to its truth. If there is no evidence at all for the truth of a proposition, or if the weight of evidence is stacked against it, it is unlikely that it is in fact true. (Although, again, it might be—because we're finite and therefore fallible.)

In order for us to have reasonable beliefs, then, we need to look for appropriate evidence for the propositions we consider. This is a crucial part of thinking well. But what counts as "appropriate" evidence? Here our earlier observations about the different kinds of propositions become particularly significant. Depending on the subject matter of these propositions, different kinds of reasons and evidence will be appropriate for helping discern their truth or falsity. The sort of evidence required to establish mathematical or geometrical propositions is quite different from what is appropriate, for example, for scientific propositions, historical claims or philosophical assertions. Along these lines Aristotle stressed that we should seek only the level of certainty or precision that is appropriate to the subject matter at hand.[4] Many confusions arise from misunderstanding just this point. A crucial part of having rational beliefs is being aware of the subject matter of the propositions in question and seeking the kind of evidence appropriate to that subject matter. So far, this is an entirely objective matter.

When we consider how much of that evidence is available to someone, however, and what he or she does with that evidence, we have introduced elements that are more subjective, in that they are more dependent on the subject. Although the truth of a belief is an entirely objective matter, the reasonableness of someone's belief will necessarily be tied to the evidence or reasons the person has for that belief. And that depends, to a significant extent, on the individual—the subject.

The proposition *The earth is (roughly) round* is true, so to believe it is to have a true belief. Whether or not it is reasonable for Fred to believe it, however, depends on the kind of evidence *Fred* has. Suppose Fred is raised in a remote village, surrounded by tall forests, in which every villager has always believed the world to be flat. Would it be reasonable for Fred, given just the evidence he has, to believe that the world is flat? Sure—even though it is a false belief!

So for finite (and fallen) thinkers like us, truth and rationality can come apart. As uncomfortable as it may be to accept this, it's actually just a matter of taking seriously the fact that we're not God, who, as omniscient and perfect, is infallible in his reasoning. And that's not a bad thing to take seriously! In fact, it's right at the heart of fearing God, which we've seen is the starting point of wisdom (Prov 9:10). But thinking and rationality need not come apart. God has intervened in our condition, revealing truth to us in the Bible and is in the process of restoring our broken relationships with him and others. Further, he influences our minds and wills by the Holy Spirit, guiding us toward what is true. This is compatible with good reasoning and seeking the best evidence we can—these are tools God has given us for truth detection and baloney detection. The Holy Spirit does not lead us to truth apart from our minds and reasoning. Rather, he works *through* them, enabling us to grasp and accept truths we would otherwise be blind to because of our spiritual condition. His role is to help us think better—not less.

KNOWLEDGE

Having defined truth and belief, let's turn finally to knowledge. The classical philosophical understanding of knowledge comes from Plato, who defined it as (rationally) *justified true belief.* There is no end to qualifications and disputes about aspects of this definition, but it remains the standard understanding of propositional knowledge, and it is sufficient for our needs.[5] On this view there are three conditions for knowing a proposition to be true: (1) you must believe it to be true (belief); (2) it must be true (true belief); and (3) you must have a rational justification, or good reason, for believing it to be true (justified true belief). Note that knowledge combines the notions of true belief and rational belief. Knowledge is both true and rational. Let's consider each of these conditions.

> ***Plato*** (429-347 B.C.)—Greek philosopher, student of Socrates, teacher of Aristotle and one of the most influential thinkers of all time. He articulated his views in dialogues, usually featuring Socrates as the main character. Platonic thought had a strong influence on early Christian thinkers, especially Augustine.

The reason for (1) is evident: I can't know a proposition to be true that I don't even believe to be true. The reason for (2) may not seem so obvious, since we sometimes speak of "knowing" something that turns out to be false. The "knowing" in quotes, however, is instructive. What we mean, I think, is that earlier we were *certain* it was true, but we were mistaken. Certainty, however, is chiefly a psychological matter; it comes and goes, and it is not necessarily connected to knowledge. I can be certain there's a monster under my bed, which is false, and I can know that 7 x 19 = 133, which is true, without being certain of it. Knowledge, classically understood, implies a success condition, an actual connection to reality. I can be convinced that the world is flat, but I can't actually know the world is flat—because it isn't.

The crucial condition is (3). The Greek word Plato used for (rationally) "justified" is *logos*. It's the term that appears three times in John 1:1, translated as "word": "In the beginning was the Word [*logos*], and the Word was with God, and the Word was God." *Logos* does mean "word," but its range of meaning is wider. In fact, it's the standard Greek term for "reason." *Logos* was used extensively in classical philosophy to refer to reason, reasoning, rational explanation and rational justification. (Notice its linguistic relation to *logic*.) The New Testament uses *logos* in some of these other senses as well, as in 1 Peter 3:15: "But in your hearts revere Christ as Lord. Always be prepared to give an answer to everyone who asks you to give the reason [*logos*] for the hope that you have. But do this with gentleness and respect." To have knowledge, according to Plato, it is not enough to have a true belief. You must also have a *logos*. Why is that?

Knowledge is more than true belief. I teach at Biola University, whose president is Dr. Barry Corey. Suppose I believe that Dr. Corey is the president of Biola University. Is this a true belief? Yes; it corresponds to reality. Suppose further, however, that I actually have no idea who the president of Biola is, although I desperately want to have a true belief in this area (as a philosopher, say, I seek to have as many true beliefs as possible). I possess a list of all of the employees of Biola, and I assume, quite plausibly, that since the president of Biola University is an employee of Biola, his or her name will appear on that list. Therefore I adopt the following plan: proceeding in alphabetical order, I work my way sequentially through the list, taking one name each day. Each day I choose, that day, to believe *this* person on the list is the president of Biola University— knowing that one day I will actually get it right. Suppose, finally, that this week I am in the Cs, and today I arrive at Barry Corey's name. So today I believe that Barry Corey is the president of Biola University. (Okay, it's a bizarre example—but this is what philosophers like to do.)

Again I ask: Is that a true belief? Yes—because it corresponds to reality. But would you say that I *know* that Barry Corey is the president of Biola? No. Something is surely missing. Although I happen to have a true belief, the emphasis here is on *happen*—it's only accidental that, today, I have that belief, that I got it right. I don't have any good reasons—reasons that would justify my believing that it is true—for holding that it's Barry Corey, as opposed to someone else. I don't have a *logos*.

If having true beliefs were all that mattered, my plan would be sufficient. But it's not. When someone asks me who the president of my university is, for example, I want to be able to say who it is. I want to know who to pray for, encourage and maybe complain to. Only those beliefs I have good reasons for do I have confidence in and actually use to get around. Those are the ones I know. Knowledge is not *just* true belief; it is *justified* true belief.

Knowledge and belief. Probably most people assume that belief and knowledge are exclusive, that if you have one you cannot have the other. They represent two separate, nonoverlapping sets (see fig. 4.4).

Figure 4.4. Beliefs and knowledge: Two separate, nonoverlapping sets

But this is not the case. On the classical understanding of knowledge, everything you know, you also believe. The reverse is not true, however: not everything you believe to be true, do you know to be true. Knowledge is more than belief, but it includes it. That is, knowledge is a subset of belief.

As figure 4.5 illustrates (it is not to scale: I'm convinced that we know much more than this suggests), I believe a range of propositions to be true (outer circle). These are my beliefs. Some of them *are* true—those that correspond to reality. So within my set of beliefs is a subset of true beliefs (middle circle). Some of them just happen to be true beliefs—I don't actually have good reasons for holding them (as in my

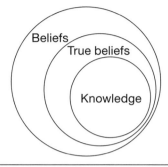

Figure 4.5. Knowledge is a subset of belief

example about Barry Corey). But others are rationally justified true beliefs—ones I have good reasons for. These are propositions that I know to be true (inner circle).

Understanding knowledge as a subset of belief enables us to recognize a further difficulty with (H), Bill's claim to have no beliefs but only scientific knowledge. Even if we grant, for the sake of argument, that Bill has knowledge of all of the propositions he holds to be true,[6] Bill still *believes* all of those propositions. Simply by virtue of having knowledge, then, Bill has beliefs—which is what (H) denies.

What counts as "rationally justified"? What exactly is required, however, before we can say that we know something? How much evidence do we need to have before our belief is rationally justified? Do we have to prove it—philosophically or scientifically? Must we be absolutely certain that it is true, beyond all possible doubt? Spelling out exactly what "rationally justified" requires is something that philosophers continue to debate, and there is no universal agreement. We can't settle matters here, but we can clear the ground by seeing what is *not* required.

Absolute proof. Do we need to prove a proposition before we can know it? It depends on what we mean by *prove*. What many people have in mind as the requirement for knowledge are grounds that are absolutely conclusive—proof that settles all disagreement, beyond all possible doubt. Let's call this *absolute proof:* proof that is capable of producing absolute rational certainty that a proposition is true. The idea is that you can't say that you know something if there remains any room for doubt about it. But very few things (if any) that we actually do know can be proved in that way.

Do I know that Barry Corey is the president of Biola University? Of course. I have very good reasons for holding it: Dr. Corey is listed as president in all of the official university literature, he presides over official functions, I have seen him introduced as president, and I have even met him and talked to him about it.

Do I know it beyond all possible doubt? No. It is *possible* that someone else is secretly president of Biola and there is a grand conspiracy to make us think it is Barry Corey. It is even possible that Martians have taken over and are deluding us! Notoriously, there exists no proof, whether philosophical, scientific or any other kind, that can absolutely rule out these possibilities. In fact, philosophers like to point out that it is logically possible (conceivable) that I am actually just a brain in a vat, hooked up to electrodes that some evil scientist has programmed to make me think everything I think, including that Barry Corey is president. There is simply no way to prove beyond all possible doubt that this is not the case.

But why should that be a problem? Is it reasonable to think that any of these bizarre possibilities is actually true? No. These are possibilities, but there is no good reason to believe any of them. For me to deny that I know that Barry Corey is Biola's president would be crazy, not to mention detrimental to my job. Radical skeptics claim that since we can't prove anything beyond all possible doubt we can't know anything at all. But why should we believe *that*? We certainly can't know *that* beyond doubt. That road is a dead end.

I agree with contemporary epistemologists who emphasize that however we spell out the requirements of rational justification for knowledge, we should start by acknowledging that we actually do know things, and quite a lot of them at that. By analyzing *how* we know those things, we can go on to develop our criteria for rational justification in knowledge. If we don't begin with what we do know—even if we don't yet know how we know it—we'll never get off the ground.[7]

Here are some things I suggest that you know, even if you don't yet know how you know them: you know that you exist, that there is an external world (it's not just an illusion), that 5 + 7 = 12, that Abraham Lincoln was shot, that Barack Obama is president of the United States, and even that torturing children for fun is wrong. I know, in addition, that Barry Corey is president of Biola University and that my wife loves me. None of these propositions can be established in the sense of absolute proof, beyond doubt, but there is no good reason to deny that we know them.

Is it because we can prove them scientifically? No, because we can't.

Scientific proof. Another requirement people commonly have in mind for knowledge is scientific proof: you can't know something unless you can prove it scientifically. True knowledge, or at least the best kind of knowledge, is scientific—apparently Bill's perspective in "I have no beliefs; I have only scientific knowledge." Not only does Bill claim that he has *only* knowledge but that *all* of his knowledge is "scientific" knowledge.

This is also confused. No doubt Bill has a great deal of scientific knowledge, which is a good thing. But not all knowledge is scientific knowledge, because not all propositions are scientific propositions for which scientific evidence is appropriate. Scientific knowledge is the rationally justified true belief of scientific propositions: truth claims about the regular workings of the physical world—the behavior of physical objects, fields and forces—that are explicable by appeal to natural laws and physical causation. Evidence for such propositions, scientific evidence, involves observation and experimentation regarding physical objects and events, and regular, natural patterns of behavior—the kind of evidence that can be quantified and tested in a laboratory. None of the propositions mentioned previously fits this description. If we have knowledge in those areas (mathematics, history, the identity of the president), as we surely do, then clearly not all knowledge is scientific knowledge.

Suppose, again for the sake of argument, that Bill has knowledge of

(H) I have no beliefs; I have only scientific knowledge.

What kind of knowledge would that be? Scientific knowledge, as he claims of all his knowledge? No, because (H) is not a scientific proposition. It does not concern the regular workings of the physical world. No experiment or appeal to natural laws could, even in principle, justify (H). This proposition is a *philosophical* proposition, a claim about belief and knowledge. That sort of proposition requires different kinds of evidence or justification altogether. In yet another way, then, (H) turns out to be not only false but incoherent. Bill's claim to have only scientific knowledge is itself something that cannot be scientifically known.

Christianity and knowledge— Philosopher Dallas Willard stresses that followers of Jesus today need to recover the historic understanding of Christianity as a knowledge tradition. The teachings of Jesus and his followers are sources of knowledge about reality, not just preferences, vague opinions or useful fictions ("faith," as it is commonly understood). Acting confidently in the real world depends on having knowledge. "Life demands a steady hand for good, and only knowledge supplies this. This is as true in the spiritual life as elsewhere."[8] *"A life of steadfast discipleship to Jesus Christ can be supported only upon assured knowledge of how things are, of the realities in terms of which that life is lived."*[9]

In order to know something, we do not have to be able to prove it beyond all possible doubt, with absolute rational certainty, nor, unless it is a scientific proposition, do we need to establish it scientifically. There is no good reason to deny that we know each of the propositions we're discussing and many more— including propositions about religious and ethical matters for which we have appropriate rational justification.

What's the bottom line? You can be much more confident about how much we can know than you probably thought. And it's important to see that opening up the scope of knowledge in the way I have just suggested does not depend on religious or theological propositions or motives. It's based on recognizing that the alternative approach is irrational: to restrict what we can know to what is proved beyond doubt or to what is scientifically established fails on its own terms. In fact it's self-refuting because *it* is a claim that can neither be proved beyond doubt nor scientifically established.

Personal knowledge. We saw earlier that truth is both propositional and personal—and that its personal aspect is most ultimate, as it is grounded in God. A similar distinction needs to be made about knowledge. So far we've spoken only of propositional knowledge, that which is expressed in knowledge statements such as "I know that it is raining outside." This, because of its importance for thinking, is our focus here. But we also speak of knowing persons—what I will call *personal knowledge.*

I have a lot of propositional knowledge about the musician Bob Dylan. I've read books about and by him, listened to his CDs, watched him on video and even seen him in concert. I know a lot about Bob Dylan. Sadly, however, I don't know Bob Dylan. I also know a lot about my wife and my friends. But, in addition, happily, I know *them*. Personal knowledge involves propositional knowledge, because you can't know a person without knowing anything about the person. But personal knowledge goes beyond this, to direct acquaintance of the person.

This distinction is particularly important in thinking well about God. Christianity is fundamentally about knowing God, which is much more than knowing that God exists or other propositions about God. Since you can't know God without knowing about him, our emphasis here on propositional knowledge still plays an important role. Indeed, the more you know about God, the better you *can* know God, just as the more you know about your friend, the better you can know your friend. But stopping with propositional knowledge is bad for relationships with God and friends. The ultimate goal of thinking well as a follower of Jesus is not the mere acquisition of propositional knowledge, but knowing and loving a Person. It is personal knowledge.

5

THINKING CONTEXTUALLY
FIND COMMON GROUND

*I have become all things to all people so that by all possible
means I might save some.*

1 CORINTHIANS 9:22

*It is absolutely disgraceful that we expect missionaries to the
Bantus to learn Bantu, but never ask whether our missionaries to
the Americans or English can speak American or English. Any
fool can write learned language: the vernacular is the real test.
If you can't turn your faith into it, then either you don't understand
it or you don't believe it.*

C. S. LEWIS, letter to *The Christian Century*

Just prior to the collapse of Communism, I taught briefly in the Soviet Union. At one point I was asked to speak at an underground church. Since my excellent translator, a Russian college student, wasn't able to accompany me, the church supplied its own interpreter. I met the new translator briefly before the service began, without checking to see how well she understood English. My lecture was to begin after the three-hour evening service concluded, but during the service I advertised it with a short teaser.

I introduced my teaser with a favorite joke that I knew worked well crossculturally—a story about a horse, which I like to embellish with animation and sound effects. As I spoke, the crowd seemed to hang on my every word. Line by line, followed by translation, I gesticulated, made noises and finally shouted my punch line: "Praise the Lord!"

Silence. The audience simply looked at me, expectantly. Knowing I was in trouble, I made a few remarks about my lecture, encouraged them to attend and hurriedly sat down.

During the break between the service and my lecture, an English-speaking Russian in attendance approached me. She informed me that the translation that was given after each line of my story bore no resemblance at all to what I said—just random, unrelated sentences in Russian. "The translation was so bad," she explained, "that the word *horse* was never mentioned." Obviously, the translator had no idea what I was talking about. As a result, neither did the audience.

THINKING CONTEXTUALLY

That night I was reminded that if we want to communicate, we need to speak the language of our audience. It's not only important for communication. Adapting to the thought contexts in which we find ourselves is essential to thinking well, more generally. This is what I mean by thinking contextually.

Our focus shifts now to thinking skills that are important to cultivate if we are to mind our faith. Thinking contextually is the first of those skills. It is essential to flourishing in college—from engaging in informal conversations with other students to participating intelligently in the classroom to dialoguing effectively with professors and other students. It's crucial for reading textbooks, examining art, watching films, and listening to music with insight and discernment.

Thinking contextually means approaching your interactions with people and ideas by striving to understand where you are and with whom you are interacting. When engaging *persons*, it's asking questions like Who am I talking to? Where is she coming from? What does she mean when she says this? What does she believe and why? What are her objections or misconceptions? Where might we find some common ground? How might I begin to build a bridge of understanding between us? Similarly, when engaging *ideas*, thinking contextually is asking questions like Where is this author coming from? What does this idea or viewpoint mean, exactly? Why does he hold this belief? What

Assumptions are underlying ideas that are not explicitly stated but are crucial for understanding those that are. Often the most important ideas are unarticulated. Thinking well involves being aware of this and asking good questions that can help bring them to the surface.

assumptions underlie it?

Being a skilled thinker is similar to being a skilled missionary. Both tasks involve asking good questions, listening carefully and thinking and learning about different languages and ways of thinking. It's especially important for followers of Jesus in the university to recognize the close connection between thinking and communicating, because in that context keeping our sanity and having an impact on other students and faculty involve both.

JERUSALEM AND ATHENS

The apostle Paul was a master of interacting effectively with people who have very different religious perspectives. In Acts 17 we see him communicate to people in two very different thought contexts. I'll call these contexts "Jerusalem" and "Athens"—names that refer to environments that are, respectively, "worldview near" and "worldview distant." We'll examine the various worldviews Paul encounters there in some more detail in chapter seven.[1] Here I'll introduce just enough to help us understand what he's doing in the two contexts, as a model for our own thinking.

In Paul's time (as today) there were two actual cities called Jerusalem and Athens. I'm using both names in a more general way to represent two kinds of thought context that correspond, roughly, to those in Jerusalem and Athens at that time. Early Christian thinkers similarly spoke of Jerusalem as representing the people of God and biblical values and culture, and of Athens, which was the academic and philosophical center of the ancient world, as standing for secular culture and pagan philosophy.

Let's specify "Jerusalem" as representing, first, an environment in which people think of God roughly along the lines that Christians (and Jews and Muslims) do: as a personal being—an agent who thinks, acts, chooses, creates and reveals himself, the creator of everything else that exists. The philosophical term for a worldview that reflects this perspective is *theism*, a term derived from the Greek word, *theos*, which means "god."

There are different forms of theism, more specific worldviews or religions that share this same general shape. All are based on a fundamental belief in a personal God, but they differ in their answers to more specific questions about who God is, how we can know God and so on. Judaism and Islam, for example, are theistic religions, although each is distinct from Christian theism (the philosophical name for the Christian worldview) in just these ways. In the university marketplace of ideas, particularly in philosophical discussions about the existence of God or "theistic belief," what is typically in view is theism as such, rather than a specific theistic religion.

Second, let's specify still further that "Jerusalem" represents *biblical* theism—a context where God is understood not only as a personal being but as the God of the Bible. Those in "Jerusalem," that is, have at least some familiarity with biblical religion and values. There is a shared way of thinking and talking about these things, among both believers and nonbelievers, that is familiar to Christian ways of thinking and talking. In this way, people and ideas in "Jerusalem" are worldview near to followers of Jesus. They speak the same language.

> "What indeed has Athens to do with Jerusalem? What concord is there between the Academy and the Church?" asked Tertullian (c. 160-c. 220), an important early Christian thinker and one of the greatest Latin writers of his time.[2]

One hundred years ago, arguably, most people in the United States lived in "Jerusalem." At that time—like the young girl who asked her father, "Daddy, are we Protestant atheists or Catholic atheists?"—even those who were not believers typically thought of God along roughly biblical lines. I've explored old American cemeteries in colonial New England and the gold-mining towns of pioneer Colorado, both areas where my ancestors lived, and I've been struck by how often the gravestone epitaphs include extensive biblical quotations and sentiments.

Times have changed. Today, not only is there far less shared biblical knowledge (among both believers and nonbelievers), the religious context is far more diverse. In fact, it's much closer to the situation faced by the early Christians. To adapt Dorothy's words to her dog in *The Wizard of Oz*, after they had been transported from Kansas to the land of Oz: "We're not in Jerusalem anymore, Toto."

Think of "Athens," by contrast, as an environment that is worldview distant: distant from biblical thought, values and language in just the ways that "Jerusalem" is near. In "Athens" another worldview besides theism is dominant, or a plurality of worldviews. In "Athens" people are largely unfamiliar with biblical religion and values. They speak a different language.

You and I live within both types of context today. If you attend a secular university, your church and campus ministry organization reflect "Jerusalem," while the thinking, language and assumptions of the university environment lie largely or entirely in "Athens." To think well, particularly as representatives of Jesus in the university marketplace of ideas, we need to be able to engage effectively in both. We need to be multilingual, to think contextually.

JERUSALEM

With these distinctions in mind, let's observe Paul in Acts 17 as he engages people and ideas in both environments. The first appears in verses 1-4.

> When Paul and his companions had passed through Amphipolis and Apollonia, they came to Thessalonica, where there was a Jewish synagogue. As was his custom, Paul went into the synagogue, and on three Sabbath days he reasoned with them from the Scriptures, explaining and proving that the Messiah had to suffer and rise from the dead. "This Jesus I am proclaiming to you is the Messiah," he said. Some of the Jews were persuaded and joined Paul and Silas, as did a large number of God-fearing Greeks and quite a few prominent women.

Obviously Paul is not in the literal Jerusalem here; he's in Thessalonica, Greece. But this is an outpost of Jerusalem: a synagogue, which is where

Jews in the first century gathered to worship when they were not at the temple in Jerusalem. And "God-fearing Greeks" were also present, non-Jews (Gentiles) who were in the process of becoming Jewish converts. They had already become biblical theists—they believed in the Bible (Old Testament) and its God, and they embraced biblical values—but they had not yet completed the process to become full-fledged Jews. Paul is in "Jerusalem."

Notice the verbs describing Paul's approach, as he seeks to communicate with these people about Jesus: *reasoned*, *explaining* and *proving*. These were common terms of Greek philosophical discourse at the time, and they imply rigorous, rational thinking and argumentation. Notice also that Paul reasons with these people "from the Scriptures" in making his case. Why does he start there? Because his audience is in "Jerusalem": they speak the same, biblical language as Paul. They know and believe the Bible and are looking for the coming of the Messiah. All this is common ground between Paul and his audience. So he takes what they already believe and reasons with them about it, helping them to discover that Jesus fulfills what the Bible teaches about the Messiah. Paul starts where they are, speaks their language and builds a bridge to where they need to be: Jesus.

ATHENS

Later in Acts 17 we find Paul in a very different context: Athens—both literally and in the sense in which we are using the term.

> While Paul was waiting for them in Athens, he was greatly distressed to see that the city was full of idols. So he reasoned in the synagogue with both Jews and God-fearing Greeks, as well as in the marketplace day by day with those who happened to be there. A group of Epicurean and Stoic philosophers began to dispute with him. Some of them asked, "What is this babbler trying to say?" Others remarked, "He seems to be advocating foreign gods." They said this because Paul was preaching the good news about Jesus and the resurrection. (Acts 17:16-18)

Athens certainly was "full of idols." It has been estimated that there were some thirty thousand gods worshiped in Athens. According to the Roman writer Petronius, it was easier to find a god than a man there: the streets and public buildings were crammed with statues of Athena, Neptune, Bacchus, Minerva, Jupiter, Apollo and Mercury.[4] Belief in many gods represents a worldview called *polytheism*, from the Greek *poly* ("many") and *theos* ("god"). Paul is not in "Jerusalem" anymore.

Paul begins engaging the Athenians in the synagogue, where he reasoned with the Jews and God-fearing Greeks. No doubt his approach in this "Jerusalem" context is the same as we saw in Thessalonica. But Paul was not content to stay with the familiar and comfortable. He also spoke "in the marketplace day by day with those who happened to be there," in the distinctly pluralist worldview context where Athenians mixed, bought and sold goods, and proclaimed and debated their views. Here, in "Athens," in addition to engaging polytheists, Paul encounters two kinds of philosophers, Epicureans and Stoics.

> ***Epicurus*** (c. 341-270 B.C.)— Philosopher from Samos, an island in the Mediterranean Sea. He founded "The Garden" in Athens, a school and philosophical community, teaching that the world was made of "atoms" moving in the "void," or empty space.

Several centuries earlier in Athens, the leading lights of philosophy were Socrates, Plato and Aristotle. At the time of Paul, however, the two dominant philosophical schools or movements were Epicureanism and Stoicism. *Epicureans* taught that all of reality, including humans, is material or physical. Human existence ends at physical death, and pleasure is the only real good, pain the only real evil. Epicurus advocated a moderate, austere life based on these ideas, teaching that one should avoid extreme, temporary pleasures as well as painful experiences. By Paul's time, however, popular Epicureanism often reflected a kind of "Animal House," party-till-you-die philosophy, similar to the lifestyle of many university students today. Epicureanism reflects the worldview of *naturalism*, which holds that all that exists is the physical cosmos.

While Epicureanism is atheistic, *Stoicism* is deeply religious. It is not theistic, however; all of reality, according to Stoicism, including humans, is part of God. God is not a personal being who creates, chooses or acts, but is a kind of rational principle that suffuses or envelopes the universe with *logos* or reason. This picture corresponds, roughly, to the worldview of *pantheism,* from the Greek *pan* ("all") and *theos* ("god"). In revised forms, both naturalism and pantheism are alive and well in the Athens of today's university.

> **Zeno** (344-262 B.C.)—Philosopher from Cyprus, founder of Stoicism. Its name comes from the *Stoa Poikilê* ("painted colonnade") in Athens, an open gallery with limestone columns at the front and painted panels at the back, where Zeno taught his disciples. Roman Stoics include Seneca, Epictetus and Marcus Aurelius.

PAUL ON MARS HILL

> Then they took [Paul] and brought him to a meeting of the Areopagus, where they said to him, "May we know what this new teaching is that you are presenting? You are bringing some strange ideas to our ears, and we would like to know what they mean." (All the Athenians and the foreigners who lived there spent their time doing nothing but talking about and listening to the latest ideas.) (Acts 17:19-21)

The Epicurean and Stoic philosophers Paul encountered in the marketplace now invite him to address what we might call the "Athens Philosophical Society." The Areopagus Court was a kind of intellectual clearing-house, a high-level marketplace of ideas in philosophy, morality and religion. It may have originally met on a hill in Athens, associated with Ares, the Greek god of war and thunder. (*Areopagus* means "hill of Ares"; since the Roman counterpart of Ares is Mars, it is also referred to as "Mars Hill.")

The verses that follow are an abbreviated record of Paul's lecture to these intellectuals. But it is extensive enough for us to catch the flavor of how he thought and communicated in this kind of context. Of course, what Paul says here applies most specifically to the task of communicating a Christian worldview within a pluralistic, "Athens" context. But we can also learn from him about how to engage people and ideas—thinking well—more broadly.

Points of contact. Let's see what else we can learn from Paul.

> Paul then stood up in the meeting of the Areopagus and said: "People of Athens! I see that in every way you are very religious. For as I walked around and looked carefully at your objects of worship, I even found an altar with this inscription: TO AN UNKNOWN GOD. So you are ignorant of the very thing you worship—and this is what I am going to proclaim to you. (Acts 17:22-23)

Notice how Paul does *not* begin. We know from verse 16 that Paul was "greatly distressed" by the idolatry of Athens. Yet he doesn't begin his address by immediately confronting and rebuking idol worship: "I see that in every way you are very religious. You certainly are, you bunch of depraved, blasphemous idolaters! Turn or burn!" In fact, rather than using the word *idol* in his initial description, Paul chooses a more neutral term *objects of worship.*

Paul is thinking contextually: he wants to *communicate* with his audience, not just talk. He cares about the people he's engaging; he wants to build bridges. He begins by finding a point of contact with them, something they hold in common. "I can see that you are very religious." In today's language Paul might say: "I can see that you're interested in spiritual things. Great—so am I. Let's talk about it."

Points of contact differ from person to person and perspective to perspective—from context to context. Finding common ground begins with looking and listening, seeking to identify ideas, commitments, interests or beliefs that we may share. Paul's statement here is not a bad place to start in seeking spiritual common ground today. Although many folks are suspicious of Christianity, they are often deeply interested in what is "spiritual." I have found that asking someone if he or she is interested in spiritual things often leads to a meaningful conversation.

The value of finding common ground goes beyond introducing a Christian worldview. If you want to understand another person or even grasp an idea, seek to identify something (commitments, assumptions, definitions, ideas, convictions, beliefs) you have in common. In a conversation, usually the best place to start is by asking questions. Often it's easy. If you're in a class with someone, play on the same intramural team, live in the same dorm or like the same music, you already share something. Begin there, ask some questions, be genuinely interested in what they think, and use that as a starting place for further discussion. If it's an idea or perspective you're trying to

Questions to establish points of contact:
- Have you ever had a spiritual experience?
- What is your take on this whole God question? What do you think God is like?
- What do you think life is about?
- What is the most significant thing that has happened to you in the last month?[4]

understand, in a book or film, you obviously won't get direct answers to your questions. Still, strive to put yourself in the author's shoes and seek to understand why she says what she says—even if you know you may not ultimately agree with her.

Learning from Nietzsche. My first graduate philosophy seminar in a secular university was on the thought of Friedrich Nietzsche, the atheist philosopher famous for asserting that "God is dead," and that, as a result, there is no objective meaning, truth or goodness. Perhaps more consistently and insightfully than any other thinker, Nietzsche thought (and lived) out the consequences of atheism. I knew, of course, that I would find much to disagree with in his views, but I wanted to understand him and his impact more fully. This particular seminar on Nietzsche, however, I took because it was taught by a Nietzschean—a scholar who not only mastered what Nietzsche wrote but passionately embraced it, with tragic personal results. I had little desire to follow the pattern of this professor's life, but I knew that learning from him would give me an unequalled chance to grasp Nietzsche. And I was right. What I learned has served me well, not only in my work as a philosopher but also for understanding others who, like Nietzsche, believe that life is meaningless. I don't recommend this particular strategy to just anyone, regardless of their background and maturity (I was older and well established in my faith when I did this). But I do commend the principle: To understand a work or idea, do your best to understand where the author is coming from and why he says what he says. Seek common ground.

Points of need. Paul not only establishes common ground with his audience, but he also uncovers a point of need that they at least implicitly recognize. Perhaps scanning the altars surrounding him as he spoke, Paul points to one of them, an image devoted to an "Unknown God," and he uses it as a bridge into a discussion of what God is like. The existence of such an altar indicates a desire among the Athenians to know (and reveals their awareness that they don't yet know) truth about God.

> *Friedrich Nietzsche* (1840-1900)— Considered by many to be the most influential thinker on the twentieth century, the philosophical father of nihilism, existentialism and philosophical postmodernism. Although not anti-Semitic himself, Nietzsche's views (along with Darwin's) significantly influenced Adolf Hitler and the Nazi movement.

There is evidence of more than one such altar in ancient Athens. Why did they build altars to an unknown god? As polytheists, the Greeks sought to appease the gods through various sacrifices and ritualistic practices in order to secure protection from disease and famine. In the aftermath of a plague or disaster, according to ancient historian Diogenes Laertes, Athenians constructed altars to as yet unknown gods in order to cover their bases, as we say, in case they had inadvertently missed any.[5] Such altars also likely reflected a sense among at least some Athenian thinkers that beyond the many finite deities of Greek religion, there must be a more ultimate God who is responsible for the existence of the cosmos and humankind, an as yet "unknown" God.

Building bridges. Paul builds on the latter possibility, appealing to what we might think of as theistic intuitions or a basic awareness of a personal God on the part of his audience. He is confident that the idea of a Creator is plausible to them, that they sense the need for such a God to explain the existence and nature of the world. Paul had philosophical grounds for thinking this, since some of the Greek philosophers, particularly Plato, had expressed and developed theistic or quasi-theistic ideas.[6]

Paul also had theological reasons for thinking this, which he spells out in his letter to the Romans:

> What may be known about God is plain to them, because God has made it plain to them. For since the creation of the world God's invisible qualities—his eternal power and divine nature—have been clearly seen, being understood from what has been made, so that people are without excuse. (Rom 1:19-20)

From a biblical perspective, because we are created by God and live in a God-created world, each of us has a sense that there is a Creator to whom we are all accountable, and for whom we were made. Our deepest longing, even when we resist it, is to be rightly related to our Creator.

Paul builds on these intuitions by unpacking their logical implications. He says to the Athenians, in effect: "You and I have the idea of an ultimate God, whom, you admit, you don't know. Let's explore that idea. Suppose there is a God who is responsible for the creation of the cosmos and human beings. What must he be like? What are the implications for knowing and worshiping him?"

> "God himself, to prevent any man from pretending ignorance, has endued all men with some idea of his Godhead, the memory of which he constantly renews and occasionally enlarges, that all to a man being aware that there is a God, and that he is their Maker, may be condemned by their own conscience when they neither worship him nor consecrate their lives to his service."
>
> JOHN CALVIN (1509-1564)[7]

In Paul's actual words:

> The God who made the world and everything in it is the Lord of heaven and earth and does not live in temples built by hands. And he is not served by human hands, as if he needed anything. Rather, he himself gives everyone life and breath and everything else. From one man he made all the nations, that they should inhabit the whole earth; and he

marked out their appointed times in history and the boundaries of their lands. God did this so that they would seek him and perhaps reach out for him and find him, though he is not far from any one of us. "For in him we live and move and have our being." As some of your own poets have said, "We are his offspring." (Acts 17:24-28)

Paul starts with what they already understand, at least implicitly, and goes on to suggest a better explanation, to tell a bigger, truer story of reality—one that acknowledges and builds on the truth that they already grasp, but also corrects the confusions and tensions in their view and fills in the gaps of what they do not yet grasp.

Points of tension. Although it follows from what Paul says here that idolatry is deeply mistaken, note that he initially communicates this indirectly—not by preaching against idolatry, but by reasoning together with them about theism and its logical implications. By exploring the theistic intuitions they share and developing them further than they themselves had done, Paul uncovers a point of tension within the Athenians' own perspective: if there is a Creator God, idolatry makes no sense. Later Paul draws the explicit inference that idolatry is not only mistaken but an offense to the true God. At this stage, however, he simply surfaces the tension embedded within their worldview. When they recognize it, they will sense yet a further need to understand what is true about God.

Every perspective that is not entirely true includes tensions, fault lines and soft spots. Often these are not evident to those who hold the view, either because they haven't fully thought them through or because they have repressed them. The tensions tend to be implicit rather than explicit. This is true of all of us, in every area of thought, not just in relation to the gospel: if we are satisfied with our own views and see no reason (yet) to call them into question, we'll tend not to consider the alternatives seriously.

This is why it seldom helps to blast away at such things immediately, by condemning what is false. Our commitment to our own view and our desire to protect ourselves naturally pushes us to build a protective wall against such attacks. It is better to build on the common ground and need that have already emerged in the conversation by allowing the implicit tensions to surface in a natural, logical way. In the interest of truth we do people a favor when we gently help them test aspects of their own position. Thinking well also means that we examine our own views and are honest when we see they are mistaken.

Speaking their language. Paul's approach was neither to accept everything others believe, so as to avoid offending anyone, nor to condemn every idea that does not come directly from a Christian source. For Paul, "all truth is God's truth." This is evident in that although everything Paul says here is biblical (it is consistent with what the Bible teaches), he doesn't quote or refer to the Bible. Unlike the "Jerusalem" audience, those on Mars Hill neither knew nor believed the Scriptures. Paul does, however, cite other thinkers: pagan poets—the philosophers Epimenides, Aratus and Cleanthes—whom the Athenians did know and believe. (At that time, popular philosophers often expressed their ideas in poetry, just as many of today's most influential thinkers are screenwriters, novelists and composers.) Obviously Paul didn't agree with everything these thinkers said. But he recognized that they got some ideas right, and he was ready to appeal to those in making his case, in order to build further bridges between his audience and the gospel.

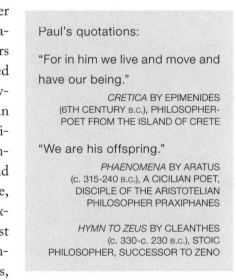

Paul's quotations:

"For in him we live and move and have our being."
CRETICA BY EPIMENIDES (6TH CENTURY B.C.), PHILOSOPHER-POET FROM THE ISLAND OF CRETE

"We are his offspring."
PHAENOMENA BY ARATUS (c. 315-240 B.C.), A CICILIAN POET, DISCIPLE OF THE ARISTOTELIAN PHILOSOPHER PRAXIPHANES

HYMN TO ZEUS BY CLEANTHES (c. 330-c. 230 B.C.), STOIC PHILOSOPHER, SUCCESSOR TO ZENO

Paul could cite these thinkers because he had studied them. He knew what people in the Athens context, including the intelligentsia, believed and why they believed it. He had thought through their worldview(s) as well as his own, and he was prepared to engage with them on their turf, in their language. Some scholars hold, in fact, that Paul used technical, philosophical language here that may have been difficult for someone of Semitic origin like Paul (a Jew, raised speaking Hebrew and Aramaic) even to articulate.[8] In any case, Paul went out of his way to understand the thinking of people outside of his own thought context and to speak to them in ways that they could understand.

Tying the knot. Paul concludes by tying the logical knot in his argument. He draws the explicit conclusion that, if there is a true, personal, Creator God, idol worship is false worship.

> Therefore since we are God's offspring, we should not think that the divine being is like gold or silver or stone—an image made by human design and skill. In the past God overlooked such ignorance, but now he commands all people everywhere to repent. For he has set a day when he will judge the world with justice by the man he has appointed. He has given proof of this to everyone by raising him from the dead. (Acts 17:29-31)

Note that even here Paul does not conclude by drilling home the inadequacies of their worldview. As in the earlier "Jerusalem" context, Paul points to Jesus.

When we engage others concerning the Christian worldview and the gospel, it is important for us to keep in mind that Jesus is always the central issue. It may be important or even necessary to answer objections or to appeal to evidence, but we do this in order to clear the path so others can consider Jesus. Apologetics is always a road, never a destination. The destination is always Jesus.

PUTTING IT TOGETHER

Let's summarize what we've seen in Paul's example and apply it to thinking well in the university as followers of Jesus. First, Paul's was a rational faith, which he expressed in reasoning with those around him. In Paul's day, no less than in ours, educated people cared about truth and thought about what they believed. Paul welcomed this and was ready to engage at that level.

Second, Paul thought contextually. Though his ultimate goal was the same in each context, he used different languages and appealed to different reasons to make his case. He cared enough about people to tailor his starting points and choose his language and reasons in that light.

This was possible, third, because Paul was intellectually prepared: he did his homework. He thought through what he believed and why he believed it, and was prepared to articulate it confidently and reasonably in different situations, to different people. But Paul also studied what others believe and why they believe it. He was conversant in the major philosophical positions of the day. He understood where he could find common ground with such positions and was prepared to use those as starting points to build bridges to the gospel. He also understood the points of tension and weaknesses of other views, and was prepared to show, rationally and gently, where they went wrong. Paul obviously read widely. He was a thoughtful, curious, inquisitive student of his culture and the thought contexts around him—as well as, obviously, a devoted student of the Scriptures.

There was only one Paul, of course; no one else has his gifts, personality or calling. But there is also only one you, with your unique package of gifts, personality and calling. During your time in the university context and beyond, seek to cultivate at least some of Paul's approach by doing the kinds of things he did.

Read, read, read—in community. How do you go about preparing to engage different contexts? I have two specific suggestions here. First, work on understanding the ideas and movements that shape the thinking and lives around you. Being in college helps, because that's the point of many of your classes. You are assigned to read and consider things you never would, left to yourself. But don't just wait for it to happen. Take the initiative to read widely, both academically and culturally. If possible, enroll in courses outside your major. Become familiar with films, music and art—both classical and current, both high and popular culture. Not merely as a passive consumer but as an informed and thoughtful student of the whole human enterprise. Of course, you need to be wise as you do so; the point is to think well.

But none of us is sufficient to do this alone. My second suggestion is to do it in community. With a few friends who share your vision, help one another in this quest. Hold each other accountable, encourage each other, share ideas and good resources (books, authors, websites, courses to take), and work together to seek answers to the hard questions that will inevitably come up as you explore alternative worldviews and viewpoints. *Mind Your Faith* can provide a starting point for this; you could read and discuss this book together, and use the MindYourFaithBook .com website and links as part of your ongoing quest.

Your Mars Hill. In many ways the "Athens" context available to you as a wired college student today is far richer and more diverse than what Paul encountered. Your Mars Hill may include a blog or website, where, with the click of a mouse, you can engage individuals and ideas from all over the world. Like the students down the hall, in your classes and at Starbucks, most of those individuals live in "Athens." As he did for Paul, may the Holy Spirit give you wisdom as you reason together with them, loving them enough to find common ground, speaking their language and building bridges to Jesus. As you think contextually.

THINKING LOGICALLY

ASK GOOD QUESTIONS
AND GIVE GOOD REASONS

"But what about you?" he asked. "Who do you say I am?"

MATTHEW 16:15

All opinions are not equal. Some are a very great deal more robust, sophisticated, and well-supported in logic and argument than others.

DOUGLAS ADAMS

According to philosopher Dallas Willard, Jesus is "certainly the greatest thinker of the human race," who "constantly uses the power of logical insight to enable people to come to the truth about themselves and about God from the inside of their own heart and mind."[1] In fact, Willard goes so far as to call Jesus a "logician." He doesn't mean by this that Jesus worked out detailed logical theories, any more than he propounded theories of particle physics. "When I speak of 'Jesus the logician,'" says Willard, "I refer to his *use* of logical insights: to his mastery and employment of logical principles in his work as a teacher and public figure."[2] Jesus thought logically.

In the strict sense, logic is the study of arguments and the structure of rational inference. However, being logical can also refer more broadly to thinking rationally—thinking that is coherent, that corresponds to the structures and rules of logic. Along these lines Paul strikingly describes worship as "logical": "Therefore I urge you, brothers and sisters, in view of God's mercies, to offer your bodies as a sacrifice—alive, holy, and pleasing to God—which is your reasonable expression of worship" (Rom 12:1, my translation). The Greek term translated "reasonable" is *logikos*—from *logos*, the standard word for reason in Greek philosophy. It means "reasonable," "rational" or, literally, "logical."[3] Paul reminds us that, given what God has done for us, offering ourselves to him in grateful worship is the only logical response—the most reasonable thing we could do. It is rational in a further way, which Paul spells out in the subsequent verse: this whole-life worship is expressed in our being transformed by the "renewing of our mind." Thinking rightly about reality changes our lives. Ideas have consequences.

THINKING LOGICALLY

When I speak of "thinking logically," the thinking skill that is our focus in this chapter, I have both broader and narrower senses in mind: thinking rationally, but with an emphasis on the basics of logic. Thinking logically is close, careful reasoning with terms that are clear, truth claims that are rationally justified, and arguments that are logically valid—tight, clear, coherent reasoning. Thinking logically is expressed in two basic activities: analysis and argument— the A-Team of good thinking. *Analysis* comes from a Greek term that means to pull apart. In this context it refers to critical thinking about ideas and arguments, breaking them down into their parts and

> **Logic for pastors** — "Some knowledge of the sciences also, is, to say the least, equally expedient. Nay, may we not say, that the knowledge of one (whether art or science), although now quite unfashionable, is even necessary next, and in order to, the knowledge of Scripture itself? I mean *logic*. For what is this, if rightly understood, but the art of good sense? of apprehending things clearly, judging truly, and reasoning conclusively? What is it, viewed in another light, but the art of learning and teaching; whether by convincing or persuading? What is there, then, in the whole compass of science, to be desired in comparison of it?"
>
> JOHN WESLEY,
> "AN ADDRESS TO THE CLERGY"[4]

examining them. *Argument*, by contrast, refers to putting ideas together to construct a coherent position. Put differently, analysis is asking good questions, and argument is giving good reasons.

Analysis. In college I was on the speech and debate team. During my senior year we held a research weekend at a mountain cabin. I arrived after others had eaten dinner, so I went to the kitchen to make a sandwich. As I was eating, an eager freshman debater, Greg, came in, wanting to talk. He asked, "Are you Dave Horner?" "That's right." "I hear you're a Christian." "That's right." "What's a Christian?"

My heart sank. For several years a cult group on campus had wreaked havoc among younger believers, convincing them that they weren't really Christians and that they needed to join this group in order to find true Christianity. The question at issue was, What is a Christian? So when Greg asked that question, I was sure where the conversation was headed. And Greg was an aggressive debater, so I anticipated a real fight. Weighing my words carefully, I produced as airtight a definition of *Christian* as I could, using every complicated theological term and distinction I knew (or pretended I knew), to cover every possible base.

Greg's response? He looked mystified and asked a few more questions. Finally the light began to dawn on me. "Wait a minute," I said. "Are you asking me what a Christian is because you want to *become* a Christian?" He replied, "Yes!"

Silently berating myself for being an idiot, I responded, "Oh! Okay, let's find a more private place." We went outside, talked through the gospel, and Greg ended up praying with me to commit his life to Jesus.

I learned my lesson. Based on what I assumed was Greg's question, I had launched into my own agenda—answering questions he wasn't asking, and not answering the crucial question he *was* asking. We were ships passing in the night. I should have thought contextually and begun by asking a few questions of my own.

What would Jesus—and Socrates—do? Asking good questions is at the heart of analysis, the first "A" in the A-Team of thinking logically. Two of history's greatest thinkers, Jesus and Socrates, are known for their skill in asking good questions. Socrates' approach to philosophy is known as the "Socratic method": seeking truth by asking questions and following the evidence where it leads.[5] Jesus also is known for asking penetrating questions, ones that cut to the heart of what is important and challenge his hearers to examine their own assumptions and motives.

In Mark 11:27-33, a group of religious leaders seek to trap Jesus about the authority he claimed for his teaching. It was a big issue for them, as they were considered the religious authorities of their time. They established *their* authority by appealing to the rabbinic traditions of biblical interpretation that preceded them. But Jesus' approach to teaching and living was quite different, and it represented a challenge. So they confronted him: "By what authority are you doing these things?" they asked. "And who gave you authority to do this?"

> In the Gospels Jesus is asked 183 questions. He asks 307.[6]

Certainly Jesus was capable of holding his own in a debate about authority, but his objective was different. He wanted these men to confront the real issues lurking below the surface of their challenge: their assumptions about authority and their motives in confronting him. So he responds by asking them a question.

> "The people were amazed at his teaching, because he taught them as one who had authority, not as the teachers of the law."
>
> MARK 1:22

> Jesus replied, "I will ask you one question. Answer me, and I will tell you by what authority I am doing these things. John's [the Baptist's] baptism—was it from heaven, or of human origin? Tell me!"
>
> They discussed it among themselves and said, "If we say, 'From heaven,' he will ask, 'Then why didn't you believe him?' But if we say, 'Of human origin' . . ." (They feared the people, for everyone held that John really was a prophet.)
>
> So they answered Jesus, "We don't know." Jesus said, "Neither will I tell you by what authority I am doing these things."

By asking the right question, Jesus turned the tables on his questioners, shifting the focus to what was most important.

ASKING GOOD QUESTIONS

As Jesus' followers today, unfortunately, we're not known as listeners so much as talkers—all mouth and no ears. At least that's the common perception, fair or not (often it *is* fair). In an increasingly skeptical and suspicious "Athens," we need to be sure that we are more like Jesus in this respect as well.

The practice of asking and listening helps us to understand people and ideas, so we are not ships passing in the night. As I was reminded in my interaction with Greg, there is no true communication without understanding. Asking and listening shows care and respect for others, including those with whom we disagree. And it can cultivate care and respect for them when we don't yet feel that way.

Asking questions also invites people to clarify and defend their own ideas, which is the best way for them to figure out what they actually believe and why, and to evaluate whether it's true. Pascal noted, "People are generally bet-

> *General life skill*—If you struggle with making friends, try asking thoughtful questions and listening carefully, and you'll find people drawn to you.

ter persuaded by the reasons which they have themselves discovered than by those which have come into the mind of others."[7] And if we are gracious in asking and listening to others, they may actually want to hear what we think!

A skill that takes practice and wisdom. Asking good questions is a skill that requires deliberate, consistent attention and practice. It is particularly helpful to work on this with others who are also honing their skills in thinking logically. Just as you improve your soccer game by practicing dribbling, passing and shooting, so you can work on asking questions in dialogue with others, sharpening and holding each other accountable.

As with any skill, asking questions can be abused. Don't take it to absurdity and *only* ask questions but never talk—like the rabbi who was famous for only asking questions. Someone finally asked him, "Rabbi, why do you always answer everything with a question?" To which he responded, "So what's wrong with questions?" There are times when we *need* to talk, as Jesus certainly did. We need to think through our own ideas and how to articulate them so we are ready to do so when that is appropriate. Asking good questions is not a dodge or a way to avoid speaking up; it's a way to put what we say in the right context.

Nor is it a technique for manipulating or bludgeoning people—something I want to stress in the strongest terms. Asking questions is a tool, but it's not a hammer to beat on people or ideas. It's more like a flashlight, to seek truth. We should always ask questions as Jesus did, "full of grace and truth" (Jn 1:14)—seeking truth passionately but treating people compassionately.

Asking good questions requires wisdom. One aspect of wisdom stressed in Proverbs is discernment. The Hebrew term *bîn* is translated into English, variously, as "insight," "discernment" and "understanding" (see Prov 1:2, 5-6). It derives from the same Hebrew root as the preposition *between*—it carries the idea of being able to see between things, to discern what is important or salient in the midst of complexity.[8] Like other virtues, discernment is a cultivated trait of character and intellect that is formed by habituation, by repeatedly engaging in certain practices or disciplines. The discipline of asking questions is particularly helpful, as it trains us to pay attention to people and to ideas.

Good questions. What counts as a good question depends on the situation. ("Where is the bathroom?" is a great question in some circumstances, but not in all.) In thinking logically, three kinds of questions are particularly important to learn to ask. They correspond directly to the three primary elements of Aristotelian logic introduced in chapter three: terms, propositions and arguments. The first (*What do you mean?*) aims at understanding and clarifying terms, the second (*How do you know that?*) at testing the truth or rational justification of propositions, and the third (*So what?*) at clarifying and testing the validity of arguments.[9] These are *kinds* of questions, which can be asked in different ways. I'll suggest several alternatives for each, and give a brief example of how each question might be used. I'll also suggest an additional strategic move or specific logical-thinking strategy that relates to each question.

Learn to ask these questions in discussions with people, but also as you read books, watch films, listen to music, listen to teachers and speakers, and as you formulate your own positions and write papers for classes. Ask them in practice sessions with friends as you seek together to develop your analytical skills. The examples I give here will focus on spiritual discussions, but the questions can be applied to logical thinking in general.

1. What do you mean? The aim of asking, What do you mean? is understanding: to clarify what is being said. It is the most important question of the three, because unless we understand what's being said we can't evaluate it adequately. Misunderstanding often results from people using terms in different ways, which usually reflects different assumptions or background contexts against which they are understood. In my conversation with Greg, I didn't so much misunderstand the words he used, as the context in which he was asking his question—what he *meant* in asking it.

Often we can simply ask the question, What do you mean by _____? There are other ways to accomplish the purpose as well, such as rephrasing the idea to see if we understand it:

- Are you saying that . . . ?
- Let me see if I've got this right . . .
- Could you explain . . . ?
- What I hear you saying is . . . Is that right?
- Can you give me an example?

Example. When someone says, "I believe that Jesus is God," should you slap him on the back and say, "Welcome to the kingdom, brother!"? Not necessarily. If you are in a "Jerusalem" context, where your language and assumptions are clearly shared, it may be appropriate. But in "Athens" more work needs to be done to make sure you understand. An atheist would not make this statement, of course, but the person need not be a theist, either. Someone who believes that everything is divine (a pantheist) can also affirm that Jesus is God but mean something quite different by it. As this example suggests, two people can affirm the same proposition or belief (*Jesus is God*), yet hold radically different understandings of it—because of their different underlying assumptions. Thinking logically asks more questions in order to uncover what's really going on.

In "Athens" an important question to ask here, one that can uncover your friend's basic (worldview) assumptions, is, What do you mean by "God"? The answer will help you see whether you're on the same page and indicate the direction you should take the conversation further.

Strategic move—paint a picture. When seeking to understand a new or difficult concept, it's helpful to compare it to another, more familiar one. This is the idea behind the strategic move, to "paint a picture": look for an analogy or counterexample to illustrate or test an idea or position, as a point of comparison. An *analogy* is a straightforward comparison between the idea and another (Is it like _____?). A *counter-example* can also test the idea, by considering an analogous case where it doesn't work (But what about _____?).

Doing this comes naturally in conversations, and most of us do it frequently. (Note that I am doing it right now; comparing the use of analogies to "painting a picture" is drawing an analogy.)

Sometimes people say things like, "If *you* believe God exists, then he exists for *you*." Unquestioned, this popular slogan relegates God's existence to the realm of subjective opinion rather than objective truth and knowledge, and so derails further serious thought about it. So it's important to question it—literally. First, make sure you understand what is being asserted. "What do you mean? Are you saying that God exists *only* if you believe he exists?" If the person agrees, then paint a picture, such as: "Does that work for other things, too—like taxes or traffic police?" "Do *they* only exist if I believe they exist?" (If not, why not?) Asking this encourages the speaker to reflect on his or her view and consider whether it is adequate, which is more likely to lead to a meaningful conversation.

2. How do you know that? Where the first question aims at clarifying terms, the second tests propositions—looking for evidence, warrant or good reasons. Again, we may ask for this in different ways:

- How do you know that's true?

- What are your reasons for saying that?

- Why do you believe that?
- What evidence do you have?
- Why might someone think that is the case?

As with the other questions, asking this can be taken too far. When my daughter Stephanee was about two years old, she asked: "Mommy, how much is two plus five?" Debbie replied, patiently, "Seven, sweetheart." Stephanee responded, "Very good, Mommy. *How do you know that?*" At that point my philosophical efforts to raise my daughter were not fully appreciated . . .

Example. "Faith is unwarranted belief"—so reads the lead statement in a guest editorial about religious faith.[10] Indeed, it serves as the author's de facto definition of faith, the starting point of his argument. Not surprisingly, he reaches the conclusion that faith is irrational. He could hardly do otherwise, when faith is so defined. But why should a reader accept this starting point? The definition needs to be challenged at the outset by asking questions: What are your reasons for saying that? Are you just defining faith this way, or do you have a rational justification for this claim? (Is this a warranted belief on your part?)

Assertions are not (yet) arguments; they need to be backed up by reasons. Winning debates by defining things in a certain way is an empty victory. Suppose I defined atheism as "The irrational belief that there is no God." It would follow logically from this that all atheists are irrational. Do you think many of them would be convinced by my "argument"? They would rightly want to know why they should accept my definition. *How do you know that?*

Strategic move—pull the rug out. A proposition is false if it does not correspond to reality. To test the correspondence of a proposition to reality, we need to identify what kind of proposition it is and look for evidence that is appropriate to that subject matter. Some propositions, however, simply *cannot* be true, and this may be evident entirely apart from exploring the reasons for or against the proposition. I'm thinking here of self-refuting propositions or positions, some examples of which we have already encountered. A self-refuting position defeats *itself*: its central claim, if true, entails that it is false. You may only hold the claim if you do not apply it to itself. Once you do, you end up having to deny it—it pulls the rug out from under itself. A bizarre but true story illustrates this.

Some years ago the American Atheist organization held its national convention in Denver (over Easter weekend), and several of us spent those days engaging attendees about their beliefs. I spoke at length with one of the atheists, Lee. During lunch I asked him, "Lee, how do you know that God does not exist?" Lee's response was unforgettable: "Because he told me so." "God told you he doesn't exist?" I asked, incredulous. "That's right," said Lee. "The Lord appeared to me in a holy vision and told me he doesn't exist."

What was the problem with Lee's view? Did he merely lack evidence? Was he simply making a factual error? No; his position *couldn't* be true. It contradicts itself. I tried, unsuccessfully, to help Lee see this (if there is no God, then he can't come to you in a holy vision; if he does come to you, then he must exist, etc.). Lee's view is self-refuting: if it is true, then it must be false. It pulls the rug out from under itself.

Few views are so transparently false. Self-refuting positions are surprisingly common, but their incoherence is usually hiding below the surface and needs to be brought into the light. Part of thinking logically is developing a nose for them, and discerning opportunities to pull the rug out.

One often hears, "Truth is relative—what's true for you is true for you; it's different for each person." Relativism about truth is another belief that, left unquestioned, undermines serious consideration of Christian truth claims (in fact, *all* truth claims). If truth is relative to individuals, then any idea is as good as any other. Which you choose to believe is simply a matter of your preference. Those who hold this are not likely to evaluate it unless they are prompted to question it.

All forms of relativism are incoherent at some level, but relativism about truth is straightforwardly self-refuting. It becomes clear when we ask the right questions: Is *that* (the claim that truth is relative) true? The speaker obviously thinks it's true or he wouldn't be asserting it. "Is it only true for you, then, or is it true for everyone?" ("If it's only true for you, why are you telling me this—since it isn't true for me? But if it's true for everyone, it must be false, since it says that nothing is true for everyone.")

3. So what? The final question is, *So what?* (Since actually saying this may easily be taken as hostile or disrespectful, some of the other ways of raising the question are often better.) It actually plays two roles in evaluating a position: determining whether it holds together logically (whether its conclusions actually follow from its premises), and determining whether it is livable (whether one can accept its implications). I'll illustrate the first role in the example below, and the second in the strategic move.

Here are some other ways of asking the question:

- What follows from that?

- How is that relevant? Explain to me how it relates to the rest of what you're saying.

- Would you explain your argument to me? How do you reach that conclusion?

- How does it follow from this . . . (for example, that God does not exist)?

- What difference does it make if this is true? What are the implications of this view?

In each case we are asking, What is the reasoning here? Does it work? Or, What does it imply?

It's not uncommon for someone, including us, to hold a position that is little more than a statement, slogan or a challenging question. We simply assume that it rests on good reasons or implies an important further conclusion—but how that actually works is never made clear. So we do ourselves and others a great service when we ask questions that bring the actual reasoning into the light, logically. That's the first role of the *So what?* question.

Example. "But science has found no more evidence for an afterlife than it has found for Santa's workshop at the North Pole."

This is another sentence from the editorial discussed previously (p. 109), the crucial move in the author's argument concerning the afterlife. The premises are not made fully explicit, but the conclusion is obvious: belief in an afterlife is irrational—because science has not found evidence for it. Believers may be tempted to respond by searching for scientific evidence or reaching for other apologetic arguments or evidence. But this would miss the essential issue: the underlying assumption that if science does not provide evidence or proof of a position, it is unwarranted. As with other views we've noted, this assumption derails serious consideration of Christian truth claims because it renders all propositions that are not strictly scientific in nature—including religious and moral propositions in general—out of the realm of objective truth, knowledge and rationality. It needs to be questioned.

The assumption is called *scientism*. In its strongest form, scientism holds that only what science can measure (the physical, material cosmos) exists, and only what science can establish (what can be, in principle, quantified and tested by scientific means) is true or can be known. Weaker forms of scientism qualify this claim in various ways. To keep it simple, we'll just speak of scientism in its strong form: the claim that a proposition or theory is true or rationally acceptable only if it is a scientific proposition or theory, one that is verifiable by reference to physical laws, according to scientific methodology.[11]

I suspect that most people hold to scientism because they assume it to be the "scientific" view: if you are committed to the value of science, you are thereby committed to scientism. But this does not follow. First, science and scientism are not the same. Scientific observation and experimentation—science—is empirical in nature, concerned with physical objects and events, and regular, natural patterns of behavior. Scientism, however, is not an empirical matter, even in principle. It is not a discovery of science or a scientific theory but a philosophical view *about* science and the nature and limits of knowledge. Second, scientism does not follow logically from science. For science to be possible, there must be a physical world, a natural order. But that natural order need not, as scientism claims, be all there is to reality. The question whether the physical universe is all that exists is philosophical, not scientific. It can't be settled by scientific investigation *within* the natural order, any more than exploring California, however thoroughly, could settle the question of whether or not anything exists outside of California. Third, it's a logical error to infer from the fact that science is a *good* source of knowledge, with which we may all agree, that science is the *only* source of knowledge—as if, since soccer is a good form of exercise, it must be the only one. It does not follow.

In fact, not only is scientism not "the scientific" view, it's demonstrably false.[12] Most important to us here is that scientism is self-refuting. Its central claim is that a proposition is true or rationally acceptable only if it is a scientific proposition, one that is verifiable according to scientific methodology. But *that* proposition is not a scientific proposition that is verifiable according to scientific methodology. Considered solely on its own grounds, scientism is not true or rationally acceptable.

Since scientism is the crucial, hidden assumption in the previous "argument" against believing in an afterlife, it needs to be brought to the surface and questioned. True, scientific experimentation has not confirmed an afterlife—because it's not a scientific question. By its nature, the afterlife is *after* this life—

> "The theorist who maintains that science is the be-all and end-all—that what is not in science textbooks is not worth knowing—is an ideologist with a peculiar and distorted doctrine of his own. For him, science is no longer a sector of the cognitive enterprise but an all-inclusive world-view. This is the doctrine not of *science* but of *scientism*. To take this stance is not to celebrate science but to distort it by casting the mantle of its authority over issues it was never meant to address."
>
> NICHOLAS RESCHER[13]

beyond the present natural order and the scientific measurements we make to describe the regular operations of things within that order. (Questions about what exists at the North Pole, by contrast, do concern the present natural order.) With the explicit premise of the author's argument we can fully agree.[14]

Here is where it is important to ask, *So what?* What follows from this? The author's (implicit) conclusion is that belief in an afterlife is irrational. But why should we think that? It only follows if we accept the unstated premise that scientific evidence is the only kind of evidence that counts—scientism. Since scientism is false, the argument falls. That's not yet evident, however, because the crucial premise is hidden. It's unstated, and so unexamined. Until the author questions it, he's not going to take Christian truth claims seriously.

How can we bring the scientism to the surface? The actual reasoning needs to be drawn out by asking questions. Here's an imaginary conversation with the author:

> "But science has found no more evidence for an afterlife than it has found for Santa's workshop at the North Pole."
>
> "Yes, that's true. But so what? What follows from that?"
>
> "Then you shouldn't believe that there is an afterlife."
>
> "Really? Why not?"
>
> "Because there's no scientific evidence for it."
>
> "But how is that relevant? . . . Are you saying that we should only believe what science can establish?"
>
> "Yes, I am."
>
> "Hmm, I see. Do you believe that?"
>
> "What?"
>
> "That we should only believe what science can establish."
>
> "Yes."
>
> "Oh. Can science establish that?" ("Which experiment would that be?")

Strategic move—take the roof off. Asking *So what?* also helps to uncover and test the actual implications of a position. This is its second role, and the point of the strategic move "taking the roof off"—a phrase that comes from Francis Schaeffer.[15] Schaeffer established a Christian intellectual community called L'Abri in Switzerland in the 1960s, where seekers and doubters from all over the world came to think and explore the Christian worldview. He stressed the need to test the "real life" or existential consequences of ideas in the life of one who holds them, to see whether they actually worked—whether one would want to or even *could* live them out consistently. We can hold false positions quite comfortably as long as they are insulated from reality. But if someone "takes the roof off" our view and exposes it to the elements, we are forced to deal with what it actually amounts to. A good way to do this, to expose a position to the elements, is to draw out its implications—logically, practically and morally. If we recognize that what is implied by our view is unacceptable, we will feel the logical pressure to change it.

Asking *So what?* questions can play this role. "You believe this is true. So what? Have you thought about the practical or moral implications of your view?" "What if your view is true? What follows, in that case?" "Do you live consistently with that?" A surprising number of comfortably espoused positions manifest deep weaknesses when we draw out their implications. An example is individual moral relativism (or subjectivism): "Morality is relative to individuals. They should be able to do whatever they want to do. What's right for you is only right for you, and you shouldn't impose your morality on other people."

Among the deep problems with this common perspective is that no one actually lives—or *could* live—consistently with it. I may well want to be a moral relativist, myself, but I certainly don't want others to be. This emerges when we take the roof off and unpack its implications. "Do you really want everyone to live this way, to do just whatever they want to do? Including Hitler, say? Or me? What if what's 'right' for me—what *I* want to do—is to impose my morality on you?" ("Are you saying I can't do that? Are you trying to impose your morality on me?")

When I had a class of students who were particularly drawn to relativism, I decided to take the roof off in a graphic way. I returned their graded writing assignment with an "F" on the front page of all the best papers (the true grade was in tiny print on the back of the paper). Handing them back to the devastated students, I pointed out that, quite frankly, I was disappointed in many of the papers. "They were well-written, grammatically tight, and logically persuasive. But I failed them. Any questions?"

Hands shot up. "Why did you fail them?"

"Because I didn't like the font you used," I replied. (I was making it up as I went.)

Several students frantically searched the course syllabus. "You didn't state that we should use any particular font."

"Well, I never know from day to day which font I'll like, so why would I put it in the syllabus?"

"You can't do that!"

"Sure I can. I'm the professor."

"But that's not fair!"

"*Fair?* Are you asking for *objective* moral standards now?"

"Welcome to the world of relativism," I went on to say. "This is what it actually looks like when we reject objective truth and value. There is nothing left to appeal to but preferences and power. Relativism sounds cool and edgy in the abstract, but in reality it's unlivable."

They got the point!

ARGUMENT: GIVING GOOD REASONS

The A-Team of thinking logically is analysis and argument: asking good questions and giving good reasons. We've examined the former; more briefly, let's consider the latter. Analysis aims at testing and evaluating terms, propositions and arguments; argument moves in the other direction. It aims to construct positions whose terms are clear, whose propositions are rationally justified, and whose arguments have a valid logical structure.[16] Argument is giving good reasons.

In chapter three I introduced the concept of an argument with this example:

If it is raining, then the streets are wet.
It is raining.
Therefore, the streets are wet.

An argument like this is a *logical structure:* a sequence of premises and a conclusion, which are organized in such a way that the conclusion "follows" logically from the premises. Assuming the premises to be true, the conclusion *must* be true—its truth follows logically from the truth of the premises. This is the case with any (deductive) argument that is logically valid.

Building on this, let's distinguish between *good* arguments and *bad* arguments. Good arguments are ones that work, where the conclusion "follows logically" from the premises—the premises support or underwrite the conclusion. Bad arguments don't work; the conclusion "does not follow" logically, from the premises. (The Latin phrase *non sequitur* means, literally, "it does not follow.")

Good arguments. There are two kinds (or two strengths) of good arguments.[17] The most basic kind of good argument, with which logic is primarily concerned, is a *valid* argument. Logical validity is a function of the form or shape of an argument. As I write these words, thankfully, I have a coffee mug in front of me, full of coffee. The mug has a particular shape. I can fill it with coffee, tea or any other liquid—or even with something like sand—and it will conform to the shape of the cup.

Logic is primarily concerned with the cup—the *form* of an argument—and only secondarily with the material poured into it, that is, with the specific *content* of the propositions that make up an argument's premises. For this reason logical arguments are often expressed in symbols that stand for the varying values that appear in specific arguments. The symbols reveal the argument's form.

For example, take the form of our simple argument:

If it is raining, then the streets are wet.
It is raining.
Therefore, the streets are wet,

It may be expressed in this way:

If P, then Q.
P.
Therefore, Q.[18]

In this case P (the antecedent) = *it is raining* and Q (the consequent) = *the streets are wet*. But any content could be "poured into" an argument of this form (it does not have to be about rain or streets), and it would remain the same *kind* of argument, logically speaking. In this case, the argument form is logically valid (the form is called *modus ponens*): whatever content you use to replace P and Q in an argument of this form, it will always be the case that *if* the premises are true, the conclusion *must* be true. (Try this for yourself by substituting different values for P and Q. You should be able to see that in each case if the premises are true, the conclusion must be true.)

By contrast, consider this argument:

If it is raining, then the streets are wet.
The streets are wet.
Therefore, it is raining.

Test this argument by assuming that the premises are true. *Must* the conclusion be true? No—while it is possible that the conclusion is true, it doesn't have to be; the streets could be wet for some other reason, such as someone watering the lawn. This argument is *invalid*. Its form is called *affirming the consequent*, symbolized as:

If P, then Q.
Q.
Therefore, P.

Whatever the content of the premises of an argument of this form, *affirming the consequent*, the conclusion will not follow logically. Non sequitur.

A good argument is, first of all, valid in its form—its premises and conclusion are connected in the right, logical ways. An argument is still better, second, if it is *sound*—when the form of the argument is valid *and* the premises are true. The right cup and the right stuff in the cup.

Consider this argument:

If Groucho Marx is president of the United States, then we're in trouble.
Groucho Marx is president of the United States.
Therefore, we're in trouble.

Is this a valid argument? Yes—its form is *modus ponens*, so if the premises are true, the conclusion must be true. Is the first premise true? I would say yes. Is the conclusion true? It may well be. But if so, we don't know it *because* of this argument. The second premise, thankfully, is false, so it is not the case that the conclusion must be true. We are not pushed logically to accept the truth of the conclusion—on the basis of the argument. It is not logically persuasive: it does not change our minds or convince us of anything.

In the best kind of argument, then, we not only have the right, logical structure—the relations between premises and conclusions are truth preserving—but we have good reasons for holding the premises to be true. Here is where evidence comes in. If we give good reasons for the truth claims that we make, *and* if our reasoning about those truth claims holds together logically, our arguments will be most powerful. That should be our aim in giving good reasons for what we believe.

Bad arguments. Bad arguments, by contrast, *don't* work: the conclusion is not logically related to the premises in the proper way (invalid), one or more of the premises is false (unsound), or both. (Uncovering problems here is one of the key roles of the *So what?* question.) A number of characteristic logical fallacies, both formal and informal, underlie invalid arguments. Developing a nose for detecting them is important for thinking logically. We just identified one fallacy, called "affirming the consequent," and we've already examined the self-refuting fallacy in some detail.

Another important fallacy to identify is "begging the question" (Latin, *petitio principii*). It means to argue in a circle: to smuggle into a premise the very conclusion you're trying to establish. Suppose that the chief piece of evidence against Bob in a murder trial is Bob's bloody knife. Imagine that Bob's defense lawyer meets with the judge and asks her to exclude the knife as evidence against Bob in the trial. "Why should I do that?" asks the judge. The lawyer replies, "Because it's not Bob's knife." "That's certainly relevant," says the judge. "On what grounds do you say that?" "Because Bob is innocent," the lawyer responds, "so it *can't* be his knife!" Obviously, this is invalid: Bob's innocence is just what the lawyer is trying to prove! He can't help himself to that conclusion as a premise in his argument—especially in order to rule out evidence against his position. It's begging the question; that is, wrongly appealing, as a premise, to the very question of Bob's innocence. Reasoning like this is surprisingly common, although not usually so close to the surface—which is why we need to continually ask good questions.

THINKING LIKE JESUS

Most important for us, in thinking logically, is not mastering the names of these logical argument forms, although that can be helpful. It is, rather, mastering the skills involved. As Dallas Willard says of Jesus as a logician: "I refer to his *use* of logical insights: to his mastery and employment of logical principles in his work as a teacher and public figure."[19] As we strive to be like Jesus in other areas, may we also be like him in this.

7

THINKING WORLDVIEWISHLY

CONNECT THE DOTS

What is man, that thou art mindful of him? (Ps 8:4)

INSCRIBED ABOVE EMERSON HALL, Harvard University

The moment we ask about the purpose of anything, we may be involving ourselves in asking about the purpose of everything. If we define education, we are led to ask, "What is Man?"; and if we define the purpose of education, we are committed to the question "What is Man for?" Every definition of the purpose of education, therefore, implies some concealed, or rather implicit, philosophy or theology.

T. S. ELIOT, "The Aims of Education"

So *what?* is a particularly important question to ask about our deepest beliefs. Several years ago my friend, an outspoken atheist philosophy professor at a secular university, announced to his colleagues that he had become a Christian. Asked what had made the difference, he replied, "The Christians have all the fun." That's not what most of us would expect to hear! My friend had concluded that the Christian worldview was intellectually credible. But he also saw something compelling in the lives of believers—in how the truth of Christianity was lived out in their values, commitments, attitudes and actions.

The consequences of ultimate beliefs are found in the nitty-gritty of life. There really is a kind of secure, spontaneous joy—"fun"—that is deeply natural to someone who sees the world as the careful creation of a rational, good and loving God, but not to those who see it as a cosmic accident, destined only for heat death. Jean Paul Sartre, an atheistic existentialist philosopher who sought to think and live seriously and consistently with his belief system, acknowledged that it ultimately led to despair. "Atheism is a cruel and long-range affair," he wrote in his autobiography. "I think I've carried it through."[1] *So what? What difference does it make if this is true?*

This is not to say, of course, that non-Christians have no fun, or that it is wrong for followers of Jesus to struggle when going through suffering. We need only read the laments that form much of the book of Psalms to see that the Bible does not advocate a superficial, smiley-face approach to life.[2] Still, if ultimate reality is a loving God who reveals himself supremely on a cross and in an empty tomb, then it is rational to live with a settled, confident joy, even in suffering. Suffering, death and struggle are real, but they're not the final word. For followers of Jesus, such a way of life is coherent.

> "Consciously or subconsciously, explicitly or implicitly, man knows that he needs a comprehensive view of existence to integrate his values, to choose his goals, to plan his future, to maintain the unity and coherence of his life—and that his metaphysical value-judgments are involved in every moment of his life, in his every choice, decision and action."
>
> AYN RAND (1905-1982)[3]

COHERENCE

Something is coherent, literally, when it "holds together" or "sticks together"—its parts are connected, consistent with each other, and they combine to form a unified, sound structure. Coherence is something we need in order to flourish as rational beings—that our thinking, acting, values, priorities and worship fit together in a unified, consistent way.

To have coherence in our thinking goes beyond putting together terms, propositions and arguments consistently (the subject of chap. 6). Our beliefs, particularly the most basic and influential, are related to each other in still further respects. They hang together in a rough unity, a weblike structure of connected beliefs.

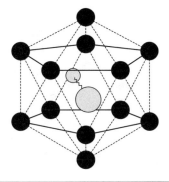

Figure 7.1. Coherence: A weblike structure of connected beliefs

The beliefs in the center are more basic and important to the web than those on the periphery, and more intertwined with the other core beliefs. To alter or eliminate a core belief produces a kind of earthquake in the overall structure.

Consider two of my beliefs. First, *It is not okay for me to lie to my wife just to get my way.* Second, *The number of moons of the planet Jupiter is greater than four.* Suppose I came to think these propositions were *not* true. How would this affect the structure of my beliefs? Switching my belief about Jupiter's moons implies little change in my other beliefs or values. But changing my beliefs about lying to my wife requires adjusting a great many beliefs about relationships, myself, my wife, truth and moral goodness. The former is more peripheral and the latter is more central to my belief structure.[4]

This picture is helpful for understanding how we actually hold our beliefs, especially about fundamental matters such as the existence of God and the meaning of life. These are not merely individual propositions we hold to be true, unrelated to other beliefs. They are essentially connected to each other in our thinking, parts of an overall structure that provides a context of meaning for each. In fact, the individual beliefs can only be fully understood and accurately evaluated in light of the structure of beliefs of which they are a part. This overall structure of beliefs is what we refer to as a *worldview.*[5]

WORLDVIEWS

Your worldview is the set of beliefs, attitudes and values that make up your orientation to the world and guide how you live your life. It's how you see "life, the universe, and everything," and live accordingly.[7] Worldviews are the largest webs or contexts of meaning in which our beliefs are found, especially our most important beliefs—our answers to the most fundamental questions about the most important things. I call these the "big questions." Our answers to them constitute the core beliefs of our worldview and give it its shape.[8]

> "A worldview is a commitment, a fundamental orientation of the heart, that can be expressed as a story or in a set of presuppositions (assumptions which may be true, partially true or entirely false) which we hold (consciously or subconsciously, consistently or inconsistently) about the basic constitution of reality, and that provides the foundation on which we live and move and have our being."
>
> JAMES SIRE, *THE UNIVERSE NEXT DOOR*[6]

Each of us inevitably lives according to some set of answers to the big questions. Often the answers are entirely implicit, unstated (and unexamined) assumptions. But some may be explicit beliefs that we have reflected on and consciously affirm. Either way, how we answer the big questions shapes our lives in their deepest dimensions—our values, our goals, our priorities, how we take tests, how we behave on dates, how we treat people, how we choose a mate, how we raise our children and more. Ideas have consequences, especially *these* ideas.

> "All beliefs are held within a context or framework of the taken-for-granted, which usually remains tacit, and may even be as yet unacknowledged by the agent, because never formulated."
>
> CHARLES TAYLOR[9]

Thinking worldviewishly is being aware of these larger structures of belief, both in ourselves and others, and thinking and acting in that light.

THE BIG QUESTIONS

Which are the big questions? Psychologist Bruno Bettelheim calls them the "eternal questions": What is the world really like? How am I to live my life? How can I be truly myself?[10] Other thinkers slice the pie differently.[11] For our purposes, three worldview questions capture what is most important.

> "Worldview . . . consists of the most general and basic assumptions about what is real and what is good—including assumptions about who we are and what we should do."
>
> DALLAS WILLARD[12]

1. What is real? Basic to every worldview is some understanding of what exists and why. Is reality exhaustively composed of physical objects and forces, or does it include the immaterial (thoughts, propositions, souls, God, etc.)? Most importantly, What is ultimate reality—the most fundamental or primary reality, which is the basis of all else that exists? Is it God, matter, nothing or something else?

2. Who are we? Every worldview represents an understanding and vision of humanity—an account of human nature, origin and meaning, and a diagnosis of the basic human problem and its solution. What is the human *telos* (Greek for "end," "aim" or "purpose")? How can humans flourish? What kind of human life is worth living?

3. What is good? Worldviews not only involve assumptions about metaphysics (the study of reality) and anthropology (the study of humanity), but also about ethics (the study of morality). What has value? What is worth desiring and pursuing? What makes it valuable? Applied to human beings: How does one become a good person?

CONNECTIONS

These big questions and their answers are essentially connected to each other. Believing that reality is only physical, for example, rules out a traditional understanding of humans as possessing nonphysical souls or minds. It also rules out the existence of good as traditionally conceived, since moral or value properties are nonphysical. The question of what makes a life worth living involves all three worldview questions. According to classical thinkers (ancient and medieval philosophers and theologians), a life worth living is one that expresses the fundamental purpose or telos of human life.[13] But what that is, or whether there is a telos at all, depends on what reality is like more generally. Are human beings intended, designed—created—or are they merely, in Bertrand Russell's words, "accidental collocations of atoms"?[14] Thinking worldviewishly sees and evaluates the connections between these questions and answers.

WORLDVIEW OPTIONS

Determining how many worldviews there are depends on the level of detail of one's analysis.[15] In one sense, because we each see the world in a slightly different way, there are as many distinct worldviews as there are individuals. But there are also *kinds* of worldviews that share a general structure based on how they answer the big questions. Each individual worldview is a more specific version of one (or perhaps a confused combination of two or more) of these kinds.

We'll limit our discussion to the four general kinds of worldview we are most likely to find in the university. We met three of them in chapter four, as they were reflected in the "Jerusalem" and "Athens" contexts Paul engaged in Acts 17. Let's briefly review and expand that picture in light of the big questions already noted.

Theism (from the Greek, *theos*—"god") is the worldview of the Jews and God-fearing Greeks Paul met in the Jewish synagogues.[16] According to theism, ultimate reality is a personal (conscious, intelligent, self-determining, active, creative, loving) God. Everything else that exists—a real universe, with physical objects, forces, natural laws and so on—was created by God and depends on God for its existence.[17]

In figure 7.2, the circle represents the cosmos (the universe or natural order—*C* stands for "cosmos"), and *G* stands for "God." According to theism, God is not a material or physical being *within* the cosmos, but an immaterial Person who is distinct in being from the cosmos, creating and sustaining it. The physical world is fully real, but reality is greater than the cosmos, more than what is physical or material. This is reflected in human nature as well: human beings are persons who, like God, are able to think, choose and love. Most theists regard humans as not exclusively physical but as possessing an immaterial mind or soul.[18] Morality, in this view, is grounded in the moral nature and will of God.

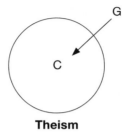

Theism

Figure 7.2. The theistic worldview

The arrow indicates that God interacts causally with (and within) the cosmos. The universe is not an enclosed "black box" operating solely on its own in an impersonal and deterministic way. Rather, God, as the Creator and Sustainer of the natural order, is actively and continually involved in its workings. Natural laws reflect God's normal ways of operating the universe. But God can make exceptions to his normal ways of operating, in order to bring about certain results. This is what occurs in the case of miracles.

In Athens Paul met Epicurean and Stoic philosophers, whose systems of thought, respectively, correspond roughly to the two most influential, nontheistic worldviews of our time: naturalism and pantheism.

According to *naturalism*, ultimate reality, indeed all of reality, is made up entirely of what is "natural"—typically understood as strictly material or physical. This includes human beings, who, in this view,

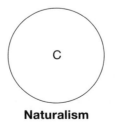

Naturalism

Figure 7.3. The naturalistic worldview

have no immaterial soul or spirit, but are solely physical entities. As figure 7.3 illustrates, there is no *G* or arrow indicating God's existence or relation to the cosmos. Astronomer Carl Sagan, a naturalist, famously asserted, "The Cosmos is all that is or ever was or ever will be."[19] There is no God, no overall creative intention or plan for the cosmos or human beings, or any transcendent or higher basis or grounding for morality. Naturalism dominates much of the university today, particularly in the scientific disciplines. Contemporary "new atheists" like Richard Dawkins and Sam Harris are naturalists.

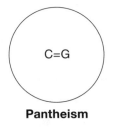

Pantheism

Figure 7.4. The pantheistic worldview

Less prominent in Western universities, but influential more broadly around the world, is the worldview of *pantheism* (from Greek, *pan*—"all"). In this view, ultimate reality, indeed all of reality, is God—though not a distinct, personal deity who thinks, chooses, acts and loves, but a nonpersonal reality that is identical to or suffuses the cosmos.

As figure 7.4 illustrates, pantheism acknowledges both God and the cosmos, but not as distinct entities, separate from each other: All is God and God is all, as it is sometimes put. For pantheists God and the cosmos are the same, seen from different angles. Strictly speaking, this is *pantheistic monism*, from the Greek word *monos*, "one." Not only is all God, all is radically *one*—there are no real distinctions, not only between God and everything else but between everything else and, well, everything else. All is God, God is all, and all is one. As there are different forms of theism (and naturalism), there are different forms of pantheism. These differences are reflected in some of the varied Eastern religions and in contemporary New Age spirituality, as well as in ancient Stoicism.

POSTMODERNISM

So far we have described the major worldviews in traditional, philosophical terms. Their names (theism, naturalism and pantheism) derive from their answer to the question, What is ultimate reality? which is a metaphysical question (about what exists). Worldviews, generally understood, are metaphysical maps of reality—descriptions of what things are, in their deepest aspects.

Many thinkers today add a fourth kind of worldview, *postmodernism*, to the list. It doesn't fit neatly into this picture (no corresponding diagram), because it's not a metaphysical perspective but an epistemological stance (epistemology is concerned with truth and knowledge). I'll say a bit more about it here, because of its current influence and because it is more difficult to describe.[20]

Postmodern can refer to different things, including art and architecture. The term is often used literally to refer to a time period with characteristic values and emphases. *Modernity*, the period from, roughly, the 1600s to the middle or end of the twentieth century, is characterized by an emphasis on science (or scientism), the individual as opposed to community, objective rationality and allegiance to metanarratives or grand ideologies like progress, democracy, capitalism or communism. *Postmodernity* is post or after modernity, and it is characterized by a rejection of these things. It emphasizes what is nonrational, experiential and communal, and it reflects an attitude of irony or suspicion toward the totalizing ideologies or metanarratives of modernity. A leading thinker of postmodern thought, Jean-François Lyotard, writes, "Simplifying to the extreme, I define *postmodern* as incredulity toward metanarratives."[21]

Our interest is in the central ideas of postmodernism—of postmodernism as a philosophy or worldview, the distinctive way of thinking reflected in the ideas of writers like Lyotard, Jacques Derrida and Richard Rorty. (This is what *postmodern* refers to in what follows.) As a way of thinking and interpreting the world, postmodernism may be considered a distinct worldview, even though it doesn't fit into the traditional categories.

Historically, postmodernism emerged from within naturalism. Its chief influence is Friedrich Nietzsche, the nineteenth-century atheist philosopher, and it represents the most recent development in a trajectory of thought beginning with Nietzsche and moving through nihilism and existentialism. The latter positions are explicitly naturalistic; they represent attempts to work out the logical implications of rejecting belief in God.[22] Postmodernism shares this history and follows its general trajectory. With postmodernism, however, there is a shift from metaphysical concerns about the nature of reality to epistemological concerns about truth and knowledge. For this reason some nonnaturalists, including Christians, have embraced postmodernist convictions.

Put simply, postmodernism is a form of conceptual relativism, a rejection of objective truth and knowledge. Postmodernists hold, typically, that all truth is relative to particular contexts: specifically, to the stories or narratives (belief systems or conceptual schemes) of particular groups or linguistic communities (groups using language in a shared way). No particular story is any truer, objectively speaking, than any other. There is no truth with a capital *T*. There are only "truths" (lowercase *t*) that are internal to, or limited to, the beliefs or language of those particular communities.

TRUTH AND TOLERANCE

In chapter eleven we'll examine how to evaluate worldviews as to their truth or falsity. But here we can consider an important part of the truth question. Thinking worldviewishly about religious beliefs helps clarify some issues that are frequently confused. We often hear that "all religions are true" or "all religions say the same thing," and that to deny this is intolerant. Let's disentangle what's correct from what is not in this perspective.

We've seen that, excluding the special case of postmodernism, worldviews are named by their answer to the most fundamental metaphysical question: What is ultimate reality—what is most real, most fundamental, which gives rise to and explains everything else there is? Is it God? Matter? Chaos? Nothing? How we answer this question defines the basic shape of our worldview and largely determines our answers to the rest of the big questions.

This can be illustrated by spelling out the major alternatives in the form of a logical tree of worldview options (see fig. 7.5). The first worldview divide concerns whether or not ultimate reality is seen as divine—whether or not there is a God (in some sense or other). *Naturalism* is the view that there is no God of any kind. If we hold that there is some sort of God(s), our views divide on further logical lines, according to whether the divine is a single, unitary deity or a plurality of deities. To believe there exist many deities is to hold the worldview of *polytheism*. The belief that God is unitary, by contrast, divides further, according to whether the divine nature is personal (having intellect and will—an agent who acts, chooses, loves, etc.) or nonpersonal. *Theism* holds that God exists and is personal. *Pantheism* holds that God exists, but is nonpersonal (not an agent, not distinct from the cosmos but identical with it). Under theism fall the different theistic religions, such as Christianity, Judaism and Islam. These differ, in turn, not in their general answers to the biggest worldview question (each is a form of theism), but in how they answer more specific questions concerning who, exactly, God is—including, most importantly, whether God has revealed himself definitively in Jesus of Nazareth.

> "More consequences for thought and action follow from the affirmation or denial of God than from answering any other basic question. They follow for those who regard the question as answerable only by faith or only by reason, and even for those who insist upon suspending judgment entirely."
>
> MORTIMER ADLER[23]

Putting this tree together makes evident that the different worldviews, however much they have in common, are importantly—indeed, logically—distinct at the most fundamental level. They represent logically different answers to the same question: What is the nature of ultimate reality?

This illustrates that statements such as "all religions are true" and "all religions say the same thing" may be well meaning, but they *cannot* be correct—as a matter of logic. This is not narrow-minded or intolerant. It's the conclusion we're driven to if we take seriously the actual

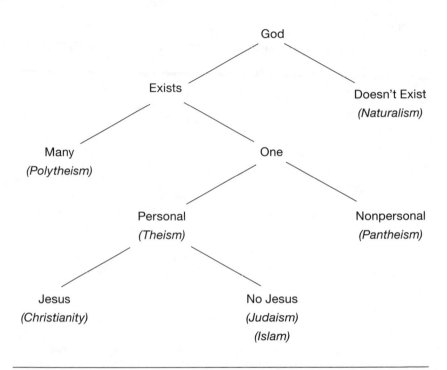

Figure 7.5. Logical tree of worldview options

beliefs of the worldviews and religions themselves. On the basis of their most fundamental truth claims about ultimate reality, not to mention other core truth claims (about, e.g., human nature, the basic human problem and how and where salvation is found), it is obvious that the different worldviews and religions do *not* "say the same thing." They differ from each other at the most fundamental level.

Because the varying core truth claims represent logically competing, mutually incompatible answers to the same questions, the different worldviews cannot all be true, *as worldviews*. If a God of any description exists, for example, the worldview of naturalism is not true, since its core truth claim is the denial of the existence of any God. And if there is no God, naturalism is true, and all of the other worldviews are false.

But don't the different worldviews and religions believe many of the same things? Yes. Although they disagree about exactly who God is, all theistic religions agree that God is personal. Because they agree in this most central truth claim, they will agree in many other areas as well. But there is significant agreement between all worldviews, theistic and nontheistic as well—especially in their specific ethical teachings (though not in their understanding of what ultimately grounds those teachings). For example, some version of the golden rule ("Do unto others what you would have them do unto you") appears in virtually all value systems, cultures and religions.[24] Facts like these, however, do not imply that all these worldviews or religions are the same or equally true.

CORE BELIEFS

Here it is important to distinguish between core beliefs and noncore beliefs. The core beliefs of a worldview are those at the center of its web—its answers to the big, worldview questions. These constitute a worldview's central truth claims, which give it its distinctive shape, making it the kind of worldview it is and distinguishing it from others. Each worldview also has noncore beliefs: truth claims that are closer to the periphery of the web. These beliefs do not define it as a worldview but are shared, to some extent, by other worldviews. Many of a worldview's particular moral views fit into this category.

This helps us to distinguish between the truth *of* a worldview as a whole, and truth *within* a worldview. Since its core beliefs are what make a worldview what it is, the truth or falsity of the worldview as a whole is determined by whether its core beliefs are true. Because there is a way reality *is*—there actually is or is not a God, for example—the different worldviews cannot be equally true, as worldviews, any more than the different answers given to question 14 on the math test can all be true. Again, this fact is a matter of logic and reality, not of religious doctrine. It holds for all worldviews, whether or not one believes in God. Among mutually incompatible propositions, at most one can be true.

A worldview that has one or more false core beliefs is not true as a worldview. But this does not imply that there is no truth *within* the worldview. All worldviews and religions must have at least some truth within them, or no one would believe them at all. (A religion that holds that 2 + 2 = 5 or that our legs grow on top of our heads, for example, will not last long.) If a personal God exists, for example, all theistic worldviews or religions will share some true core beliefs, even though the different religions cannot all be ultimately true. And all worldviews will have some, perhaps many, true noncore beliefs, such as *The world is round* and *It is wrong to torture children for fun*.

There is no reason to think, then, that if you believe one religion to be ultimately true you must hold all the beliefs of alternative religions to be false or regard all their adherents as bad. Nor, on the other hand, need you assume that if there are true ideas or good people within a worldview, then it must be a true worldview. None of these conclusions follows. We should not confuse the truth of a worldview with truth within a worldview, or the behavior of those who hold a worldview with what makes the worldview true or false (reality).

A BIBLICAL PERSPECTIVE

In fact, on strictly biblical grounds, followers of Jesus should not regard all viewpoints they differ with as entirely false, much less consider all adherents of other views as bad. We've seen that the Christian intellectual tradition proclaims that "all truth is God's truth," wherever it is found. Theologians distinguish between *general revelation*, truth that God reveals in and through creation, and *special revelation*, more specific truth that God reveals through his mighty acts, the words of the biblical prophets and the life, actions, and words of Jesus, all recorded in the Bible. Although the Bible has unique and final authority as God's specific and direct message to humankind, Christians also recognize *both* general and special revelation to come ultimately from God.

Because of general revelation, all human beings, created in the image of God and living in a

> "It is superstitious to refuse to make use of any secular authors. For since all truth is of God, if any ungodly man has said anything true, we should not reject it, for it has also come from God. Besides, since all things are from God, what could be wrong with employing to His glory everything that can be rightly used in that way?"
>
> JOHN CALVIN[25]

God-created cosmos, may reason and discover significant truth about the cosmos, themselves and even God (see Rom 1:18-20). This is true even if they hold to what is ultimately a false worldview. On Mars Hill, Paul drew true insights into the nature of God and creation from pagan philosophers. Their theistic intuitions were based in general revelation. There was truth in their worldview, even though their worldview as a whole was false. Because of general revelation, then, we should expect to find truth within other religions and worldviews.

Similarly, we should expect to find exemplary people in different religions and worldviews. Theologians also teach that all human beings share in common grace, or the benefits of God's goodness—physical and moral goods which God extends to all those he has created and cares for, even those who are alienated from him. Because they are created in God's image and share in the blessings of creation, human beings of all worldviews and religions can, to some extent, understand and embrace basic moral values and obligations, including the Golden Rule (see Rom 2:14-16). Of course, people who hold to other worldviews will not live in perfect consistency with what they know to be true—for the same reason that followers of Jesus are not perfectly consistent with their values and commitments: we are all fallen, sinful people. Being a Christian should make a significant difference in our character, but it's not a reward for being better than everyone else, much less for being perfect. Following Jesus begins with acknowledging that we're not, and placing our trust in the only One who ever was.

Christians need not fear ideas that come from outside a Christian worldview. God's truth can be discovered throughout the created order and within all the academic disciplines. We need to be discerning, however, because not all truth claims *are* true. Thinking worldviewishly, especially distinguishing between the truth of a worldview and truth within a worldview, is an important part of that discernment. Nor should we feel threatened or defensive toward those with whom we disagree. It can be liberating to realize that the truth of the Christian worldview is not determined by us but is grounded in reality. God does not depend on us for his existence! We can be confident in what we believe, but also open to engage and learn from those who disagree—to defend our faith without being defensive, "with gentleness and respect" (1 Pet 3:15).

TOLERANCE AND "TOLERANCE"

Should we be tolerant of other worldviews and religions? Yes—but we should be clear about what that means. *Tolerance*, particularly in contemporary thought, has come to mean something very different than what it referred to in the past. The popular understanding these days is that tolerance means that opinions are created equal, everyone is right in whatever they believe or practice, and no one is wrong. To think otherwise, to view anyone's belief or behavior as mistaken or false, is considered intolerant. I'll call the popular view, "tolerance" (in quotation marks). Although well-intentioned, it's a false understanding of tolerance—a bad idea that has very bad consequences. It derails serious consideration of religion, morality and worldviews as matters of objective truth, and it contributes to the anti-intellectual temper of our time.

To hold that all propositions are equally true (2 + 2 = 4, 2 + 2 = 5, etc.) is to commit intellectual suicide. Taking "tolerance" seriously means the end of education, including the university. What would be the point of learning if all beliefs, including all those the students already hold, are already equally true? In fact, "tolerance" is self-refuting. It amounts to saying it is wrong to say that anything is wrong. If true, that statement itself is intolerant and therefore wrong. "Tolerance" pulls the rug out from under itself.

TRUE TOLERANCE

But there is such a thing as true tolerance, which is not a matter of how we treat beliefs (as true or false), but of how we treat people. True tolerance is respecting people and treating them with dignity, even when we disagree with them about what is true or false. In fact, true tolerance involves respecting people enough to recognize and acknowledge such disagreement—not trying to minimize it or to claim, for example, that "all religions say the same thing" when they don't.

True tolerance is compatible with holding a strong view of objective truth, even in matters of religion, morality and worldviews. In fact, it *requires* such a view because tolerance itself is a moral value, one that only makes sense if understood as objective. To say, "I'm committed to tolerance, but I don't see it as any more true or good or important than any other idea or value, including intolerance," is not to be committed to tolerance!

As American culture becomes increasingly coarse and nasty in handling disagreements, there is an ever-greater need for followers of Jesus to be different, to model true tolerance. (It's something that needs to be seen, not just heard.) True tolerance means

"Tolerance is not indifference, but a generous regard and even provision for those who differ from us on points we deeply care about. To support tolerance—which is not the same as lacking intolerance—more is required than just a lack of certainty concerning differences at issue. We must also care about people."

DALLAS WILLARD[26]

disagreeing agreeably with those who hold other views, and being consistently respectful and patient—even when accused of being intolerant. But it also means, at the same time, commending and defending what is true. It's being like Jesus, "full of grace and truth" (Jn 1:14).

Part Two: *Faith*

Furious with rage, Nebuchadnezzar summoned Shadrach, Meshach and Abednego. So these men were brought before the king, and Nebuchadnezzar said to them, "Is it true . . . that you do not serve my gods or worship the image of gold I have set up? Now . . . if you are ready to fall down and worship the image I made, very good. But if you do not worship it, you will be thrown immediately into a blazing furnace. Then what god will be able to rescue you from my hand?"

[They] replied to him, "King Nebuchadnezzar, we do not need to defend ourselves before you in this matter. If we are thrown into the blazing furnace, the God we serve is able to save us from it, and he will rescue us from Your Majesty's hand. But even if he does not, we want you to know, Your Majesty, that we will not serve your gods or worship the image of gold you have set up." . . .

So Shadrach, Meshach and Abednego came out of the fire, and the satraps, prefects, governors and royal advisers crowded around them. They saw that the fire had not harmed their bodies, nor was a hair of their heads singed; their robes were not scorched, and there was no smell of fire on them.

Then Nebuchadnezzar said, "Praise be to the God of Shadrach, Meshach and Abednego, who has sent his angel and rescued his servants! They trusted in him and defied the king's command and were willing to give up their lives rather than serve or worship any god except their own God." . . .

Then the king promoted [them] in the province of Babylon.

DANIEL 3:13-18, 26-28, 30

Part two is about faith. Contrary to popular opinion, faith is essentially connected to the life of the mind. Flourishing as followers of Jesus in the university requires both thinking well and believing well—a life of reasonable faith and faithful reason.

8

THE NATURE OF FAITH

GETTING IT CLEAR

Without faith it is impossible to please God, because anyone who comes to him must believe that he exists and that he rewards those who earnestly seek him.

HEBREWS 11:6

[Faith] affects the whole of man's nature. It commences with the conviction of the mind based on adequate evidence; it continues in the confidence of the heart or emotions based on the above conviction, and it is crowned in the consent of the will, by means of which the conviction and confidence are expressed in conduct.

W. H. GRIFFITH-THOMAS (1861-1924), *The Principles of Theology*

This book is about minding your faith. So far we've concentrated on the mind. Some believers may be nervous at this point. What about faith? The big problem for students in college, they think, is losing their faith, not their mind. But the two go together. Those who lose their faith in college do so precisely because they have lost their mind. Thinking well about these matters—including faith—is essential to sanity and flourishing in the university. Only when I began to think better did I recover the faith I had lost.

FAITH VERSUS REASON

We usually think of faith in contrast to reason. The titles of innumerable books such as Sam Harris's recent bestseller *The End of Faith: Re-*

ligion, Terror, and the Future of Reason, attest to this.[1] Contrasting faith
and reason is a given; it sets the terms of the discussion. But the Bible
doesn't talk this way, and for good reason. Not only does it never pit
faith and reason against each other, it doesn't even contrast them. I
won't discuss what the Bible does contrast to faith until chapter ten.
First we need to build the foundation. We'll start with the usual contrast, however, in order to understand what faith and reason actually
are and imply. Getting clear on both is crucial.

Broadly speaking, there are two options for relating faith to reason:
marriage and *divorce*. Faith and reason are friends, intimate partners
who belong together "till death do us part," or they have irreconcilable
differences and should separate. Within the marriage option, as within
actual marriages, different arrangements are possible—different ways
to understand the respective roles faith and reason play. But they all see
faith and reason as compatible.

FIDEISM AND RATIONALISM

The majority view is divorce. Within this view are two opposed options. Both agree that faith and reason are incompatible, but disagree
over which side is right. We'll call them, in more technical terms, *fideism* and *rationalism*. These terms are also used in other ways.[2] I use
them here in a strong sense (i.e., *strong* or *hard* fideism and rationalism), to represent the extreme options of "all faith, no reason" and "all
reason, no faith" respectively. For simplicity, I focus on the extremes,
rather than more nuanced possibilities that may lie between them,
since analyzing extreme cases clarifies the issues and sets the context
for evaluating more moderate positions. I also do this because much of
the discussion today (with new atheist writers, for example) actually
does reflect the extremes.

Rationalism is based on the Latin word *ratio* ("reason"). For rationalists, reason alone is important. To have faith, on this view, is to deny
reason—to be *ir*rational. Like Bill (in chap. 4), who claimed to have no
beliefs (probably meaning "faith") but only "scientific knowledge," rationalists consider faith incompatible with knowledge of any kind, especially scientific knowledge. At best, faith is a kind of opinion or pref-

erence; at worst, it is wishful thinking. Either way it's not rational and should be rejected outright.

On the other extreme, fideism, from the Latin word *fides* ("faith," "faithfulness"), agrees that faith and reason are incompatible, but opts for faith as what's important. Many religious believers are fideists, including many Christians. But its influence extends far beyond traditional religious believers. It reflects the assumptions of contemporary popular culture (think of Oprah Winfrey and many of her guests) concerning "spiritual issues."

I'm convinced that rationalism and fideism are both misguided. Each is based on misconceptions about faith and reason, and how they relate to each other. Both positions fail on their own terms: neither takes faith *or* reason seriously enough. Thinking, believing and living well demand a fully rational faith and a fully faithful reason.

Our focus in this chapter is fideism. We'll use it as a bridge to construct a more adequate account of faith. Only a biblically and philosophically robust understanding of faith will be sufficient for a flourishing life in the university, where the faith and reason question is constantly in view.

WHY FIDEISM?

People usually adopt fideism with little thought. As the popular culture, "person-on-the-street" approach to such matters, it's in the air we breathe, culturally and intellectually. Most people have simply never thought otherwise. For religious believers there is an additional factor: the "person in the pew" is often *taught* a fide-

> **Søren Kierkegaard** (1813-1855)— Danish Christian philosopher and theologian. His life was tragic and lonely, which is reflected in his writings (he's been called "the brooding Dane"). Kierkegaard emphasized the "infinite qualitative distinction" between God and humanity, and described faith as "passionate inwardness."[3]

istic outlook from the pulpit. A quick Internet search reveals more than one church sign proclaiming, "Reason is the greatest enemy that faith has." Whether it's taught or caught, many students raised in Christian families assume that faith and reason are incompatible. When confronted with rational objections to faith in college, they have little capital to draw on. Typically, they end up either rejecting their faith or else relativizing it by sealing it off in a separate sphere from reason—no longer a biblical faith that engages, informs and energizes all of life. Either way, the students have lost their faith, and it's because they lost their mind.

Fideism has its thoughtful defenders, however. For example, in the nineteenth century Søren Kierkegaard criticized the role of reason in relation to faith. He described faith as a leap into the dark, necessarily full of risk and rational uncertainty. Whether Kierkegaard should be considered a strong fideist is debated.[4] But the sorts of considerations he and other thoughtful fideists raise are important, as they identify aspects of faith that are important in constructing an adequate understanding.

Before we address some of those considerations, I should note the most commonly cited (and notorious) rationale purportedly given for fideism. It is widely attributed to the early Christian thinker Tertullian (c. 160-230). He is reported as saying, on behalf of faith in Jesus: "I believe it because it is absurd."[5] This seems as clear a rejection of reason in favor of faith as we could find. In fact, it implies that faith isn't really faith unless reason is *entirely* rejected—until one believes what is rationally absurd. That would be the goal, apparently, for the believer.

> "[Tertullian's] style is caustic and highly memorable, though unfortunately his words have often been distorted or taken out of context by readers unable to appreciate his deep sense of irony. For example, he never said, 'I believe because it is absurd,' and his famous 'What has Athens to do with Jerusalem?' was not meant to be read as an anti-philosophical remark. On the contrary, Tertullian was deeply engaged with philosophical issues."
>
> GERALD BRAY[9]

But if the chief criterion for faith is that it be absurd, then surely anything goes. Why limit oneself to religious matters? I can think of far more absurd candidates for me to believe, such as *I am the Queen of*

England. It's difficult to imagine someone of Tertullian's stature seriously commending such a position.[6]

In fact, he didn't. The statement is a mistranslation of what Tertullian said, and it distorts his actual position. The original context from which it is taken is actually an argument in *defense* of the rational credibility of Jesus' identity.[7] True, Tertullian was not a fan of the pagan schools of philosophy of his time, but he was trained in philosophy and engaged in extensive rational argumentation.[8]

In fact, Tertullian elsewhere explicitly *affirmed* the use of reason as a way of honoring God:

> Obviously reason is something that belongs to God, because there is nothing which God, the creator of all things, did not foresee, arrange, and determine by reason. Nor is there anything he does not want to be investigated and understood by reason.[10]

Tertullian was not a fideist.

REASONS FOR FIDEISM

But some reasons for fideism should be taken seriously.[11] Faith and reason appear, for example, to play very different, even opposite roles in our thinking and living. Reason measures, examines and tests things in order to determine what is true or reliable. By contrast, faith trusts and commits. They pull in different directions. You will never trust or commit yourself to something or someone as long as you are examining it and testing it.

Think of a door. Reason *tests* the door—it examines, measures and determines what it is made out of and how strong it is. Faith, by contrast, walks through the door—it makes a commitment. And commitment inevitably involves risk. No matter how much we've tested the door, there are no rational guarantees about what we'll find on the other side, if only because the outcome is still in the future.

Probably the best example of faith is getting married, although the same is true, to lesser degrees, for all relationships. A marriage relationship can be entered into only by trust and commitment. When you marry someone, you place your trust in him or her to be who the person says he or she is, to commit to you in "good faith," to be "faithful" to you for a lifetime, and so on. Your trust is expressed in committing yourself to your partner, where you promise to be and do the same things for him or her, for a lifetime. The marriage ceremony is a public enactment of your pledge of trust and commitment. That's what marriage *is*: a covenant relationship, based on—constituted by—trust and commitment.

The stakes are high and the risk is considerable. Marriage changes your life, in almost every respect, for the rest of your life. There are no guarantees in advance about what life will hold for you as a family, what challenges and opportunities you will face together, and how each of you will handle them. Marriage is walking through the door—for better or worse, for richer or poorer.

PROBLEMS WITH FIDEISM

Considerations like these stress the differences between faith and reason. They are right—up to a point. The differences provide important insight into what faith is and how it differs from its cousin, belief, as we analyzed it in part one. Faith, unlike belief (holding a proposition to be true), involves *trust* and *commitment*. We explore this more fully later.

But fideism is wrong to reject reason entirely. True, as fideists stress, faith involves putting your trust in and committing yourself to someone or something. But a crucial question looms: What are you trusting *in* or committing yourself *to*—what is the object of your faith? Not everything is worthy of trust and commitment. If we reject reason and rational testing entirely, we have no way to determine where to put our faith.

Reason is necessary. Fideism fails for three reasons. First, reason is necessary to evaluate the object of our faith.

During my junior year of college, the Christian groups on campus joined forces and invited a noted Christian apologist to give a public lecture defending the historical credibility of Jesus' resurrection. I invited the debate coach, a communications professor and not a religious believer, to attend. When we spoke afterward, I was stunned. "I think the important thing is not *whether* Jesus rose from the dead," he said.

"The important thing is whether you *believe* he rose from the dead." Here is unvarnished fideism—in one who is not a believer. In his view, what's important is not the object of one's faith, but that one has faith.

Of course, it does matter whether I believe that Jesus rose from the dead. It changes everything about how I live my life, and why. It's at the core of what it means to follow Jesus, according to Paul: "If you declare with your mouth, 'Jesus is Lord,' and believe in your heart that God raised him from the dead, you will be saved" (Rom 10:9). But, as we saw earlier, Paul also argues that if Jesus did not actually rise from the dead, our faith is worthless (1 Cor 15:14). Paul is no fideist. Biblically, believing that Jesus rose from the dead is important only because he actually did so.

I doubt the debate coach reasoned this way about other areas of life. Make a simple replacement in his statement: "I think the important thing is not *whether* you have a million dollars in your checking account. The important thing is whether you *believe* you have a million dollars in your checking account." Would he agree? Of course not. Why, then, does he throw rationality aside when it comes to matters of religion? Like many others, he assumes that when it comes to such things, reason, truth and knowledge are no longer applicable. He's a fideist.

Let's continue to compare the two cases: It also matters whether I believe I have a million dollars in my checking account. Believing that would also change my life. It would radically alter how I write checks, for example. But if I actually have only $35 in my checking account, I'll run into reality pretty quickly, and it will be painful.

Whether we believe something—whether we trust and commit ourselves to something—matters. This fideists stress. But what matters even more is whether the object of our trust and commitment is true or trustworthy. Faith, religious or not, is only as good as its object. Only an object that is true and trustworthy can be and do what we trust it to be and do. Ultimately, even minimal faith in a true object is worth more than passionate faith in one that is false. If we can't evaluate the potential objects of our faith, we have no idea where to place our trust and commitment. Fideists are right to stress that reason's role is to test and examine. But testing and examining where we place our faith is essential.

Reason is inescapable. Second, reason is inescapable. Even die-hard fideists must choose what or whom to place their faith in, and there's always more than one candidate available. Possible objects of faith are presented to us every day: friends, potential spouses, courses of action, career paths—not to mention chairs, bridges and airplane pilots. Or the multitude of logically distinct religions and worldviews competing for our trust and commitment.

On what basis can the fideist choose between these alternatives? Even to close our eyes and arbitrarily jump is to choose for a reason. It's to see blind leaping as the correct approach to take to such matters. But reaching that conclusion involves reasoning—in this case, reasoning that concludes that we shouldn't employ reasoning! It's one thing to acknowledge that marriage requires trust and commitment that go beyond what can be conclusively established by evidence and argument. It's another to infer from this that rational thought plays *no* role in choosing a marriage partner, so we might as well marry the next person you see. That, again, involves reasoning—bad reasoning. Reason is inescapable. Insofar as they give reasons for fideism, thoughtful fideists implicitly acknowledge as much. As rational beings, we always reason. The only question is whether we do so well or poorly.

Fideism is unbiblical. For followers of Jesus, fideism faces a crucial, third problem: it's unbiblical. We've seen that Paul rejected fideism when it comes to the resurrection of Jesus, and earlier we saw him employ reason and logic in arguing for the truth of the gospel. But valuing thinking and evidence is not unique to Paul. Indeed, we would expect the same from Jesus, given what we've seen. And we are not disappointed. To give one example, when John the Baptist was experiencing doubts about Jesus' identity, he sent his followers to ask Jesus whether he was in fact the Messiah they had been waiting for. Jesus replied, "Go back and report to John what you hear and see: The blind receive sight, the lame walk, those who have leprosy are cleansed, the deaf hear, the dead are raised, and the good news is proclaimed to the poor" (Mt 11:4-5).

Note how Jesus does not respond to John's questions: "Don't ask questions, just believe," or "The important thing is not *whether* I am the Messiah. The important thing is whether you *believe* I am the Messiah." Instead, he confirms his identity by appealing to evidence that he is fulfilling messianic predictions.[12] In so doing, Jesus affirms both the legitimacy of John's questions and the importance of using evidence to answer them.

Faith and wisdom. We can see in another way that fideism is unbiblical. Part of the difficulty we face in dealing with faith and reason these days is that we inherit inadequate understandings of both. Although understanding reason is our focus in chapter nine, to set the stage I'll introduce a central component of my account of reason into our discussion here. In contrast to most modern approaches, the classical (ancient and medieval) understanding of reason embraces what I call the wisdom model of rationality.

When I speak on the subject of faith and reason in secular university environments, I like to hold up a Bible and point out that although this book is thought to be about faith (and certainly it is), it also has a lot to say about reason. I explain that the Bible contains a whole genre of books called "wisdom literature," about how to live a rational, intelligent life. It reflects an approach to reason that is embraced by a growing number of contemporary philosophers.[13] On a wisdom model, such as we see in the Bible's book of Proverbs, being rational is more than just looking for good reasons for holding the beliefs you do, although that's part of it. Being rational—being wise—includes the whole package of one's moral and intellectual habits and patterns of thinking and acting. Wisdom concerns all of life. Hence Proverbs discusses a wide range of issues, such as how to use money intelligently, how to speak wisely and how to lead effectively. Being rational, on the wisdom model, includes being wise in friendships, in work relationships, in marriage and in raising children.

Particularly relevant to us here is that each of those areas inevitably involves trust and commitment. A wise person doesn't seek to avoid all trust and commitment. That's impossible and foolish to attempt. A wise person trusts and commits him- or herself to appropriate people, projects and courses of action. But he or she does so wisely, not fool-ishly. And that rules out fideism. Proverbs explicitly rejects faith that is not examined by reason: "The simple [naive persons] believe any-thing, / but the prudent [wise persons] give thought to their steps" (Prov 14:15).[14]

The wisdom model of rationality illuminates how rationality and trust and commitment can go together. True, no philosophical argu-ment or scientific proof can guarantee in advance that someone you marry will not turn out to fail you, but it doesn't follow that rationality has no place in your choice of a spouse. You do your best to make sure you're making a wise choice, based on the sorts of evidence appropriate to making such decisions. For example, you strive to determine whether you and the person are really compatible—by spending time with the person, meeting his or her parents, asking lots of questions, watching how he or she responds to different situations, and talking through important issues together. The process involves judgment and discern-ment, which are further components of wisdom, as Proverbs teaches.

At some point, however, you must make a commitment, one way or the other. Making a choice is unavoidable. If you do not choose to

Childlike faith—Aren't we supposed to have the "faith of a child," uncomplicated with reason, study and rigorous thought? No. It's true that Jesus teaches repeatedly (Mt 18:1-14; 19:13-14; Mk 10:14-16; Lk 18:15-17) that we must "become like children" in order to enter the kingdom of God. But what does this mean? Jesus explains this further only in the Matthew passage, where he says, literally, "Whoever takes the lowly position of this child is greatest in the kingdom of heaven." He's speaking of a child's humility, not the content of his faith or qual-ity of his thinking. The word *faith* is used in none of these passages. Nor do the expressions "childlike faith" or "faith of a child" occur elsewhere in Scripture. When the Bible speaks of a child's thinking or the content of his or her faith, it's always in warning or condemnation: "Brothers and sisters, stop thinking like children. In regard to evil be infants, but in your thinking be adults" (1 Cor 14:20).[15]

marry this person, you've chosen not to be married to them. And *that* choice has significant implications and consequences as well. In this and many other areas of life, trust and commitment are unavoidable. You probably know unwise people who tend to make foolish choices in marriage, friendships or careers. But you likely know others who make wise choices in these matters. Faith can be unreasonable—we can place our trust and commitment in the wrong object. But faith can be reasonable, too.

Faith and belief. Fideists are right to stress that trust and commitment are central to faith. But reason is also necessary. An accurate understanding of faith can pull these elements together, along with what we've seen about truth, belief and knowledge, into a coherent picture.

How does faith relate to belief or holding a proposition to be true? We've noted that scholars often consider faith and belief as different concepts (see sidebar on p. 73).[16] But what does the difference amount to? Fideists and rationalists see faith as belief *minus* something—as belief without reason, evidence or rational grounds. This is reflected in Mark Twain's quip: "Faith is believing what you know ain't so."[17]

Instead, we should see faith as belief *plus* something—as belief plus trust and commitment. What distinguishes faith from belief is not what faith lacks but what it adds to belief. On this understanding it's perfectly possible for faith to be reasonable, even to include knowledge. If your beliefs about the object of your faith are reasonable beliefs—if you have good reason to see the object of your faith as true or trustworthy—then it's reasonable to place your trust in that object.

I have faith in my wife, Debbie; our relationship is grounded in trust and commitment. But that faith is by no means ignorant or irrational. My trust in Debbie is based on good reasons. In fact, it's based on knowledge—of Debbie and her character and commitments. Over the years, my faith in Debbie has grown as my knowledge of her has grown. And it continues to grow. The better I know her, the more I trust her and commit myself to her. It's a fully rational faith, solidly grounded in reasonable beliefs and knowledge. But it goes beyond those beliefs and knowledge, to trust and commitment.

WHAT IS FAITH?

Let's now gather the distinctions we've made into an understanding of faith that can integrate these insights. Every instance of faith, religious or not, has four elements. To illustrate, let's use a decidedly nonreligious example mentioned already: sitting in a chair. It could be any chair, but assume it's the chair in which you now sit, which, let's imagine, is in a college classroom. As with every instance of faith, your sitting in this chair has four parts or elements.

Object. First, every instance of faith has an *object*—something or someone you put your faith in. By "object" I don't mean a physical object, like a door or a chair. In this illustration, it *is* a physical object, a chair. But the object of one's faith may be a person or even an idea, such as justice or the theory of evolution. In each case, the object of your faith is whatever fills the blank in: "I have faith in _____," or "I trust in _____." This is faith's most important element because, as we've seen, our faith is only as good as its object. I may trust passionately in the million dollars in my bank account, but I'm not rich unless the money's actually there.

Content. Second, every expression of faith has *content*. The content of your faith is the set of propositions you believe (or know) about the object of your faith. It's what fills the blank in "I believe that _____." Here

> ***Talking about faith***—In actual conversations with nonbelievers, I try to avoid the word *faith*, because it has strange connotations for many people. It's easier to use a different term altogether. I usually simply define *faith* as "trust": placing your trust in something or someone. Trust is the most obvious of the four elements, the easiest to understand, and it's virtually synonymous with faith. Most people understand that they regularly put their trust in things like chairs, that there's nothing religious about it, and that what makes their trust reasonable or not is what they put their trust *in*.[18]

what we've said about belief and knowledge comes in. Trust *in* an object always presupposes or includes propositional beliefs or knowledge *about* the object. If you believed nothing about the object of your faith, you wouldn't be putting your faith in it. You wouldn't know that it exists! These beliefs may be largely implicit rather than explicit, which is probably the case as you sit in the chair. Chances are you haven't consciously reflected on the chair or made factual assertions about it. Still, you believe certain propositions about the chair: that it exists, that it is made of durable materials, that it will hold you up and so on. If you didn't hold these propositions to be true, you wouldn't be sitting in the chair.

If you doubt that you have beliefs about the chair, imagine that last night a nefarious art student confided to you that she and her friends have planned a prank for class today. In the classroom in which you now sit they've removed several chairs and replaced them with identical chair look-alikes, made out of flimsy papier-mâché. Hidden video cameras will record the hapless students who attempt to sit in the fake chairs and fall to the floor. Would that knowledge make any difference in your behavior today as you come into the classroom and sit down? Of course. You'd check your chair very carefully before taking your seat. Why? You now have reason to doubt your earlier implicit beliefs about the chair and its ability to hold you up—which means you do hold those beliefs.

Trust. As fideists stress, however, faith, even in a chair, goes beyond merely having beliefs about it. The first element faith adds to belief is *trust.* When you sit in a chair, you trust it to hold you up. You put confidence in it, you depend on it. And so, as in all cases of trust, risk is involved. In this case, you put *all* of yourself, your whole body weight, into the chair—and you trust it to hold all of you up.

Commitment. Finally, faith adds *commitment.* You don't fully express faith in the chair until you actually sit in it. Indeed, putting all of yourself in the chair is *how* you express your trust in it. You may claim you have faith in the chair, but if you refuse to sit in it you don't really trust it. Sitting—making a commitment to it—seals the deal; it ties the knot. Commitment is how we express our trust.

Understanding faith in terms of these four elements embraces the correct insight of thoughtful fideists, that faith involves trust and commitment. Faith is more than just believing certain things to be true; it's more than belief. But this understanding also recognizes that faith is not less than belief. It includes it. The belief or content component is extremely important, because it's where *reason* comes in. Reason's role

"He does not believe, that does not live according to his Belief."
THOMAS FULLER (1608-1661)[19]

is to evaluate faith's object, to determine whether it is worthy of our trust and commitment. The belief component is also important for growing in our faith.

The better we know the object of our faith, the stronger will be our confidence in trusting and committing ourselves to it.

FAITH AND CHRISTIAN FAITH

Most people see faith as solely a religious matter. But nothing in what we've seen about trust and commitment is limited to religious believers. Whatever our worldview or religious commitments, we regularly trust people, bridges, chairs and maps. We commit ourselves to such objects by marrying them, listening to them, engaging in economic transactions with them, crossing them (bridges), sitting in them (chairs), following them (maps) and committing our futures to them (academic projects, career paths). If we didn't exercise trust and commitment in these ways, we couldn't function in the world. Religious faith is not something radically unique. It's the same kind of thing we all express, when we trust and commit ourselves in the ways just mentioned. What distinguishes each specific form of faith, including religious faith, from others, such as faith in a chair, is its object. In every expression of faith, its object determines what form of faith it is and thus what degree of trust and commitment is reasonably called for.

So far, our analysis of faith has been largely philosophical in nature, aimed at making sense of how, upon reflection, we understand and apply the concepts of belief, faith, trust and commitment in all of life. But this picture also fits specifically Christian faith, faith as it is taught and modeled in the Bible. Christian faith has the same four elements. What sets it apart is its object: the God of the Bible, as revealed supremely in Jesus. Of course, as in every instance of faith, the object makes all the difference. When we're talking about faith in a chair, all the content needed are some mundane beliefs about the chair and its properties, and all that's required for expressing one's trust and commitment is simply to sit in it. Placing our faith in God is far more extensive. Its content includes beliefs about who God is and what he's like, about Jesus' death on the cross, about his promises to those who trust and follow him, and so on. And expressing our faith in God requires far more than a simple physical action. It involves everything about us—trusting him with our life, including our eternal life, and committing ourselves to follow him and his will in obedience for the rest of our life. Christian faith is much more like a marriage commitment than it is like sitting in a chair. But the same four elements are involved.

Moreover, just as faith in a chair is rational or irrational, depending on whether the chair is worthy of our trust, the Bible's understanding of faith stresses the truth and trustworthiness of God as the object of our faith. In fact, Scripture acknowledges that some religious faith is irrational and strongly warns against it. This type of warning is at the heart of biblical arguments against idolatry (worshiping and trusting idols or false gods). I suggest that you read the critique of idolatry in Isaiah 44, for example. You will not find fideism ("The important thing is not *what* you place your faith in. The important thing is that you place your faith in *something*"). Instead, Scripture reasons along these lines: There is only one true God, the Creator and Sustainer of the world, who alone is worthy of your trust and commitment. Faith in idols (which *you* made!), trusting *them* to care for you and sustain you, makes no sense. It's stupid! Idols can never be or do what you're trusting them to be or do. Only the true God can. Idolatry is irrational faith. Trusting the true God is rational faith.

GROWING IN FAITH

To advance in our faith we need to grow in each of the areas of belief, trust and commitment. They work together. Growing in *belief* means learning more about God, especially through studying the Scriptures. Thinking well and loving God with our minds is an important part of the life of faith. The more we know about God and his purposes, the more we can trust and obey him. If our faith ends there, however, we become bloated, arrogant and cynical (1 Cor 8:1). We have to take what we know about God and *trust* him with it. Do I believe that God is good, that I could never improve on his will for my life? Then I need to actually trust him with my life, to see him as *my* good (Ps 73:28). *Commitment* is putting that trust into action by living it out, by obeying what God says about life. It's not enough to say that I believe that God is my highest good, or that I trust that his will is what is good, pleasing and perfect (Rom 12:2), unless I actually make choices to live that way, trusting him with the results—to "trust and obey," as an old hymn puts it.

> "Disobedience blinds the conscience; obedience makes it keen-sighted and sensitive. The more we *do*, the more shall we trust in Christ."
> JOHN HENRY NEWMAN (1801-1890)[20]

When we step out in obedience, our belief and trust increase as a result. One of the great benefits of identifying yourself as a Christ follower at your university, by reaching out to your fellow students with the gospel, serving the suffering or defending the truth of the Christian worldview, is that it forces you to trust God with the results. That's when you come to see experientially, not just theoretically, that God is true and trustworthy. Faith in God is not something we express only once, when we initially place our trust in Jesus. It's a choice of trust and commitment that we're to replicate every day for the rest of our earthly lives. As a friend puts it, walking with Jesus is saying yes to him once—and saying "uh-huh" every day thereafter.

THE NECESSITY OF FAITH

FAITH AND REASON

*Now faith is the assurance of things hoped for, the
conviction of things not seen.*

HEBREWS 11:1 ESV

*I think a case can be made that faith is one of the world's great
evils, comparable to the smallpox virus but harder to eradicate.
Faith, being belief that isn't based on evidence, is the principal
vice of any religion.*

RICHARD DAWKINS, "Is Science a Religion?"

When my daughter Stephanee was about five years old, we attended
a family reunion in the Colorado mountains. On Sunday morning I
gave a devotional talk at our outdoor worship service. As an illustration
I asked Stephanee to come to the front. I had her turn away, so she
couldn't see me. "Sweetheart," I said, "I want you to trust me. I'm going
to ask you to fall backward. I'll catch you, but you'll have to trust me.
Okay?" She obeyed without hesitation, and I caught her in my arms.

Stephanee exercised faith. Her faith included each of the four elements we identified in the previous chapter. I (and the promise I made
to her) was the object of her faith. Its content was her knowledge of me.
She trusted me to do what I said I would do, and she expressed that
trust in commitment by doing what I asked.

Was Stephanee's faith reasonable? Everyone I've told this story over the years has agreed that it was—because of the faith's content. Although Stephanee couldn't see me at that moment and didn't fully understand why I was asking her to do this, she knew *me*. She knew I loved her dearly and that I would never try to hurt her. She also knew I was strong enough to catch her. In short, she knew my character (that I *would* catch her) and my capability (that I *could* catch her). Given what she knew, based on her experience over the five years of her life, it was wholly reasonable for her to trust me. Things would be far different had I been a stranger, an abusive father or another five-year-old.

Given the understanding of faith we have developed, we could multiply examples of rational faith. The prospects of a happy marriage between faith and reason look good. The remaining pole of the "divorce" view, rationalism, however, denies that possibility. This is what I'll address in this chapter. As we used fideism to develop a more adequate understanding of faith, we'll examine rationalism in order to arrive at a more sensible understanding of reason.

RATIONALISM

Rationalists agree with fideists that faith and reason are incompatible, but they opt for reason. (Recall that, as with fideism, I'm addressing solely strong or hard rationalism.) Faith is irrational, they believe, and should be rejected entirely—"All reason, no faith." This perspective has a long history, but it has received new life recently in the popular, in-your-face writings of new atheist authors like Richard Dawkins, Christopher Hitchens and Sam Harris. I'll use the writings of these three as representative of rationalism because they're so influential and their rationalism is strong and explicit.[1] According to Dawkins, an Oxford biologist, faith is "a kind of mental illness."[2] It "means blind trust, in the absence of evidence, even in the teeth of evidence."[3] "Faith is the great cop-out, the great excuse to evade the need to think and evaluate evidence. Faith is belief in spite of, even perhaps because of, the lack of evidence. . . . Faith is not allowed to justify itself by argument."[4]

Notice that Dawkins's claim is an "in principle" one. He does not say, "Some expressions of faith are irrational. Let's look at this or that instance of faith and examine whether, in that case, the faith is reasonable." Dawkins rejects *all* faith as unreasonable—in principle. Faith *cannot* be reasonable.

What could justify such a claim? As I said earlier, given the understanding of faith we have developed, we can multiply examples of rational faith. To reject all faith as irrational, then, rationalists need to provide either an alternative understanding of faith that is at least as plausible as our account, but which renders it essentially incompatible with reason, or an account of reason that shows it to be essentially incompatible with faith. I'll call this the *rationalist project*—the attempt to understand faith and/or reason in such a way as to rule out all faith as irrational. I'm convinced that the rationalist project is doomed to fail. Let's see why this is so.

Rationalists on faith. Can the rationalist analysis of faith underwrite the rationalist project? Unfortunately, the rationalists we're considering provide no analysis of faith. Their standard approach to faith, as evidenced in Dawkins's statements, is simply to assert or define faith as "irrational belief"—along the lines of Mark Twain's purported definition: "Faith is believing what you know ain't so." That's not a conclusion, for Dawkins, to an investigation or demonstration. It's the starting point. So defined, of course, faith *is* irrational. It could hardly be otherwise. But why should we accept this characterization? It simply begs the question of whether faith is essentially irrational.

To be plausible, or even intellectually responsible, an account of faith must begin with a careful analysis of what faith actually is and provide a fair evaluation of its possible credentials—particularly if it is to be the basis of critiquing faith as essentially irrational. It needs to examine a form of faith that thoughtful believers actually embrace. (If you're committing a language to writing you need to find out what actual language users mean by a term.) If the account addresses Christian faith, in particular, it needs to deal with an understanding of faith that reflects what the Bible actually teaches and that thoughtful defenders of the rationality of faith like Augustine, Aquinas and contemporary Christian philosophers would recognize and endorse. To understate things significantly, we find none of this in the authors under consideration.[5]

Can rationalists develop such an account? It's not logically impossible, but I certainly wouldn't hold my breath. In chapter eight we developed the understanding of faith we did precisely by taking seriously the things just mentioned. Other careful accounts of faith throughout history have similar features and likewise understand faith to be compatible with reason, in principle. No plausible analysis of faith is going underwrite the rationalist project. If rationalists are to succeed, it will need to be on the basis of their account of reason and rationality.

St. Augustine (354-430)—A North African (from present-day Algeria), one of the most influential thinkers of all time, and certainly one of the greatest Christian minds. A university professor of rhetoric in Milan, Augustine examined the dominant philosophies of his day: Manichaeism, neo-Platonism and Christianity, and explored a lifestyle of sexual freedom. Influenced by the prayers of his Christian mother, the thoughtful preaching of Ambrose (c. 340-397) and his own intellectual investigation, Augustine became a Christian in 386. He started a small community of intellectually oriented friends who studied and prayed together, and he eventually became a bishop. He wrote numerous books, articles and sermons on philosophy, theology and ethics.

Rationalists on reason. Unfortunately, our writers say even less about reason than they do faith.[6] The chief (or sole) attribute of reason, as they use the term, appears to be that it is incompatible with faith. But to reject faith as irrational on this basis also begs the question.

As examples such as Stephanee's show, nothing in a commonsense or uncontroversial understanding of reason rules out all forms of faith. Rationalists need to impose further conditions on rationality that can do the job. Since they do not specify what those conditions may be, we'll have to suggest our own. We need not examine every possible candidate, however. Like Dawkins's objection, my primary argument here will be an in-principle one. I claim that all such conditions will fail—that any attempt, whatever its particular details, to construe rationality in a way that could justify the rationalist project *cannot* succeed. If I'm right, rationalists face a dilemma. Any understanding of reason that is strong enough to rule out all faith as irrational will be implausible, even irrational. But any conception of rationality that is plausible will not rule out all faith.

WHAT'S WRONG WITH FAITH?

To justify their project, rationalists need to impose conditions on rationality that are incompatible with one or more essential aspects of faith. Which aspect(s) of faith would rationalists reject? I have identified four elements: object, content, trust and commitment. That there are objects of faith is not in dispute—what is debated is whether it is rational to put our faith *in* such objects. This leaves the other elements. Rationalists can't sensibly reject belief, the holding of a proposition to be true, since it is basic to all rational activity.[7] What is in question, then, are those elements of faith that distinguish it from (mere) belief or knowledge: the fideist's favorites, trust and commitment. These, the elements that involve risk, presumably represent the rationalist's target.

Of course, if rationalists require only that we reject *unwarranted* trust and commitment (placing our trust and commitment in an object we have insufficient reason to believe is true or trustworthy) there is no dispute, because this is exactly what the Bible itself commends. Rationalism, in that case, would be indistinguishable from a biblically and philosophically informed understanding of faith. (It would be inconsistent with fideism, of course. But so is biblical faith.) Whether or not particular instances of faith, including religious faith, are reasonable would have to be assessed on a case-by-case basis, which is exactly the position I'm commending. But since Dawkins and company claim that *all* faith is irrational, they need to say more than this. To justify the wholesale rejection of faith, rationality must exclude trust and commitment entirely, *in principle*. But what conditions could rationalists put on rationality that are strong enough to warrant this?

As I say, these writers do not specify. I'll not try to guess which ones, if any, may actually be operating as unstated assumptions in their views (although scientism is almost certainly lurking in the background), but I'll illustrate the problems briefly with what I take to be the two most popular candidates for such conditions. We met them earlier (in chap. 4) as commonly espoused requirements for having knowledge: *absolute proof* and *scientific proof.* The motivation is similar here. According to the absolute-proof condition, we may rationally accept only what can be conclusively established by strict philosophical (or mathematical or geometrical) demonstration, a method that produces conclusions with absolute rational certainty. The scientific-proof condition requires that we rationally accept only what can be established by scientific verification (scientism, in other words). Both conditions are strong enough to rule out all trust and commitment—faith's "walking through the door" goes beyond what can be established by strict philosophical demonstration or scientific verification. But we've seen that these two conditions also rule out accepting most of what we actually do know or rationally believe. In fact, they're self-refuting, since neither condition can itself be established on the grounds it demands. Although philosophical demonstration and scientific verification are excellent methods for justifying appropriate kinds of propositions, not all rational matters are of those kinds. As conditions on all of rationality they fail on their own terms.

RATIONALISM IS IMPOSSIBLE

There is good reason to think that what we see in the case of these two possible conditions holds for all attempts to justify the rationalist project. Rather than examine and critique all of the other possible candidates for the job, I'll turn to my in-principle considerations. We'll see that trust and commitment, and the risks they entail, are unavoidable. In fact, they are necessary to rationality itself. The rationalist project is both impossible and irrational.

Relationships. To see that eliminating all trust and commitment is impossible, consider, first, relationships. Marriage is the chief example, but it applies across the board. Having any relationship, whether a friendship, a working relationship among colleagues, an employer-employee relationship or a marriage, requires that you trust and commit yourself to the other person to the extent appropriate to the kind of relationship it is. You trust them to be who they claim to be, to do what they claim to do, to fulfill their obligations, to tell you the truth, and so on. In turn, you commit yourself to the other person, pledging (implicitly or explicitly) to be and do these same things for them. To have a relationship at all, as opposed to being an isolated hermit in a cave, it is necessary to trust and commit yourself in those ways. And that always involves risk: it goes beyond what we can rationally guarantee in advance by philosophical demonstration, scientific verification or any other such procedure. Sometimes the relationship does not work out, when one or more of the persons turn out not to be trustworthy, after all. It is an unfortunate and regular fact of life that relationships are destroyed, marriages end in divorce and hearts are broken. Such experiences, hopefully, teach us to be wiser in our trust and commitment. But the risk is unavoidable if we are to have relationships at all.

The rationalist's wholesale rejection of faith, then, requires rejecting all human relationships. Suppose Walt, a rationalist, acknowledges this. He bites the bullet and goes to live as a hermit in a cave. Walt won't avoid trust and commitment altogether, since in order to get around he'll have to trust his senses and perceptual capacities, memory, beliefs, the stability and continuity of the natural order, and so on. These are things that, notoriously, can't be established by strict philosophical demonstration or scientific verification (or any other condition sufficient to rule out all trust and commitment); all such demonstration and verification already presupposes them.[8] Even apart from that, however, Walt's life would hardly be a supremely rational one. We don't regard someone who avoids all human relationships, who is unable to trust people or commit him- or herself to friendships as an ideal of human life or rationality. We consider this person stilted, incapable of living a fully human life. We don't commend someone like Walt; we recommend him for therapy. Seeking to avoid all relationships is foolish and irrational. Relationships are a central and unavoidable part of a flourishing, rational human life. An account of reason that rules them out is unacceptable.

Economics. Economic relationships represent a second, very practical arena of relationships. Economic exchange—relationships between buyers and sellers, employees and employers, stockholders and boards—is built entirely on trust. Think of the levels of trust involved in my simply buying a coffee at Starbucks. I trust that what I mean by "venti half-caf" is the same as what the barista means by that term. I trust that he or she is following sanitary regulations and has not slipped arsenic into my cup, that the register or computer is working properly, and that he or she is honestly (and capably) calculating my bill and giving me the proper change. (While it is wise to double-check such things, life is far too short never to trust people in such situations.) Likewise, the barista trusts me—that I am using language in the same way he or she is, that my money is genuine, and that I am not buying the coffee in order to throw it in his or her face. Without such trust, even this simple sort of economic transaction is impossible. And such transactions are pervasive in each of our lives. The fact that sometimes such trust is misplaced just proves the point, which is that economic transactions are *built* on trust and cannot occur without it.

> "One of the most important lessons we can learn from an examination of economic life is that a nation's well being, as well as its ability to compete, is conditioned by a single, pervasive cultural characteristic: the level of trust inherent in society."
>
> FRANCIS FUKUYAMA[9]

There is more. The employer trusts the baristas to follow the regulations, to be honest, and to do their job well. And the baristas trust the employer to fulfill his or her commitments to pay them for their work, to provide health benefits when needed, to pay the employer's portion of their Social Security tax, and so on. It works like this all the way up the Starbucks chain of command. At the top, the stockholders, who have invested in the company, trust its officers to obey the law and to fulfill their promises. Economic life is impossible without trust. It necessarily involves commitments to persons, projects and promises that go beyond any form of rational guarantees, philosophical, scientific or otherwise.

As I write this, the United States is in the midst of a severe economic crisis. Why? Not because of technological limitations or lack of resources, but because of a widespread breakdown in the webs of trust. People at all levels of the economy have failed to be trustworthy. They've been dishonest or foolish, pursuing short-term, unethical strategies, motivated by greed rather than fulfilling the obligations that investors and clients have entrusted to them. The consequences have been disastrous. What is the solution to such problems? *No* trust? That would be impossible. It would put an end to economic transactions altogether, eliminating all buying and selling and exchange. In fact it would rule out currency itself, which is based on a government's promise to honor it with value. Trust is unavoidable. What is needed, rather, is trustworthiness, which is a matter of character, at every level.

Language. A third element of relational life is the use of language. Language is also built on trust. The practice of discourse is only possible if there exists a general trust in the truthfulness and trustworthiness of what people say. Even the possibility of lying, as Immanuel Kant noted, presupposes a general practice of truthfulness.[10] In other words, communication is a matter of trust.

To acquire a language requires trust.[11] Typically it is learned from our parents. This requires (implicitly) trusting our parents to be consistent in pointing out and applying terms to various objects, and trusting that our concepts of these things correspond to those terms—not to mention trusting that all of this fits into an intelligible ordered reality. None of these assumptions can be established by either philosophy or science. The point is not that we can't rationally analyze and evaluate language. It's that we can never do so until we've already learned the language to a reasonably competent level. And *that*, unavoidably, requires trust.

This is particularly clear when it comes to learning a new language. For my doctoral work in philosophy at Oxford, based on medieval philosophical texts, I had to learn Latin. How did I begin? I bought a standard text, Frederic Wheelock's *Latin Grammar*, and began to work through it, learning declensions, conjugations and vocabulary.[12] At the beginning, since I didn't already know the language, I had no choice but to trust what Wheelock said about these things, that he was giving me accurate information. I committed myself to understanding Latin as he presented it. It was a reasonable trust since Wheelock is highly regarded as an authority in such matters, but it was trust nonetheless. I could not establish any of these things in advance, because that would require that I already *knew* Latin.

Of course my language learning did not end merely in trust. Eventually I came to grasp Latin well enough to understand it in its own right, not simply "because Wheelock says so." Someday, in fact, I may know it well enough to be able to evaluate Wheelock and conclude that he got a few things wrong. (I'm not there yet.) But I could never get to that point without initially trusting Wheelock or some other text. I could never *learn* Latin without trust. As we'll see, this is true for all learning.

Fides quaerens intellectum ("Faith seeking understanding")—A famous dictum about faith by St. Anselm (1033-1109), echoing Augustine.[13] The point is not that faith is a kind of ignorance or believing things we don't understand at all—as in fideism. The Latin word for "understand" (*intellectus*) refers to grasping the essential nature of something. In all knowledge and learning, we begin by trusting authorities. But our goal is to come to understand the subject matter in itself, to grasp its essential nature. Properly understood, faith does not preclude education, learning and scientific research. It motivates and makes them possible.

Each of these central arenas of human life and thought is ruled out if we understand reason in a way that rules out all faith. To be consistent, the person who rejects trust and commitment entirely must reject all relationships, including all economic relationships, and all language. (Walt, in his cave, must forswear all reading and writing, which are language dependent, as well as all knowledge derived from reading and writing.) This is not yet to mention the fact, which I don't have space to develop (you can think it through for yourself), that a consistent rationalist would also not be able to sit in chairs, cross bridges, fly on airplanes or ride buses, since these involve trust and commitment. May I suggest that this would not be a more rational life? Faith is unavoidable. The "no faith" view is impossible.

RATIONALISM IS IRRATIONAL

Ironically, it's also irrational. This is because rationality itself, understood broadly (and uncontroversially) as thinking, reasoning, weighing propositions as true or false, making inferences and so on, requires trust and commitment. This can be shown in several ways, but I'll give you one line of argument that builds on what we've already seen.

We saw that learning a language begins with trust. But this is true of all learning, whether languages, history, biology, geography or physics. Because we are finite and therefore limited in our awareness of things, we have to learn them from those who already know—teachers, textbooks, maps and the like. That requires trust. To reject all trust is to reject learning itself and therefore to reject all reasoning about subjects that need to be learned—*all* subjects, in other words, for normal human beings.

Trust continues to be essential for mature thinkers, even experts in the field, who no longer operate at the level of wholly trusting authorities in order to learn the basics. Even at an advanced point most of what they know depends on sources of information that go beyond what they themselves have experienced or established. Reasonable scientists do not restrict themselves to information they have personally validated by experiment. If they did, they would have to begin by proving everything that precedes their own work, including reinventing the wheel and discovering that water is H_2O.[14] The scientific enterprise is cumulative. Each new scientist depends on the reports of previous scientists concerning the results of their discoveries. But this involves trusting that those records are accurate and truthful. Richard Dawkins could do none of the work he does in biology if he actually rejected faith of every kind.

This is the case for most, perhaps all, knowledge. Virtually everything we know about the world, we know on the basis of testimony of others.[15] How do you know, for example, where Australia is and how it is shaped? Such knowledge is based on maps (which, by the way, pilots must trust in order to fly there). Most of us know that the sun is the center of our solar system and that water boils at 212 degrees Fahrenheit, but few of us are able to prove it. Nor do we need to. We know these things because someone has discovered or established

"Do not be scared by the word authority. Believing things on authority only means believing them because you have been told them by someone you think is trustworthy. Ninety-nine per cent of the things you believe are believed on authority. I believe there is such a place as New York. I have not seen it myself. I could not prove by abstract reasoning that there must be such a place. I believe it because reliable people have told me so. The ordinary man believes in the Solar System, atoms, evolution, and the circulation of the blood on authority—because the scientists say so. Every historical statement in the world is believed on authority. None of us has seen the Norman Conquest or the defeat of the Armada. None of us could prove them by pure logic as you prove a thing in mathematics. We believe them simply because people who did see them have left writings that tell us about them: in fact, on authority. A man who jibbed at authority in other things as some people do in religion would have to be content to know nothing all his life."

C. S. LEWIS[16]

them and we trust their reports. Even those who *are* able to prove such things can't prove everything they know, and it would be silly for them to try. To make any progress they must trust the testimony of others. As philosopher Robert Audi concludes, "It may be that no normal human being would know anything apart from dependence on receiving testimony."[17]

The entire enterprise of learning, experiment and knowledge is founded on trust and commitment. In the real world (not Walt's cave) rational pursuit is inherently social. Scientists, scholars and academics commit themselves to academic projects and collaborate with other thinkers in common academic endeavors such as laboratories, think tanks and common research projects. The subject of this book involves the most substantial academic project of all: the university. As are all other relationships and endeavors, the university is constituted by trust and commitment. Those who commit to the university community and its relationships do so because they trust the value of truth, knowledge, science and intellectual progress, which cannot be established by philosophical demonstration or scientific verification. They pledge themselves to abide by honesty and fairness, moral values that also cannot be established in these ways, but without which the enterprise would be impossible. Members of the university promise each other to honor such commitments, and they trust their colleagues in the university community to honor them as well. Finally, at the heart of the intellectual enterprise, for a scholar, is a commitment to search for results that cannot be guaranteed in advance but lie entirely in the future—a search that involves risk, requires language and relationships, and builds on the testimony of peers and the records of those who have gone before.

Simply by virtue of being part of a university, then, one is embedded in multiple webs of trust and commitment. Those who are truly committed to the life of the mind cannot consistently reject trust and commitment. They can only, as the wisdom model of rationality advises, seek to be wise in their trust and commitments.

RATIONALISM REJECTED

A rationalism that rejects all faith should itself be rejected. It is incompatible with reason, learning and an intelligible life. The rationalist project fails on its own terms. It may be objected that I've only shown the impossibility and irrationality of rationalism, *as I have interpreted it here*—as the rejection of all trust and commitment. My conclusions would not follow if one held to a less extreme understanding of rationality, one that allows for the possibility of reasonable trust and commitment.[18] That's true, but it's exactly my point. A more modest and nuanced—a more plausible—conception of rationality is compatible with faith. Faith is not irrational in principle. Once the possibility of reasonable trust and commitment—faith—is allowed, which is what strong rationalism denies, the focus turns from faith as such to evaluating particular cases of faith, including cases of religious faith. Whether faith is

rational in such cases depends on the object of that faith, not merely
that it is faith. And that is how it should be.

REASONABLE FAITH AND FAITHFUL REASON

Both poles of the divorce view—fideism and rationalism—are dead
ends. The more reasonable—and faithful—view is marriage. Faith and
reason are friends and partners. They go together. They need each
other and cannot flourish or even survive apart. Our faith should be a
reasonable faith, and our reason should be a faithful reason—one that
recognizes the inevitable and rationally necessary presence of trust and
commitment. Trusting and committing yourself to what you have good reason to think is true and trustworthy, in those cases when doing so is appropriate or unavoidable, is the most reasonable thing you can do. Refusing to trust a chair that you have good reason to think will hold you up is irrational. As Oxford philosopher Sir Anthony Kenny observes, "That way neurosis lies."[19]

St. Thomas Aquinas (1225?-1274)—
Italian monk, theologian, philosopher and poet (possibly the originator of the limerick). One of the most influential Christian thinkers, Aquinas wrote over one hundred works on a wide variety of subjects. He is best known for his arguments for the existence of God, his accounts of natural-law morality and virtue ethics, and for holding a strong, positive doctrine of creation. God's grace does not "destroy" nature, according to Aquinas; it completes or perfects it. His massive *Summa Theologiae* may be considered the most ambitious attempt in the Christian intellectual tradition to develop a detailed, comprehensive Christian worldview.

Followers of Jesus living in the context of the university have every reason to be confident that theirs is a rational faith. (More on its credentials in chap. 11.) We can fully embrace our Christian faith and at the same time embrace a fully rational understanding of reason. We have no reason to suspect science—although we should reject scientism. We have no reason to fear philosophical analysis and argument—although we should reject philosophical conclusions that are based on faulty assumptions such as rationalism. And we should embrace biblical faith—but reject fideism.

We can and should do this because all truth is God's truth. All that is legitimate in science (or technology or history or philosophy) is entirely and fully compatible with the Christian worldview, and should be wholeheartedly embraced and practiced by those who follow Jesus. Biblical faith does not reject truth. Rather, it gives us confidence to pursue it.

The virtue of faith. Classical Christians like Augustine and Aquinas thought of faith as a virtue—a disposition or cultivated habit of discerning, trusting and committing oneself to what is worthy of trust and commitment. Along the lines of Aristotle's (and Aquinas's) understanding of the virtues, we could say that the virtue of faith avoids two opposite vices: fideism, or irrational and unbiblical trust and commitment, on the one hand, and rationalism, the impossible and irrational rejection of trust and commitment, on the other.

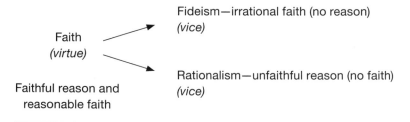

Figure 9.1. Faith, fideism and rationalism

In this view, proper faith is an inescapable part of wisdom. That's just as we would expect, given the picture of thinking, believing and living that has emerged in these chapters, particularly on the wisdom model of rationality. British pastor and poet G. A. Studdert Kennedy (1883-1929), a scholar trained in the classics, summarized well the implications of this view of faith for the academic enterprise:

> The faculty of faith is not meant to kill the faculty of criticism and the instinct of curiosity, but rather to keep them keen and alive, and prevent them dying of despair. Faith is the mark of those who seek and keep on

seeking, who ask and keep on asking, who knock and keep on knocking until the door is opened. The passive, weak-kneed taking of everything on trust—which is often presented as faith—is a travesty of its truth.

True faith is the most active, positive, and powerful of all virtues. It means that a man, having come into spiritual communion with that great personal Spirit Who lives and works behind the universe, can trust Him, and, trusting Him, can use all his powers of body, mind, and spirit to cooperate with Him in the great purpose of perfection; it means that the man of faith will be the man of science in its deepest, truest sense, and will never cease from asking questions—never cease from seeking for the reason that lies behind all mysteries.[20]

10

CHALLENGES TO FAITH

HANDLING DOUBTS AND OBJECTIONS

We live by faith, not by sight.

2 CORINTHIANS 5:7

Faith . . . is the art of holding on to things your reason has once accepted, in spite of your changing moods.

C. S. LEWIS

Doug, a freshman at Stanford University, was actively involved in Christian fellowship and ministry. One day he met with me to discuss the doubts he was experiencing about his faith. He announced that he was choosing to withdraw from Christian community in order to have time to "work through" his doubts. I was taken by surprise when almost immediately Doug joined the party scene in his dorm and effectively disappeared, his faith, by all appearances, a distant memory. I can see now that Doug's doubts were multidimensional in their origin. Most of ours are. Dealing with them appropriately and turning them into opportunities to grow also needs to be multidimensional.

Some of our struggles with faith are intellectual. Others are more sociological or relational in origin—particularly powerful factors in a secular university, where we live in a tight social context in which followers of Jesus form a minority community in belief, values and practice. Still other struggles have a moral basis. Much of the time, as is likely in Doug's case, all of these factors may be involved. The biblical understanding of the heart suggests this, as it implies that there are multiple aspects to why we believe and choose and live as we do. The wisdom model of rationality suggests this as well.

CHALLENGES TO FAITH

In this chapter we examine three kinds of challenge to faith: objections, doubts and practical difficulties in living by faith. Each has intellectual, relational and moral dimensions. Part of handling challenges wisely is discerning these dimensions. *Objections* come from the outside, from others—professors in the classroom, students or others we engage in conversation, or other sources such as books or films. *Doubts* are challenges from the inside—our own questions and struggles about our faith. The two overlap, since we often struggle with the same questions as others, and their objections may prompt our own doubts. Sometimes our struggles result simply from the *practical difficulties* of living out our faith in the midst of daily pressures and temptations. All three kinds of challenge are inevitable for believers, especially college students. As Paul says concerning temptation or testing (the word he uses refers to both), "No temptation has overtaken you except what is common to mankind. And God is faithful; he will not let you be tempted beyond what you can bear. But when you are tempted, he will also provide a way out so that you can endure it" (1 Cor 10:13). Challenges to faith ebb and flow in different seasons of life and vary in different circumstances. But they often come to a particular focus in college, as they did for me. Struggles with faith don't end when you graduate, however. They're still a part of my life—and that of anyone who takes seriously the call to follow Jesus in a fallen world. On the positive side, these challenges play a crucial role in God's process of maturing us to be like Jesus. But unless we think and believe well as we face them, they will drive us crazy.

RESPONDING TO OBJECTIONS

Explicit objections are obvious, stated and primarily intellectual in nature. They range from trivial misrepresentations of Christianity to genuine, important challenges to Christian faith. Implicit objections lie below the surface, unstated and usually unrecognized assumptions, values or pressures that erode our vision. They are often the most destructive to faith.

Explicit objections. There are well-known intellectual objections to Christian faith, such as the problem of evil and suffering. We who desire to love God with our minds and represent Jesus in the marketplace of ideas need to think them through and respond to these objections appropriately. This requires hard work in prayerful study, reflection and practice. Thankfully, there is no lack of resources in this area, which informed and wise Christian thinkers have developed and made widely available.[1] Here are some suggestions for how to think about responding to objections.

First, do it in community. Otherwise the task can seem overwhelming. None of us has the time and ability to master all the objections that can be raised to Christian faith, and few of us feel fully adequate to answer even a few of them. We need to work together. Individuals naturally focus on those objections they have personally encountered. If your roommate seriously challenges you about the "intolerance" and "narrow-mindedness" of Christianity ("How can *any* religion claim to have 'the truth'?"), the issue of religious exclusivism will become important to you, and you'll be motivated to seek answers to it. Once you've thought and prayed through it, you can become a go-to person for helping others respond. Other believers struggle with different questions, and they can become resource persons to the community in those areas. We were made to live and grow together, and facing these things as a community makes the challenges manageable.

The importance of this came home to me several years ago, as I taught at the European Leadership Forum, made up of like-minded followers of Jesus from all over Europe, particularly the former Soviet Bloc countries in central Europe, where there are few mature believers and Christian resources. These leaders gather once a year, at great personal expense, to worship and fellowship together, and to network, be trained, and develop common strategies and resources for addressing crucial issues and objections to the faith. In their own countries these leaders may be the only person, or one of two or three, seeking to engage the marketplace of ideas. For them, developing a broader community with like-minded friends is a matter of survival. The same is actually true for us, whether or not we recognize it. At the very least, if we don't engage objections together, we'll be less effective. More realistically, however, the task is daunting and we're likely to become discouraged and give up if we attempt it alone. I urge you to take advantage of the natural opportunities you have in college to find like-minded believers and commit together to study, research, and engage objections as a community.

Wired community—The possibilities of broader community today are huge. Take advantage of opportunities, electronic or otherwise, to network with like-minded students at other universities and believers in other countries, especially those with few believers and resources.

Second, if an objection is raised in the context of a conversation, remember that first and foremost you're dealing with a person, not an objection. Seek to win the person, not merely the argument. Jesus' ministry was characterized by "grace and truth" (Jn 1:14), and his followers should be like him in both respects. First Peter 3:15 calls us to give a rational defense of our hope, but to do so "with gentleness and respect." Sometimes this means shutting up and listening, rather than jumping in with responses and objections of our own.

Third, as Doug's example suggests, keep in mind the biblical understanding of the heart, according to which our thoughts and beliefs are bound up with our values, motivations, loyalties, commitments, character and choices. "The heart has its reasons of which reason knows nothing," according to Pascal.[2] Faith issues touch all of these elements, which is why doubts and struggles are multidimensional. In fact, the central faith question is really a worship issue: In what or whom will I put my ultimate trust and commitment? Will I trust, love, serve and commit my life to God or to something or someone else? Everything is at stake in how we answer this question. Issues of God's existence and the truth of the Christian worldview are never merely theoretical matters.

Keep these things in mind when responding to objections. Only God knows exactly what factors prompt someone's questions. When I dialogue with someone, I assume that their questions or objections are honest intellectual queries and should be answered in good faith, to the best of my ability, unless or until it becomes evident that something else is going on. If I sense the objections are merely dodges or excuses, I begin to ask questions that challenge them more pointedly. Or it may emerge that beneath their objections are deep personal hurts or struggles that I need to be sensitive to. In any case, asking questions is crucial because they can uncover the deeper issues. And I need to be gracious to the person and sensitive to the guidance of the Holy Spirit throughout.

Blaise Pascal (1623-1662)—French physicist, mathematician, philosopher and deeply committed Christian. A child prodigy, Pascal had no formal education, including college, but he pioneered probability theory, developed the barometer and invented a mechanical calculator. On November 23, 1654, he had a two-hour religious experience that led to his conversion. Pascal's most famous work is his *Pensées* ("thoughts"), many of which were collected from scraps of paper on which he jotted his reflections.

Implicit objections. Often the most powerful objections lie below the surface, operating at the level of implicit assumptions, values and social pressures. Here relational and moral factors are particularly salient. But intellectual challenges also play a role at this level, often in their most powerful form. Here, for example, is where we see the chief effect of two ideas we've explored at length: scientism and "tolerance" (the faulty current understanding of tolerance). I've noted that these ideas typically derail serious consideration of the Christian worldview as a matter of truth and rationality. It's important to see that they play this role, not as surface, explicit objections to faith, but as implicit, usually unconscious assumptions.

Wheelbarrows. A story told by former Soviet premier Nikita Khrushchev illustrates how implicit objections work.[3] It concerns a period in the Soviet Union when there was rampant petty theft. To prevent workers stealing from the factories, the authorities posted guards at the exits. The guard assigned to the timberworks in Leningrad knew many of the workers personally.

The first evening, out came a worker, Pyotr Petrovich, pushing a wheelbarrow carrying a large, suspicious-looking sack. The guard said, "Okay, Petrovich, what've you got in the sack?" "Just sawdust and shavings," replied Petrovich. The skeptical guard told him to tip it out and empty the sack. Sure enough: just sawdust and shavings. Petrovich stuffed the contents back into the sack, and wheeled it away. The next evening, the same thing happened: Petrovich with his wheelbarrow and a suspicious-looking sack. "What's in the sack, Petrovich?" "Just sawdust and shavings." "Tip it out." Again, just sawdust and shavings.

It happened every night for a week. Finally the guard's curiosity overcame his frustration: "Look, Petrovich, I know you're smuggling something out of here. Just tell me what it is, and I'll let you go." Petrovich's reply? "Wheelbarrows."

Sometimes what is most important is not what we see, but what lies beneath what we see—like the wheelbarrow. Implicit objections act as "wheelbarrows" in our thought. As underlying ideas, assumptions or values, they are often more important than our explicit beliefs—they "carry" them. Usually we're not aware of the wheelbarrows, but they're at work in our thinking, nonetheless. Assumptions like scientism and "tolerance" carry our train of thought away from serious engagement with important truth. For example, although few people have ever heard the term *scientism*, many hold scientistic assumptions. They assume that only what science validates can be a matter of truth or knowledge. So when they encounter ideas about religion or morality, which fall outside the scope of science, the wheelbarrow of scientism carries these ideas away from serious consideration as matters of objective reality. If they were to embrace one of these ideas, such as belief in God, while under its influence, they would accept it as an optional add-on, a kind of spiritual truth or "what's true for you." But not as honest-to-goodness, objective truth about reality, something that *must* be engaged. It would be a matter of faith, in the fideistic sense, not something that can be known.[4] The only way to deal with wheelbarrows is to make them visible: they need to be uncovered, examined and questioned. Asking good questions, especially *So what?* is often the most effective strategy.

Plausibility. Another distinction is helpful here. Implicit objections operate as part of what sociologists of knowledge call a *plausibility structure*, a context of unquestioned assumptions that govern what a person regards as being possibly true.[5] The idea is that unless we assume that something *could* be true we won't seriously consider evidence or reasons that it *is* actually true. It's not believable; the soil is too hard for the seed to penetrate. Dealing with implicit objections involves intellectual agriculture work: softening the ground and removing stones. Until one's implicit objections are dealt with, one will not take the Christian worldview fully seriously, as a matter of actual truth and reality. Explicit objections are claims that the Christian worldview is false. Implicit objections prevent one from seeing it as fully true.

Plausibility structures are not merely (or chiefly) matters of ideas. The values, priorities and assumptions of the communities in which we live—what those around us find plausible—shape what we find believable. The process works in subtle, usually unconscious and implicit, ways. This is why it's a struggle to be part of a minority community in belief and practice —and why it's so devastating for Christians to abandon the university. The presence of thoughtful believers in the university community makes the Christian worldview plausible, softening the soil, making Christian faith believable so that one can see it to be true. Our *not* being in the university's marketplace of ideas has the opposite effect. It hardens the soil, perpetuating the sense that Christian faith is, at best, a kind of useful fiction. This lies beneath many of the doubts believers have, especially in the university, as well as the objections of nonbelievers. One of the most im-

> Making the gospel plausible:
> - Be a community: follow Jesus in community with other believers, acting as a body.
> - Be a counterexample: be intelligent, loving, "full of grace and truth."
> - Be a blessing: serve others, meet needs, care about the poor.

portant elements in recovering my faith as a college student was being introduced to books of robust thinking and scholarship written by Christian intellectuals. It wasn't just that they answered many of my questions. They also made me aware of a greater, intellectually engaged Christian community, and gave me a vision for seeing myself as part of that community. This made the Christian worldview plausible for me.

DOUBTS

Our faith is also challenged from the inside, from our own doubts. As noted, doubts and objections often converge. Here are a few additional suggestions for handling doubts wisely.

First, recognize that doubt is inevitable. Because we're finite, we don't know everything. There will always be questions. Because we're fallen, we're inclined to distort and misinterpret even what we do know. The biblical understanding of the heart is relevant to us as believers as well. We all tend toward idolatry, toward seeking our basis of significance and fulfillment in something other than God (Rom 1:18-23). And we're usually unaware of it. According to Jeremiah 17:9:

> The heart is deceitful above all things
> and beyond cure.
> Who can understand it?

Because we're finite and fallen we need faith. Our limited reasoning is not enough to get us to all the truth we need, especially about the most important things. But what makes faith necessary also renders doubt inevitable. The only way to escape doubt is not to think at all, which is impossible. And to attempt it is an offense to the Creator of our minds. Instead, face your doubts honestly and seek to deal with them wisely.

"The inescapable presence of doubt is a constant reminder of our responsibility to truth in a twilight world of truth and half-truth."

OS GUINNESS[6]

Second, some doubt is good. It's part of thinking, seeking truth. *Logical doubt* is not simply accepting everything, but testing truth claims, examining their warrant and seeking to be wise. I was recently interviewed for a television program described as a cutting-edge analysis of important topics from the perspective of "healthy skepticism." But I quickly discovered that there was little healthy or balanced about the skepticism of the host. His agenda was to debunk all religious belief.

There is such a thing as healthy skepticism, an attitude of questioning that seeks truth. But much skepticism is *un*healthy, in either (or both) of two directions: it's either too skeptical or not skeptical enough. We are too skeptical when we make doubt our aim, rather than seeking truth. This is not logical doubt but *psychological doubt*—doubting everything, being unwilling to believe even what we have good reason to believe. This is often portrayed as "open-mindedness." But that's a misunderstanding. As G. K. Chesterton remarked about H. G. Wells, "I think he thought that the object of opening the mind is simply opening the mind. Whereas I am incurably convinced that the object of opening the mind, as of opening the mouth, is to shut it again on something solid."[7] Open-mindedness is a virtue when you are looking for truth, but not when you have found it. There's a big difference between being open-minded and being empty-headed.

The other form of unhealthy skepticism is not being skeptical enough, which, ironically, may accompany being too skeptical. Skeptics often doubt everything but their doubts; their skepticism doesn't go far enough. In fact, the radical skeptic who rejects all truth and knowledge does so on the basis of certain skeptical assumptions about truth and knowledge which operate, in effect, as knowledge claims he or she accepts and uses to guide life—including reaching skeptical conclusions. Such skeptics aren't skeptical enough. They need to doubt their doubts.[8]

And that's my third piece of advice: doubt your doubts. As we struggle with doubt, we can easily make the same kind of mistake as the radical skeptic. The assumptions that are prevalent in the thought contexts in which we live affect us too, and often motivate our doubts. They need to be brought to the surface, identified and questioned. When you doubt, ask yourself: What about my doubts? Are they based on assumptions that I have *less* reason to believe than I do the beliefs I am doubting?

Fourth, stay in community. We need to do this for many reasons, but it's especially important in dealing with doubt. By the grace of God, when I was going through my own season of doubt in college, I sensed that bailing out of Christian fellowship was not going to help, that if I was to find answers to my questions, it would not be in a bar or the party scene. I can see now that those environments would more likely pull me away from logical doubt toward psychological doubt, a condition where I no longer cared about the questions. It's probably what happened with Doug when he chose to withdraw from Christian community. Where better to struggle with one's questions and try to find answers than with those who actually know God and who may have faced the same struggles and worked through them?

"A faith without some doubts is like is like a human body without any antibodies in it. People who blithely go through life too busy or indifferent to ask hard questions about why they believe as they do will find themselves defenseless against either the experience of tragedy or the probing questions of a smart skeptic. A person's faith can collapse almost overnight if she has failed over the years to listen patiently to her own doubts, which should only be discarded after long reflection."

TIMOTHY KELLER[9]

We need each other. When I'm in a desert of doubt, you may not be. When you're faltering in your faith, I may be walking strong and can help you. Listen to the wisdom of Hebrews 3:12-13, which stresses the importance of community in keeping our perspective sane: "See to it, brothers and sisters, that none of you has a sinful, unbelieving heart that turns away from the living God. *But encourage one another daily,* as long as it is called 'Today,' so that none of you may be hardened by sin's deceitfulness."

Fifth, remember that God has a bigger plan for you, even in your doubt. His ultimate goal is not to erase all doubts or give us absolute rational certainty about everything. His goal is to make us like Jesus. Sometimes he uses seasons of doubt, just as he allows times of suffering, to draw us away from our idols so we can *truly* learn to trust and worship him.

For the past few years, I've struggled with chronic illness. My immune system is damaged, and my condition has developed to the point where, ironically, I have become "allergic" (actually, I have a strong toxic reaction) to paper—particularly to books. It sounds like a joke, especially for an academic, but it's serious. As I write this, for example, I'm able to read my (physical) Bible only while wearing a mask and rubber gloves. And these are my *new* books. All the older ones, the thousands of books I accumulated over the course of thirty years in academic contexts, are now entirely off-limits to me, sealed in plastic and sitting in storage. As you can imagine, this is quite a blow to someone whose vocation is bound up with books. (And it makes writing this one quite a challenge.) But it's more than that for me. I don't just use books: I love them. Quite honestly, this has been very hard. I continue to pray that this condition will not be permanent (I'm seeing gradual, slow improvement).[10] But I wouldn't trade what I've learned through this experience. God has used it to change my life in deeply significant ways—weaning me from idols, shaping my character, purifying my trust in him and drawing me to himself in ways that I had never before experienced.

> "It is not as a child that I believe and confess Christ. My hosanna is born of a furnace of doubt."
> FYODOR DOSTOYEVSKY (1821-1881)[11]

Doubt can play this role in our lives. The most effective representatives of Jesus in the marketplace of ideas are not those who have never questioned their faith or have airtight but superficial answers to every question. They are individuals who have been through the furnace of doubt and have emerged with a gracious, seasoned, confident trust that is grounded in a personal experience of God himself. There are no shortcuts to that kind of faith.

Finally, in your doubt don't lose sight of what you do know. Don't be perpetually "open-minded," but commit yourself to what you do know about God, even in the furnace or desert. Don't hold off on trusting God until all your questions are answered or all your doubts are erased.

That will never happen in this life. It's also foolish to pursue. It's like saying, "I don't have enough to save money now. I'll wait until I have lots of money, and then I'll start saving." Obviously you'll never have lots of money unless you start saving—now. Think of faith, similarly as an investment. You may feel like you don't have much faith, and that you don't know much about God or yourself. Start where you are, by trusting and committing all you do know about yourself to all you do know about God—however little that may be. Invest what you've got, and let God build and multiply it in his time.[12]

Early in the twentieth century, Charles Spurgeon, an influential British pastor, compared trusting God with how engineers (before the age of helicopters and heavy equipment) could begin the process of building an iron bridge across a large canyon.

> Years ago they wanted to put a suspension bridge across a mighty chasm. From crag to crag it was proposed to hang an iron bridge aloft in the air, but how was it to be commenced? They shot an arrow from one side to the other, and carried across the gulf a tiny thread. The connection was established; by-and-by the thread drew a piece of twine, and the twine carried after it a small rope, the rope soon carried a cable across, and all in good time came the iron chains. Faith is often weak but it is still of utmost value.[13]

LIVING BY FAITH

If we left our account of faith here, it would be misleading. The biblical picture of faith is not primarily one of accruing beliefs or getting answers to questions. It's *living* in a certain way: trusting God and what he says about reality, and acting accordingly—trust and commitment, lived out in the nitty-gritty of life, in every decision and action. As C. S. Lewis observes, the biggest struggles of faith are often not intellectual objections but the daily challenges of staying true to what we believe, despite our emotions and appetites—fueled by social pressures—pulling us in other directions.[14] Confidence in faith ultimately comes only to those who follow that path.

What has been particularly helpful to me in this area is to discover how the Bible understands faith and its contrast. As I noted in chapter eight, Scripture never contrasts faith to reason. What it does contrast to faith is *sight*. This way of thinking underlies the most famous of all biblical descriptions of faith: "Faith is the assurance of things hoped for, the conviction of things not seen" (Heb 11:1 ESV). It's explicit in Paul's summary of his approach to life and ministry: "We live by faith, not by sight" (2 Cor 5:7).

But is this just another way of making the same point? Does it mean that biblical faith is irrational, blind faith? No. The biblical picture is not of closing your eyes and leaping into the dark. It's of *opening* your eyes to see more than what is merely visible—to recognize a reality that is bigger than that. As it is sometimes put, faith is not a leap into the dark, but a walk into the light.

> "It is not reason that is taking away my faith: on the contrary, my faith is based on reason. It is my imagination and emotions. The battle is between faith and reason on one side and imagination on the other."
>
> C. S. LEWIS[15]

Sight. "Sight" in the previous passages stands for two things. First, for what is immediately present or obvious to us in the world around us. In particular, it refers to what we directly perceive with our five senses: sight, touch, smell, hearing and taste. That is, the empirical world. We seldom doubt what is visible in these ways: it's just there, in our face. Second, sight refers not only to what is present to our senses but also to what is present in time. The here-and-now is visible; what's in the future is not.

Biblical faith relates to both of these. First, God is not "in our face," physically. We don't perceive him with our five senses, because he's not a physical object. Many refuse to believe in God simply for that reason, saying that they will only believe what they can see, what is empirically verifiable. But that assumes that reality is limited to the physical or empirical world, and that knowledge is limited to what we can experience with our five senses—which is just what these biblical passages deny. But are those assumptions true? No. They would also rule out the existence of thoughts (including thoughts about what is empirically verifiable), propositions and states of consciousness—things we know to be real but are not visible in this way. Moreover, the demand that we restrict our knowledge to what we can experience with our senses is self-refuting, since we can't know that empirically. God is not a physical object but is no less real for that. Second, the fulfillment of what God is up to in our lives and the realization of his plans and promises for us lie in the future. We can't see them yet. But they are no less true for that.

A larger vision. The biblical contrast between living by faith and living by sight is all about perspective. Paul makes this clear in the immediate context of his statement in 2 Corinthians 5:7, "We live by faith, not by sight," where he's giving the rationale for his life and ministry, explaining why he has chosen a life that involves shipwreck, hunger, persecution and struggle. He concludes:

> Therefore we do not lose heart. Though outwardly we are wasting away, yet inwardly we are being renewed day by day. For our light and momentary troubles are achieving for us an eternal glory that far outweighs them all. So we fix our eyes not on what is seen, but on what is unseen, since what is seen is temporary, but what is unseen is eternal. (2 Cor 4:16-18)

Paul lives as he does, in the circumstances he faces, because of his understanding of those circumstances—his perspective. He recognizes that what he *sees*—his outward, physical condition, his sufferings and setbacks—is not all that is real. What's happening "behind the seen" is actually far more important. Paul understands that God is actively at work in his life, shaping his inward life, his character, and that he is using him to introduce others to Jesus, people with whom he will share eternity. Paul is living for the big picture, the long view—what is eternal, still in the future, and not just what's "in his face," right now. He has an eternal perspective. His "eyes" (note the deliberate paradox) are fixed "not on what is seen, but on what is unseen." Paul's vision encompasses more than physical sight. His eyes aren't closed. They're open to a larger reality.

> "Brothers and sisters, now we believe, we do not see. The reward of that faith will be to see what we believe."
>
> AUGUSTINE[16]

From faith to sight. Older Christian thinkers describe heaven as the *visio Dei*—as seeing God (see Mt 5:8; 1 Jn 3:2). There we'll also be able to see "the rest of the story," the bigger reality lying behind our limited perspective here. All of this is part of what Paul fixed his eyes on, in faith. In heaven the shades will open, the mists will evaporate and everything will become clear. We'll understand what God was up to, why he allowed what he did, and what it all meant.

Even now, however, as we trust God and live accordingly, our perspective grows. Our vision becomes more acute and we come to see the world differently. I'm now old enough to have attended several of my high school reunions. Much of what used to be faith to me is now sight. In the lives of my high school classmates I can *see* the results of bad decisions they've made, especially about sex—choices based on ideas that once appeared so attractive but now are seen to be disastrous. We make our choices and then our choices make us. The results of our values, decisions and actions become increasingly evident in our lives, even in our personal appearance. As George Orwell said, "At fifty everyone has the face he deserves."[17]

LIVING FAITHFULLY IN THE UNIVERSITY

The contrast between faith and sight is not the same as that between faith and reason, because not trusting your "sight" can be the most reasonable thing to do. Pilots know that it can seem to them, when flying by the "seat of their pants," that their plane is climbing when it's actually diving. So when flying at night or in a storm with no visibility, trusting their instruments is the rational thing for a pilot to do. Similarly, if reality is actually bigger than what we can "see" at the moment, the most reasonable thing we can do is trust our instruments—the bigger perspective God reveals in the Scriptures—and live accordingly.

In the university, what's "in your face" can be overwhelming. College provides ample opportunities to live "by the seat of your pants," to follow your feelings and hormones and to conform to social pressures. Plenty of voices and values around you encourage you to experiment with sex or to seek your significance solely in academic achievement. These things are immediate: what you see, feel, taste and touch. But if

God is real and what the Bible says is true, then living according to that limited perspective is insanity.

A FIERY FAITH

A vivid picture of living by faith is found in the story of Daniel's college friends, Shadrach, Meshach and Abednego, who faced death by fire because they remained faithful to God and refused to worship the king (see p. 139). What was "in their face" must have been nearly overwhelming. But they had a bigger perspective, as revealed in their words to the king:

> If we are thrown into the blazing furnace, the God we serve is able to deliver us from it, and he will deliver us from Your Majesty's hand. *But even if he does not*, we want you to know, Your Majesty, that we will not serve your gods or worship the image of gold you have set up." (Dan 3:17-18, emphasis added)

They didn't make deals with God or hedge their bets. They trusted God to do what he knew was best, whatever that would be. And they acted accordingly. God did deliver them, and they experienced his presence in an unprecedented way (see Dan 3:21-25).

What will be the results of *our* choices to live by faith, not by sight? Now, only God knows. But someday we will too, when we see the rest of the story.

THE CREDIBILITY OF FAITH

WORLDVIEWISH APOLOGETICS

*But in your hearts revere Christ as Lord. Always be prepared to
give an answer to everyone who asks you to give the reason for
the hope that you have. But do this with gentleness and respect.*

1 PETER 3:15

*I don't see myself as so much dust that has appeared in the
world, but as a being that was expected, prefigured, called forth.
In short, as a being that could, it seems, come only from a creator;
and this idea of a creating hand that created me refers me back
to God.*

JEAN PAUL SARTRE, "Conversations with Jean-Paul Sartre"

When I recovered my faith in college, I was motivated to defend it to
others. I discovered *apologetics*. Eventually I also discovered why that's
a bad word to some people, especially those who've been badgered by
apologetics junkies looking for an argument. I'm afraid I've contributed
to the problem myself.

But pointing to the truth of the Christian worldview is a good thing.
In fact, it's a crucial part of thinking and believing well in the marketplace of ideas, especially the university. Yet it needs to be done in the
right way and for the right reasons. In previous chapters we've covered
much of what that involves. What I'd like to do in this one is pull some
of those strands together, with a few needed distinctions, into an integrated picture of the credibility of Christian faith.

APOLOGETICS

Apologetics is the art and science of explaining and defending the truth claims of Christian theism. The name is drawn from the Greek term *apologia*, translated in 1 Peter 3:15 as "give an answer" or "make a defense." It referred in the first century to giving a defense, as in a court of law. So Christian apologetics is typically conceived as "giving a rational defense" of the Christian worldview. But we should understand it more broadly than what this may suggest.

First, apologetics has both negative and positive roles. *Negative apologetics* is like "playing defense" in football—defending Christian truth claims against objections and misconceptions. It involves clarifying the Christian worldview in light of misconceptions, and answering questions and responding to objections. *Positive apologetics* is "playing offense"—making the case for Christian theism, pointing to the truth about God and the gospel. "Giving an answer" can refer to both roles; we shouldn't restrict apologetics to defending Christian theism in the strictly negative sense. When we discussed how to respond to objections to faith in chapter ten, we were talking about negative apologetics. In this chapter we'll focus on the positive apologetic task.

Most people think of positive apologetics solely as presenting philosophical or historical arguments. This is important, but making the case for faith is more than that. If we think of apologetics more broadly as pointing to the truth about God, it's obvious that it can take many forms. In fact, if God is the Creator of everything else that exists, then *everything*, in some way, reflects God and his truth. Apologetic pointers may be drawn from any or all of it.

The good, the true and the beautiful. We've seen that the Bible paints an integrated picture of the human personality and human reasoning, where our beliefs are bound up with our loves, values and desires. This suggests the possibility of an integrated understanding of apologetics as well. Here's one way to approach such a model. Ancient philosophers and theologians described the most ultimate values as truth, goodness and beauty: truth as ultimate in the cognitive domain, goodness in the moral domain and beauty in the aesthetic domain. Classical thinkers also understood these three values as bound together in a dynamic unity, as ultimately *one:* truth is good, goodness is beautiful and so on. The unity of these values makes perfect sense, from a Christian perspective: they are ultimately bound together in the nature of God. God himself is the ultimate ground of goodness, truth and beauty. As God's creatures, created in his image, we are drawn to these properties. But they also point beyond themselves, to their fulfillment in God.

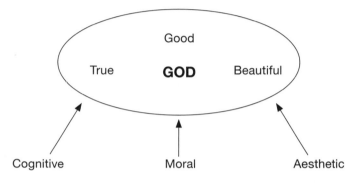

Figure 11.1. The unity of goodness, truth and beauty with God as the ground of goodness, truth and beauty

An integrative vision of apologetics takes this into account. Depending on our particular gifts and personality, each of us may be drawn toward God by one (or two) of these pointers more than the other(s). Most apologetic efforts focus on the cognitive domain. They seek to show, with arguments and reasons, that Christian truth claims are true. But some people are more drawn through reflections of God's goodness or beauty in the world. This suggests that we should broaden our understanding of apologetics to include all three domains. C. S. Lewis, who developed arguments and pointers in each category, was perhaps the most balanced of any recent Christian apologist in his approach. It may be why his writings remain particularly effective, even at a time of skepticism about truth and rationality. In Lewis's own journey to God, beauty was arguably the most important aspect.[1] And for many readers his imaginative writings are his most compelling.

Pointers to truth about God can take many forms, then, reflecting the mosaic of individual gifts and personalities God has given his people. Thinking of apologetics in a broader way is freeing for many believers—to realize, for example, that living a truly good life can point to-ward the goodness of God, or that creating beautiful art can draw our gaze toward the beauty of God (J. R. R. Tolkien called us "sub-creators" who reflect God's image in our own creating).[2] Arguments and expla-nations are needed, of course. But apologetics is not restricted to those who are so gifted. In fact, when Jesus identified our chief pointer to him, it was not an argument but a behavior: "By this everyone will know that you are my disciples, if you love one another" (Jn 13:35). Considerations like these make particular sense in light of what we saw in the last chap-ter about plausibility structures. Whereas arguments and more tradi-tional reasons provide direct evidence that Christian faith is true, these less direct pointers serve primarily, I think, to make the message plau-sible. They soften and enrich the soil; they make it believable.

Arts and sciences. What does it mean to say that apologetics is an "art" and a "science"? *Science*, from the Latin *scientia*, refers to "knowledge"—specifically, to systematically organized knowledge. *Art*, from the Latin *ars* (*artis*), refers to skill. Sciences, such as history and the physical sci-ences, are systematic bodies of information we master by knowing (learning facts, principles, data and so on). The arts, such as fine arts, music and communication, are skills we master by doing. The two are related, of course, which is why a complete college education includes both arts and sciences. Each discipline includes something of each. A competent historian not only knows many facts about history but also how to *do* history—how to analyze data and interpret various historical sources. A competent musician also learns music theory, a body of knowledge. But that's not at the heart of what it is to be a musician. Arts require practice, because that's the only way to become skilled.

The science of apologetics involves mastering a body of knowledge: studying arguments and evidences, and thinking through questions and objections. The art of apologetics is learning to apply this knowledge effectively to those who need it. It includes many things we've empha-sized here: asking good questions, learning the language of your audi-ence and thinking worldviewishly. Both art and science are necessary.

I once attended a public panel discussion at a secular university on the problem of evil, featuring a Christian apologist and a philosophy professor from the university, an atheist. It was attended by some three hundred students and faculty. After the apologist made a presentation on the topic, the philosopher aggressively attacked him and his presentation, reviling the apologist's adherence to the Bible and his belief in the reality of hell. The professor was obviously very emotionally invested in the issues, and his attack was, frankly, unfair to the apologist. If you were the apologist, how would you respond to this? I've reflected on that question quite a bit, since I saw what actually happened. The Christian slammed his Bible down in front of the professor and yelled, "Read it!" And he informed the professor, among other things, that he would eventually know exactly what hell is like, since that's where he was headed.

I was stunned and ashamed. I think most of the audience thought the apologist had provided better reasons and stronger arguments. But they wanted nothing to do with him or what he stood for. He may have won the argument, but lost both his opponent and the audience. He won the battle but lost the war.

I've made similar mistakes, though none as egregious (or public) as that, as far as I know. It's a temptation at times, particularly if you like to argue or are driven to win. But it's wrong. As you and your friends—rightly and importantly—seek to develop your skills as apologists, pay as much attention to the art as you do the science. Seek always to be like Jesus, "full of grace and truth" (Jn 1:14).

WORLDVIEWISH APOLOGETICS

There is, as I have suggested, no single, correct method of apologetics. But how we think about making the case for the credibility of Christian faith is crucial. I have found it most helpful to extend what we've seen about thinking worldviewishly to this area as well. In my view the best way to think about the truth of the Christian worldview and to commend it to others is to do it worldviewishly—"worldviewish apologetics."

The Loch Ness Monster. How do we evaluate worldview beliefs like "God exists"? A typical approach is to treat them as independent, isolated claims: add up the evidence for and against each proposition and accept it or reject it solely on that basis. Taking this approach, naturalists often claim that theists bear the burden of proof when it comes to belief in God.

The idea is that belief in God is like belief in the Loch Ness Monster. All people hold roughly the same set of beliefs about lakes, aquatic life and Scotland. But some folks (call them "Lochies") have an *extra* belief: that in one of the Scottish lakes, Loch Ness, lives a large creature, the Loch Ness Monster. What's the reasonable way to proceed in evaluating this belief? Should we assume the Monster exists, until it can be proved that it doesn't? Or should we assume there is no such creature, until Lochies provide conclusive evidence that there is? The latter is the reasonable approach. That there is a Loch Ness Monster is an extra belief, one that only Lochies have. Surely the burden of proof (in Latin, *onus probandi*) lies with them. It's up to the Lochies to show that there is a Loch Ness Monster. It's not up to the rest of us to prove there is none.

> "It is by reference to this inescapable demand for grounds that the presumption of atheism is justified. If it is to be established that there is a God, then we have to have good grounds for believing that this is indeed so. Until and unless some such grounds are produced we have literally no reason at all for believing; and in that situation the only reasonable posture must be that of either the negative atheist or the agnostic. So the onus of proof has to rest on the proposition."
>
> ANTONY FLEW (1923-2010),
> *THE PRESUMPTION OF ATHEISM*[3]

This is how naturalists often portray belief in God. We all share the same basic set of beliefs, it is argued, which amounts to naturalism. But theists have an extra belief—that God exists. So the burden of proof is on theists to prove their position.

Extra belief: "God exists."

Naturalism

Figure 11.2. A naturalist portrayal of belief in God

Naturalism, in this perspective, is the default view. It's the rational one to hold, unless and until theists come up with a sufficiently compelling proof for God's existence. (Interestingly, in the last few years of his life, Antony Flew, the philosopher who most influentially argued for this approach, abandoned naturalism. He concluded that recent cosmological evidence for a Designer *does* provide a sufficiently compelling proof for the existence of God.[4])

The entire approach is mistaken, however, and it's important and instructive to see why. The reasoning works in the case of the Loch Ness Monster because virtually everyone really *does* hold roughly the same set of beliefs about lakes and aquatic life. Belief in the Loch Ness Monster really *is* just an extra one added on to that general set of beliefs. But that's not the case with belief in God. Belief in God's existence is not merely a belief about an extra entity in the world. It's a worldview belief. In fact, it's a core worldview belief logically embedded in a web of related beliefs within a conceptual structure. As such, it can't be evaluated accurately or even fully understood in isolation from the rest of the worldview.

Figure 11.3 illustrates the more accurate picture, which we've seen already (see chap. 7).

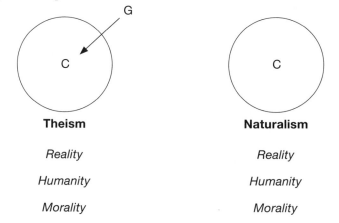

Figure 11.3. Worldviews of theism and naturalism

Theism and naturalism are entirely different belief systems, based on entirely different answers to the big questions. Belief in God is not a mere extra belief in the theist's inventory of beliefs. It's the theist's answer to the most fundamental worldview question, the central belief of the theistic web.

It is not the case that naturalists have no belief about ultimate reality. They have a *different* belief from theists—the belief that there is no God, and that ultimate reality is entirely physical and nonpersonal. From their different central claims, theism and naturalism unfold as fundamentally different, competing conceptions of reality, with different views of the origin, existence, and nature of the universe, of human beings, of morality, and of much more. The two worldviews differ, not in a single belief but "all the way down."

> "Religious belief should be assessed as a rounded whole rather than taken in stark isolation. Christianity, for example, like other world faiths, is a complex, large-scale system of belief which must be seen as a whole before it is assessed. To break it up into disconnected parts is to mutilate and distort its true character. We can, of course, distinguish *certain* elements in the Christian faith, but we must still stand back and see it as a metaphysical system, as a world view, that is total in its scope and range."
>
> WILLIAM ABRAHAM[5]

Because theism and naturalism are worldviews, descriptions of reality at the deepest level, they need to be evaluated as such, in comparison to each other. Each worldview needs to be evaluated as to whether its description of reality corresponds to reality. No single worldview, whether theism, naturalism, pantheism or any other, bears a special burden of proof. Nor does any get an automatic pass. All should be judged honestly at the bar of reality. In sum, worldview beliefs should not be treated as isolated claims but seen in their logical relations to other beliefs within worldviews. And those worldviews should be evaluated in relation to other worldviews. That is, we need to compare and evaluate worldviews *as* worldviews.

How do we do this? I'll illustrate the reasoning involved with two analogies and then sketch the tests for truth that are relevant to evaluating worldviews.[6]

Maps. Suppose we have two, quite different maps, A and B, of the same terrain. How do we evaluate them to see which (if either) is correct? The answer is obvious: unfold each map and see what it says the terrain is like. What should we expect to find on the ground, according to A? according to B? We compare the two descriptions with each other, and then examine the terrain to see which, if either, corresponds to reality. If we don't find the town that A says is there, or if we find major features like lakes and mountains that don't appear on A, we don't consider A to be a credible description of the terrain. If we find what map B leads us to expect, and we don't discover major features that are missing from B, we consider B credible. Only a map that accurately describes what it purports to describe is a true or correct map.

We evaluate competing maps *as maps*—in comparison to each other and in light of reality. Now think of worldviews as maps—large, metaphysical maps—that describe reality in its deepest aspects. They should be tested in terms of those descriptions. As with other maps, we unfold or unpack each worldview to see how it describes reality. What are the worldview's core beliefs, its answers to the big questions (What is real? Who are we? What is good?)? This is, in effect, what we did in our brief treatments of theism, naturalism, pantheism and postmodernism. Based on their answers to the big questions, what should we expect to find (and not find) in reality if this worldview is true? The worldviews give very different pictures. How do they compare to reality? Which makes the best sense of what we actually find, with the fewest difficulties? There will always be question marks and difficulties because we don't know everything. Our data are incomplete. But we want to know which worldview map makes the *best* sense of the most data we do have, with the fewest difficulties.

A court of law. There is nothing mysterious about this type of reasoning. In fact, the way we evaluate worldviews is similar to how we evaluate complex, competing explanations in a range of disciplines, including higher-level scientific theories, historical explanations, philosophical theories and literary interpretation. But it's probably most obvious as the kind of reasoning that occurs in jury trials. This is our second analogy.[7]

Suppose a jury must determine whether Joe killed his wife. The prosecuting attorney claims that Joe did it, the defense attorney claims Joe didn't. How does the jury decide? Typically, no single argument or piece of evidence can settle the issue, and no single proof could establish it beyond all possible doubt. What needs to be explained is a range of evidence, including fingerprints, DNA evidence, eyewitness testimony, alibis and motives. The jury is presented with competing explanations of that evidence. The prosecuting attorney provides one explanation (the guilt hypothesis), which, he argues, best explains the range of evidence. The defense attorney presents a competing explanation (the innocence hypothesis), which, she argues, best explains the evidence. Both explanations cannot be true, because they contradict each other. The true explanation is the one that corresponds to reality, the one that fits what really happened. The jury's job is to determine which, if either, that is.

But how do the jurors reach that determination? They look for the explanation that best fits the evidence as a whole. Which explanation is

- *Nature* of truth: correspondence to reality
- *Tests* for truth: ways to determine if an explanation corresponds to reality

able to account for all of the important evidence, without leaving major gaps? Can it do so without adding extra, ad hoc elements that don't really fit with the rest of the story? Is one explanation able to account for the same evidence as the other, but in a less cumbersome and complicated—a simpler and more natural—way? Which explanation holds together more coherently?

These questions represent tests for truth such as coherence, explanatory power and simplicity—the same sorts of criteria regularly appealed to in other high-level explanations. In the case of a straightforward, meteorological proposition like *It is raining,* a simple, empirical test for truth is sufficient: look outside. Even in science, however, not all propositions are that simple. Higher-level scientific theories (theories about entropy, gravitational fields, quarks, etc.) involve a number of truth claims and cover a range of phenomena. No single observation is sufficient to test their truth. As in the courtroom, they are tested in terms of these broader kinds of criteria.

The jury does not look for proof beyond all possible doubt. That is available only in abstract areas like geometry and mathematics. "Who done it?" questions are factual matters, where proof of that kind is impossible. The jury looks for what best explains the evidence beyond a reasonable doubt, or what explains the preponderance of evidence.

WORLDVIEW TESTS

In evaluating worldviews, as in the courtroom, a range of evidence needs to be explained. The different worldviews represent competing explanations of that evidence. Similar questions are relevant in evaluating these explanations. Which worldview, if any, can account for the whole of the relevant evidence, without leaving major gaps? Can it do this without adding ad hoc elements that don't fit with the rest of the worldview? Is one worldview able to account for the same evidence as the others, but in a simpler and more natural way? Which worldview is more coherent?

Worldview explanations go beyond even high-level scientific theories or courtroom explanations, however. They are the highest-level explanations of all—explanations of why there is a physical cosmos at all, of what human beings are and why they behave the way they do. Most worldview analysts agree on at least three tests for truth as specifically relevant to evaluating such explanations: *consistency* (or logical coherence), *factuality* (factual adequacy, explanatory power), and *livability* (experiential viability).[8] We'll look briefly at each, and I'll note their relevance to some features of the worldviews we've discussed.

Consistency. The first worldview test is *consistency*. Here we look for how well a worldview holds together in a logically coherent way. Minimally, we ask whether its *core beliefs* are logically compatible with each other. Consistency functions as a minimal condition, a deal-breaker. If the central tenets of a worldview are logically inconsistent, that worldview simply *cannot* be true as it stands. Contradictory propositions cannot be true.

Suppose you are talking with Peter, who informs you that he was born in Boulder in 1992. A few minutes later he mentions that he was born in Kansas City in 1994. What do you now know about when and where Peter was born? Nothing! He may have been born in Boulder in 1992 or in Kansas in 1994—or somewhere else at some other time. But it can't be the case that both of his statements are true. You know that already, even if you don't know what the truth actually is, because his statements are logically incompatible with each other. This is why contradictory testimony in a court of law is simply ruled out of court. It *can't* be true.

This test raises serious problems for pantheistic monism. Its core truth claim is radically monistic, which entails the denial of *any* real distinctions—including the distinction between truth and falsity. But to hold to pantheistic monism is to consider it to be true, which presupposes the distinction between truth and falsity. It's inconsistent.

It may be objected that appealing to logical consistency as a test for worldviews is circular—it begs the question against those perspectives, such as Eastern worldviews that do not recognize such logic. Of course these worldviews violate this test for truth, one might say, but that's because Western, Aristotelian logic is part of the thinking they reject. We only accept the consistency test as valid if we have already bought into Western thinking (theism, naturalism). It's not legitimate to judge the truth of worldviews by a test that already assumes the truth of one of those worldviews.

The law (principle) of noncontradiction (principium contradictionis): "The same attribute cannot at the same time belong and not belong to the same subject in the same respect" (Aristotle).[9] The idea is that two logically contradictory propositions can't both be true: It cannot be the case both that God exists and that there is no God (meaning the same thing by "God," "exists," etc.).

This objection fails. For one thing, notice that it is itself a logical objection—to the logical inconsistency of circular reasoning. Without a prior commitment to the validity of logic, the objection has no point. In fact, such a commitment is inescapable. The fundamental principle here, the law of noncontradiction, does not depend on a Western way of thinking. It's presupposed in all thinking and all language. Aristotle may have first formulated it as a law, but its truth no more depends on Aristotle than electricity depends on Benjamin Franklin or Thomas Edison. Suppose you affirm the proposition "It is raining." Doing so presupposes that you also, at the same time, *deny* any proposition that logically contradicts it, such as "It is not the case that it is raining." If you do not, then your original assertion makes no sense. This is true for all thinking, Western or otherwise. In fact, it holds for *rejecting* Western logic. I can't sensibly reject Western logic and at the same time and in the same respect *accept* Western logic! Logical consistency is inescapable as a test for truth.

Postmodernism rejected. The consistency test is also sufficient, in my view, to rule out the truth of postmodernism as a worldview. A number of the noncore beliefs and values of postmodern thinkers are valid and important, but at the core of philosophical postmodernism is a logical contradiction. It is a form of conceptual relativism, and all relativisms face coherence problems at some level. Postmodernism's central thesis (truth claim) is that all truth is relative to particular linguistic communities, that no proposition is true for all conceptual schemes. But what about *that* proposition? Is *it* true? Obviously a postmodernist thinks so; what else could asserting it mean? Is it only true for postmodern relativists or also for those who are not? If the latter, as I think most postmodernists actually believe (that is, they believe it's a fact about reality that *all* truth is relative to particular linguistic communities), then the postmodern assertion is objectively true. But that means it's false, because it's the claim that there *is* no objective truth. Postmodernism is self-refuting.

If a postmodernist recognizes this problem, and says, "Well, actually, this proposition is relative too. It's just what postmodernists believe, in their community," then I would ask, "Why, then, are you asserting it? Why are you telling *me* that all truth is relative? It's only true for you. It's not true for me, because I'm not a postmodernist." As philosopher Roger Scruton says, "A writer who says that there are no truths, or that all truth is 'merely relative,' is asking you not to believe him. So don't."[10]

Factuality. As they stand, inconsistent worldviews are false. Suppose that so far as we can tell, two or more worldview options are logically consistent. In that case we focus on other tests for truth. The second test for truth is *factuality*. It's what we most often appeal to in comparing and evaluating the remaining worldviews. Here is where we look at the worldview maps, see how they describe reality and test that against reality. Is the worldview factual? Does it explain the data or evidence we find in the world? Does it have explanatory power? Is its explanation simple or ad hoc? Standard apologetic arguments and evidence fit here. They appeal to features of reality a worldview needs to account for and explain, and they argue that the best explanation of those features is given by Christian theism.

There are various features that worldviews need to explain. I'll mention only one: the existence of *persons*. Arguably, this is the central aspect of reality needing explanation. On nontheistic worldviews like naturalism and pantheism, ultimate reality—the most fundamental feature of reality—is *non*personal. Personality is not, for those worldviews, in any deep or obvious way, on the map. How then can there *be* persons such as human beings? A river can't rise above its source. How can nonpersonal reality give rise to persons? Persons are not merely more complex organizations of nonpersonal matter. They are of a higher order of reality altogether. At best, the existence of persons is a kind of ad hoc addition to nontheistic worldviews, something unexpected. Various proposals have been put forward to deal with this problem, particularly in naturalism. Some naturalists bite the bullet and deny that human beings *are* persons in any recognizable sense. But only persons can write books and make such arguments. It's a nonstarter. No account of persons in merely physical, materialistic terms has yet been generally accepted, and for good reason. Because physical properties and personal properties are fundamentally different *kinds* of things, the search for personhood in the merely physical realm simply cannot succeed. It's not just that we don't yet have enough scientific data, as if personhood could be discovered someday in a test tube. The problem is much deeper than that. Reality is bigger than what can be found in test tubes, and this is the deepest example. By contrast, persons are exactly what theism leads us to expect. Personality is at the center of the map.

Livability. The final test for truth is in some ways a further application of both consistency and factuality: *livability.* This is not a test we would apply to scientific theories or legal cases, of course, because how to live is not part of what they are designed to explain. But it *is* an important part of worldviews. A worldview needs to be consistent, not just in what it asserts in its core truth claims or in how it describes the world, but also with life. Some views sound fine on paper, but they simply cannot be lived consistently. A true worldview makes sense not only of the data of history and science, but also of human life.

We need to ask, then, of worldview maps: Does this make sense of human life? Does it account for and can it answer the deepest of human hungers and longings—for meaning, significance, love and hope? *Can* we live consistently with it, with honesty and integrity? This is the *So What?* test. It "takes the roof off" worldview claims. What are the logical, moral and practical implications of this vision of reality? Do those implications fit our deepest understandings of ourselves and our lives?

Here again nontheistic worldviews face the difficulty that their vision of ultimate reality is nonpersonal. But meaning, significance, love and hope are all personal categories. They are features that make sense and are satisfied in a personal universe—they're just what a personal map leads us to expect to find. These hungers could merely be illusions, of course, desires for something that does not exist. But why are they so deep and so universal?[11] The most obvious hunger that points to theism is the hunger for spiritual reality. Despite his atheism, toward the end of his life Jean Paul Sartre admitted that he viewed himself not "as so much dust that has appeared in the world," which is the perspective he advocated in his writings, "but as a being that was expected, prefigured, called forth. In short, as a being that could, it seems, only come from a creator; and this idea of a creating hand that created me refers me back to God."[12]

Cumulative case. The features I have mentioned here, and many others, point to a single, coherent explanation, one that makes sense of *all* these lines of data. There remain questions and difficulties in Christian theism, as in any worldview. They give rise to various objections and questions. But there are far fewer here than in the alternatives. The Christian worldview does the best job, by far, of explaining the most evidence with the fewest difficulties. I've painted in broad and incomplete strokes here, of course. There is much more to say in each case, and further features of reality to be explored, which I leave to you.

CHOOSING A WORLDVIEW

In a trial the jury must reach a decision. So also in evaluating worldviews. We can't simply suspend judgment about these matters. Not only are the different worldviews logically distinct visions of the world, the worldview options are logically exhaustive. Their core truth claims cover every option. There is a God or there is not. If not, naturalism is true and all other worldviews are false. If God does exist, then God is one or many, nonpersonal or personal. If God exists and is personal, then he has either revealed himself definitively in Jesus or not—either Jesus uniquely provides (through his death and resurrection) the way to enter a relationship with God, or he does not. Logically and ultimately, only one of these worldviews can ultimately be true *as* a worldview.

This means there is no neutral ground when it comes to choosing a worldview. If you choose not to believe in the Christian God, you have not chosen to believe in nothing. You believe in some other worldview, probably naturalism. Naturalism is a worldview, too, with its own set of beliefs about a whole host of things. It's not true by default. So the question needs to be asked: Is *it* true? Does it provide a *better* explanation of reality? Choosing a worldview always needs to be understood in light of the alternatives.

Once again we may compare this to marriage. Suspending judgment with respect to marriage is impossible. If you don't choose to marry Susan, you've chosen *not* to marry Susan. Both alternatives (marriage and nonmarriage) involve risk; both go beyond what we can have absolute rational certainty about; both are open to doubt. But the choice can't be avoided.

Choosing a worldview, then, is a matter of faith. Not as fideism suggests, where faith is an arbitrary leap, entirely apart from rational considerations. Choosing a worldview is very much a rational matter, based on evidence concerning what makes the best sense of reality. But as with almost everything else in life, choosing a worldview involves trust and commitment that go beyond what can be proved or rationally established beyond all doubt. There will always be room for question marks and doubts, whichever option we choose. We need to approach the choice according to the wisdom model of rationality, recognizing that trust and commitment are necessary and unavoidable, and examining the evidence in that light—seeking to make the wisest choice possible, given all the data available.

Finally, because it involves faith, the question of the credibility of the Christian worldview is connected to what we've seen about living by faith. There are eminently good reasons for believing the Christian worldview to be true. Like marriage, however, the "proof" is ultimately "in the pudding"—in living it out, in following Jesus. Our deepest convictions that God is real, that Jesus is who he said he is and that the gospel is true, come *after* we trust and commit ourselves to him, not before. God reveals himself most ultimately and finally, to those who, like Shadrach, Meshach and Abednego, place their trust in him, and live accordingly.

If you have not yet done so—if you are attempting to suspend judgment or are waiting, unrealistically, for all questions to be answered and all doubts erased before you act—I urge you to place your trust in Jesus, and begin to follow him in obedience.

Part Three: *Character*

The king assigned [the young men] a daily amount of food and wine from the king's table. They were to be trained for three years, and after that they were to enter the king's service. Among those who were chosen were some from Judah: Daniel, Hananiah, Mishael and Azariah. The chief official gave them new names: to Daniel, the name Belteshazzar; to Hananiah, Shadrach; to Mishael, Meshach; and to Azariah, Abednego.

But Daniel resolved not to defile himself with the royal food and wine, and he asked the chief official for permission not to defile himself this way. Now God had caused the official to show favor and compassion to Daniel, but the official told Daniel, "I am afraid of my lord the king, who has assigned your food and drink. Why should he see you looking worse than the other young men your age? The king would then have my head because of you."

Daniel then said to the guard whom the chief official had appointed over [them], "Please test your servants for ten days: Give us nothing but vegetables to eat and water to drink. Then compare our appearance with that of the young men who eat the royal food, and treat your servants in accordance with what you see." So he agreed to this and tested them for ten days.

At the end of the ten days they looked healthier and better nourished than any of the young men who ate the royal food. So the guard took away their choice food and the wine they were to drink and gave them vegetables instead.

To these four young men God gave knowledge and understanding of all kinds of literature and learning.

DANIEL 1:5-17

In part three we bring the vision we have been developing of mind and faith into a focus on character. The ultimate consequences of ideas are seen in how we live. Thinking well and believing well are expressed in living well.

COLLEGE LIFE AND THE GOOD LIFE

A MORAL VISION

*Therefore I urge you, brothers and sisters, in view of God's
mercies, to offer your bodies as a sacrifice—alive, holy and
pleasing to God—which is your reasonable expression of worship.
Do not be conformed to the pattern of this age, but be transformed by the renewing of your mind, so that you may discern and
come to understand and accept by testing and experience what is
the will of God—that which is good and pleasing and perfect.*

ROMANS 12:1-2, author's translation

A good man is hard to find.

TOM WAITS

College can be a tough place to keep your moral sanity. Opportunities abound to lose your character and more. Followers of Jesus belong
to a minority community, and the social pressures to conform to other
beliefs, values and practices can be intense. But college life can also be
the good life—a time of significant moral formation and flourishing, a
season of cultivating your character instead of losing it. In this chapter
I cast a vision for such a life. A moral vision. It builds on what we've
already explored. Flourishing in our character requires more than good
thinking. But it's essential that we think well about it, for living well is
a reflection of thinking and believing well in action.

Every year in American colleges
- 44 percent of students are heavy drinkers; 1,700 die from alcohol-related causes.
- more than 97,000 students experience alcohol-related sexual assault or date rape.
- nearly 5 percent of student women may be sexually victimized. Up to 25 percent may be assaulted during their college years.[1]

JUST SAY NO

Leaving home to go to college can be like entering a huge candy store, with more options and varieties of sweet stuff than you ever imagined and without the presence of stern parents telling you to eat vegetables instead. But a diet of candy can't sustain life, because it provides little or no nourishment. In fact, it's destructive. It produces obesity and eventually debilitating and even deadly diseases like diabetes. As attractive as "eating whatever you want, whenever you want" can sound, it's incompatible with a healthy, flourishing life.

So what? Who wants a healthy, flourishing life?

I hope that question sounds crazy. But it may not. It's possible to reach a state where you don't care about living a healthy, flourishing life, where you don't see health as something worth aiming at as a goal. This can come about in at least three ways. First, you can become addicted to what is unhealthy—where your appetite is so habituated to candy, say, that you don't want anything else, no matter how sick it makes you feel. Second, you may have never had an adequate understanding or experience of health. Your dietary training may have been: Don't eat candy, don't eat this or that. Do eat broccoli (which you hate). But you never got the point of *why* eating the right food is a good thing—that being healthy opens up a realm of possibilities, like participating in sports or being more effective in other things you do. Or third, it could be that you never caught a compelling vision for doing those other things, like sports. You never imagined a life beyond sitting and watching TV or surfing the Internet—a life spent in pursuing a greater cause or ambition that being healthy would serve. So why not just eat candy? At least it feels good!

My point is not to give health advice or rail against candy. But the analogy helps us to think about the moral life. And how we think about it is crucial. For the most part, knowing what is morally right and wrong is no more a mystery to us than knowing what is physically healthy and unhealthy. Our challenge is usually in *doing* it. What's typically lacking is our motivation, which is bound up with our character. But our motivation and character are also bound up with how we think about the moral life.

These days most people understand ethics or morality as a set of constraints, as limits on what we can do. "Just say no" to X, Y and Z— that's what morality and the moral life are all about. The basic difference between followers of Jesus and other people is just that Christians have a bigger list of things to say no to, and they're more serious about saying no to them. Sometimes.

SAYING YES

This is not how we should think about morality. It's not how Christians of the distant past thought about it, nor is it the understanding of morality in the Bible. And it's not surprising, given those facts, that it doesn't work. In the heat of the moment, far from home, given social pressures to do otherwise and with passions and hormones raging, "just say no" is just not enough. Rationally and for the long haul, I am convinced, we will not say no to things that are attractive to us—things that our culture and peers value—without saying yes to something bigger and better. Saying no only makes sense in light of a more compelling yes.

In high school I competed in track. But I started late, not until the spring of my junior year. I had a lot of catching up to do; I was not used to all the training and discipline required. It was brutal. Early in my first season I was at an extended family gathering, pigging out on a large piece of rich pie. My older cousin asked how track was coming. "Hmpff," I grunted ("Okay"), my mouth stuffed with pie. "Are you winning any races?" "Hmpff," I responded ("No"). "Well, you never *will* win any if you keep eating pie like that." "Hmpff? ("Really?")

He was right. As I started to develop more strength and speed, and began to catch a vision for running well and achieving some goals in

> "The essential thing about chastity is not a renunciation of pleasure but an all-encompassing orientation of life toward a goal. Where there is no such orientation, chastity inevitably deteriorates into the ridiculous."
>
> DIETRICH BONHOEFFER (1906-1945)[2]

track, I came to see the point of saying no to things that would keep me from excelling. Saying no makes sense, depending on what you say yes to.

THE GOOD LIFE

Seeing the moral life as saying yes is part of the wisdom model in the Bible and ancient and medieval thought. Classical philosophers spoke of it as the *good life*—not in the superficial sense in which we sometimes use the phrase "Living the good life." They didn't mean self-absorption, material wealth or physical pleasures. They meant being a good person, flourishing as a human being—living a fully human life. On this understanding, morality is not primarily about saying no, although it inevitably includes that. It's about saying yes to what is actually good. From a biblical perspective, it's living life as a good, loving and wise God created us to live it. It's sanity.

FLOURISHING

The Greek word classical philosophers like Aristotle used to identify the good life is *eudaimonia*. It represents the fundamental human telos or goal, what we're meant to aim at or strive for as human beings. Traditionally *eudaimonia* was translated into English as "happiness." This can be misleading in our time, since we typically regard happiness as something subjective and superficial, the way we happen to feel. That's not at all how classical thinkers saw it. *Eudaimonia* was an objective matter, an actual condition of well-being. A better translation, the more common one these days, is "flourishing." Its meaning is similar to that of the Hebrew term *shalom*, used frequently in the Old Testament concerning God's will for his people.

According to Aristotle, *eudaimonia* is what everyone ultimately wants. It's what we all are really—and rightly—looking for, beneath, behind and beyond all of our lesser aims and wants: a flourishing, meaningful life. *Eudaimonia* is what we say yes to—however we understand what it amounts to, specifically. And that is the crucial question around which different worldviews and philosophies divide: What *is* a flourishing life, exactly? Where is such a life to be found? A worldview's answer will depend on its answers to the three big questions, its views of reality, humanity and morality. One's vision of the good life brings all of one's worldview considerations to a focus.

The central concern of ancient philosophers was to determine what the good life consists of. According to Christian philosopher Dallas Willard, describing the good life is what Jesus was up to in his Sermon on the Mount (Mt 5–7).

"The webbing together of God, humans, and all creation in justice, fulfillment, and delight is what the Hebrew prophets call *shalom*. We call it peace, but it means far more than mere peace of mind or a cease-fire between enemies. In the Bible, shalom means *universal flourishing, wholeness, and delight*— a rich state of affairs in which natural needs are satisfied and natural gifts fruitfully employed, a state of affairs that inspires joyful wonder as its Creator and Savior opens doors and welcomes the creatures in whom he delights. Shalom, in other words, is the way things ought to be."

CORNELIUS PLANTINGA JR.[3]

> As outstanding thinkers before him have always done, Jesus deals with the two major questions humanity always faces.
>
> First there is the question of which life is the good life. What is genuinely in my interest, and how may I enter true well-being? . . . The second question Jesus deals with in the sermon concerns who is truly a good person. . . . It is for very good reason that Jesus' teachings here in response to these two great questions have proven to be the most influential such teachings ever to emerge on the face of this weary planet.[4]

Older Christian writers like Augustine and Aquinas, in fact all Christian thinkers until the late Middle Ages, understood the moral life in these terms.[5] Morality, they believed, is chiefly about what is good, what is worth living for. Rules, duties and saying no are often necessary, but they are secondary. They get their point from what we say yes to.[6]

TOO EASILY PLEASED

Thinking this way about ethics changes the way we understand our moral struggles and challenges. On this perspective our fundamental problem as humans is not that we have desires. It is not even that our desires are too strong. It's that they are too weak—that we settle for too little.

We tend, that is, to exchange our greatest and deepest good, which is God, for lesser goods. We get these out of order. Things like health, sex, meaningful relationships and accomplishment *are* good. They are part of God's good creation. But they are not *the* good. In biblical terms, our problem is idolatry: we try to find our deepest source of value, significance or satisfaction in something other than God himself. And that distorts and disintegrates everything else.

Only if you and I are captured—*captivated*—by a vision of God as our good, and of our relationship with him as the good life for us, as the source of our true flourishing, will we be willing and able to say no to

"If there lurks in most modern minds the notion that to desire our own good and earnestly to hope for the enjoyment of it is a bad thing, I submit that this notion has crept in from Kant and the Stoics and is no part of the Christian faith. Indeed, if we consider the unblushing promises of reward and the staggering nature of the rewards promised in the Gospels, it would seem that Our Lord finds our desires not too strong, but too weak. We are half-hearted creatures, fooling about with drink and sex and ambition when infinite joy is offered us, like an ignorant child who wants to go on making mud pies in a slum because he cannot imagine what is meant by an offer of a holiday at the sea. We are far too easily pleased."

C. S. LEWIS, "THE WEIGHT OF GLORY"[7]

other gods, to very attractive but lesser things. St. Augustine understood this, and it defined his entire orientation to life. In the first paragraph of his autobiography, *Confessions*, he writes one of my favorite lines in all of literature: "You have made us for yourself, O God, and our heart is restless until it finds its rest in you."[8] King David's worship leader, Asaph, after struggling with questions of suffering and injustice, reached the same conclusion: "The nearness of God is my good." (Ps 73:28 NASB)

Thinking this way helps us see how Scripture can describe all of life as worship. For to worship God is to see him as our greatest good and highest value. It's to regard him as the chief object of our affection, and thus the highest priority of our lives. It is because God is our good that saying yes to him, offering him all that we are, have and do, is the only reasonable response (Rom 12:1). Worship is everything and everything is worship.

WHY DOES GOD GIVE COMMANDS?

In this view, doing what's right makes sense. It's how we flourish. But many people, Christians included, have a very different view of biblical morality, especially biblical laws and commands. They see them primarily as restrictions on human behavior and desire ("just say no"), and as arbitrary, unconnected to human flourishing. Most people think of saying no to sex outside of marriage, for example, as an arbitrary limit religion puts on us and our pleasure, for no particular reason other than God forbids it. And God forbids it for no particular reason. But not only is this incompatible with the classical vision of morality, it's a distortion of what Scripture actually teaches.

The Bible itself characterizes the purpose of God's laws and commands very differently. The Old Testament Law is recorded in the Pentateuch or "book of the law"—the first five books, Genesis through Deuteronomy. The last of these books, Deuteronomy, is particularly helpful on this point because it serves as a review or summary of the law (*Deuteronomy* means "repetition of the law") given by Moses to the people of Israel just before they head into the Promised Land.[9] As Moses summarizes the laws, he comments on their purpose. It's far

> "See, I set before you today life and prosperity, death and destruction. For I command you today to love the LORD your God, to walk in obedience to him, and to keep his commands, decrees and laws; then you will live and increase, and the LORD your God will bless you in the land you are entering to possess. . . . This day I call the heavens and the earth as witnesses against you that I have set before you life and death, blessings and curses. Now choose life, so that you and your children may live and that you may love the LORD your God, listen to his voice, and hold fast to him. For the LORD is your life."
>
> DEUTERONOMY 30:15-16, 19-20

from arbitrary. In his commentary Moses consistently points out to the people that the law is to be obeyed *for their good*, so they will be blessed and flourish in fulfilling the life God has given them in the Promised Land. For example, he tells the people to "observe the LORD's commands and decrees that I am giving you today for your own good" (Deut 10:13), "so that it may go well with you and your children after you" (Deut 4:40), "so that you may live and prosper and prolong your days in the land that you will possess" (Deut 5:33), and "so that the LORD your God may bless you in all the work of your hands" (Deut 14:29).[10] Indeed, Moses says that obeying God's law is a matter of life and death.

Take to heart all the words I have solemnly declared to you this day, so that you may command your children to obey carefully all the words of this law. They are not just idle words for you—*they are your life*. By them you will live long in the land you are crossing the Jordan to possess. (Deut 32:46-47, emphasis added)

In the Bible's picture of morality, arguably, the deepest contrast is not between right and wrong, although that is obviously there, but between life and death. This is a particular emphasis in the biblical wisdom literature, in its model of the "path." In this view, each of us is offered a fundamental choice between two paths of thinking, character and behavior. One leads to life, flourishing and blessing, and the other to death, destruction and cursing (see, e.g., Prov 2:7-22). God's way of life is, literally, a "way of life" (Prov 6:23).

LIVING RATIONALLY, BY FAITH

God's will for us, including his moral will, is "good, pleasing and perfect" (Rom 12:2). His commands are part of his blessing his people (see chap. 13). They are aimed at our *shalom*, our flourishing. The reason I'm stressing this way of thinking about morality is that we can't flourish in our character if we don't think and believe well about the moral life, if our understanding of morality does not correspond to reality. And much of what contemporary followers of Jesus think about these things is misconceived. From a fully biblical perspective, doing the right thing makes sense. The moral life is not arbitrary but eminently rational. It fits reality—the way we are made and how we will actually flourish as God's people. But living this way also involves living by faith rather than by sight. What we "see"—what it *feels* like to us much of the time, given our desires and hormones, not to mention the cultural values and social pressures around us—can be quite different. As in the rest of life, living by faith morally means trusting God and what he says about the good life and living accordingly.

If we seek to follow Jesus, we will face tensions and situations, even the occasional crisis, where we may be called on to take a moral stand in the face of pressure to do otherwise. To do so at the right time and in the right way requires not only courage but wisdom. Both courage and wisdom are matters of character. Traditionally, character traits like these are called "virtues." This is how Aristotle and most other classical thinkers spelled out the good life—as a life of virtue. Virtues are stable dispositions to act, feel and be motivated in certain ways, even to see things in a certain way. A kind person, for example, reliably cares about people, feels compassion for individuals when he or she sees that they are hurting, and can be counted on to act in helping them. Because this person is kind, he or she sees needs that other people miss. Character traits are cultivated over time, as a result of the choices we make, the examples we follow and the power of the Holy Spirit at work in our lives.

CRISIS AT THE KING'S TABLE

A helpful example of wise character expressed in living by faith is found in Daniel 1 (see p. 207), where we see the first moral crisis faced by Daniel and his three Hebrew friends after they are taken to Babylon as captives. Part of their three-year "university" training for leadership in Babylonian society involved eating the finest Babylonian cuisine, food from "the king's table." Unfortunately, however, this diet included foods that violate Jewish dietary laws. Immediately the young men are faced with a crisis of conscience: between being faithful to follow God and his ways, on the one hand, and seeking to do a good job and please their new teachers and authorities, on the other. I noted earlier that Daniel's approach to his time in Babylon was to be an insider who excelled at his work and won respect and influence on that basis. But we see here the very possibility of doing that brought into question. If these men compromise their conscience simply to fit in, they will indeed be insiders, but they will lose the distinctiveness that makes them stand out and be effective as God's people. But if they don't compromise, they may lose the opportunity to be insiders.

> "You are the salt of the earth. But if the salt loses its saltiness, how can it be made salty again? It is no longer good for anything, except to be thrown out and trampled underfoot.
>
> You are the light of the world. A town built on a hill cannot be hidden. Neither do people light a lamp and put it under a bowl. Instead they put it on its stand, and it gives light to everyone in the house. In the same way, let your light shine before others, that they may see your good deeds and glorify your Father in heaven."
>
> MATTHEW 5:13-16

This sort of tension is inevitable for all of us who pursue a biblical vision of the good life. Jesus identified it when he stressed that we are to be *in* the world but not *of* it. (Our tendency is to be of the world but not in it.) Jesus called his followers, metaphorically, "salt" and "light." Salt is a preservative and a seasoning; it prevents decay and it adds flavor. Light illuminates and exposes: it uncovers what is hidden and it shows the way to go. Both salt and light are effective only if they are introduced into the environment they are meant to serve *and* they retain their distinctiveness.

The situation the Hebrews faced is a common one for Jesus' followers in the university. Of course, the tension *can* be avoided. Students who adopt the survival mode in college, hoping merely to get through without actually engaging people and ideas, will not face it. They are not *in* the world. And those who jump into everything the university environment offers without being faithful to follow Jesus will also avoid the tension, but in the other direction. They are *of* the world. Either option represents a failure to be who we were created to be and to do what we were created to do, in the environment where God has placed us.

FAITH AND WISDOM

So how do we handle this tension? We are confronted with two very practical questions: *How do we know when to take a stand?* And *How do we take that stand without unnecessarily alienating the very people among whom God has placed us to represent him?* Let's take notes on how Daniel and his friends handled this first crisis. It fits the faith and rationality picture we have developed. These young men lived by faith, not by sight. And they did so wisely.

What did they see in this case? What was "in their face"? I suspect that the food at the king's table looked awfully good—not typical dorm food, shall we say. But more was at stake. Not only was eating Babylon's finest cuisine attractive, the likely cost to the Hebrews of *not* eating it, of not fitting in to the official program, was sure to be high. At the very least, raising the issue with their superiors would be socially awkward and uncomfortable. But the text implies that it would have been far worse than that. If they opted out of the standard routine, the Hebrews would probably lose their privileged university status. Minimally, that would mean having to live the menial life of the average captive. More likely, given the standard "zero tolerance" Babylonian practices we see reflected in the rest of the book of Daniel, disobeying their captors would result in prison or death.

TAKING A STAND

The social pressure was intense. "But Daniel resolved not to defile himself with the royal food and wine, and he asked the chief official for permission not to defile himself this way" (Dan 1:8) While the account focuses specifically on Daniel and what he does, the context indicates that his three friends were included in the situation as well (Dan 1:11-17). And we know from a later passage that the four men acted in community, sharing their concerns with each other and praying together (Dan 2:17-18).

Why did Daniel choose the food issue as a place to take a stand? The text indicates that the Babylonian captors had already changed the names of the four young men from their Hebrew names, which had biblical significance ("Daniel," for example, means "God is my judge"), to Babylonian names that had pagan associations. There is no indication that the Hebrew men objected to their name change. Why didn't they take a stand there?

How do we determine when we need to take a stand, and when we need to fit in? There is no single, simple answer to this question. Not every possible area of tension between biblical values and the values of those around us is a place we should take our stand as believers. Otherwise, we could not be *in* the world; we would be isolated and unable to relate to anyone but those just like us. Again, however, if we always fit in, if nothing is distinctive about us, or we hide our distinctiveness entirely, we have become of the world and our presence there is entirely unnecessary.

Determining when to take a stand is a matter of wisdom. It involves thinking well. But as the wisdom model of rationality stresses, wisdom includes the character trait of good judgment: the disposition and ability to carefully consider the circumstances and discern what is at stake, who are the people involved, and how best to be firm but winsome. Whether or not to take a stand in a particular situation depends on all of these factors. Obviously, the question of what exactly is at stake is crucial. Some things are so important that we should always stand up for them—although, even there, *how* we do so differs from situation to situation, and discerning what that is also requires good judgment. Apparently, the situation where Daniel and his friends were given new names was not one of those occasions. We may assume that while their Hebrew names had great significance to them, they did not think it was essential to following God to be called them by that name. The dietary laws of Israel, by contrast, played a central biblical role in distinguishing God's people from the nations around them. Following Yahweh faithfully, as a Jew, was to be radically distinctive in certain key ways, and one of them was to follow a very specific set of dietary practices. Wisdom involves insight and judgment, the ability to make appropriate distinctions in determining which issues are central and nonnegotiable, and which are not.

> **Must followers of Jesus observe Jewish dietary laws today?**—"'Don't you see that nothing that enters a person from the outside can defile them? For it doesn't go into their heart but into their stomach, and then out of the body.' (In saying this, Jesus declared all foods clean.)"
>
> MARK 7:18-19

What if you don't already have good judgment? Well, recognizing that you are not yet wise is a good sign that you're on the way. Like other virtues, wisdom, including good judgment, is developed over time, through practice. If you face a situation calling for wisdom, I suggest, first, that you pray for wisdom and God's guidance, which he promises to give (Jas 1:5). Second, look for those who *are* wise and ask them for advice. Here the role of community is crucial. The right sort of friendships is key to the pursuit of wisdom. As C. S. Lewis put it, "The next best thing to being wise oneself is to live in a circle of those who are."[11] That's because wisdom rubs off; being around wise people is the best chance we have to become wise ourselves. When you're young (but not only then), it's particularly valuable for at least one of those friends to be older, a mentor. When the first universities, like Oxford, were created, they operated on a guild or apprenticeship model, where a student was trained and guided by a master in the discipline. This picture also lies behind the biblical wisdom model of rationality. We learn wisdom from being with wise people who model it, who help us come to see things we wouldn't see on our own by asking us questions and sharing insights, and who hold us accountable. Over time, as we walk faithfully through such situations, learning from both mistakes and successes, we increasingly become wise.

Besides hanging around wise people, I recommend two general strategies for a lifelong pursuit of cultivating a wise character. First, study prayerfully the wisdom literature of the Bible, particularly Proverbs. An excellent practice is to read a chapter a day. (Proverbs has thirty-one chapters, so it fits well into a regular routine.) As you read, notice what wisdom is, as it is described there. What are the different aspects or constituents of wisdom? What does wisdom look like in the different areas of life? Pray that God will transform your character as your mind is being renewed (Rom 12:2) in this way. Second, read stories and biographies of wise people. This is an extension of hanging around wise people. Wisdom is best learned not by reading treatises or arguments about it but by *seeing* it—not only in the lives of those around us but also in the stories of those beyond our own circle of friends.

ACTING ON OUR CONVICTIONS

We need wisdom to determine when to take a stand, but also *how* to take it. Daniel not only "resolved not to defile himself with the royal food and wine"; he also "asked the chief official for permission not to defile himself in this way" (Dan 1:8). Thankfully, "God had caused the official to show favor and compassion to Daniel" (Dan 1:9). This suggests at least two things. Daniel and his friends had surely prayed extensively about this situation (Dan 2:17) and trusted God to go before them in this way. No doubt they saw the official's favor toward them as a specific answer to prayer. But they also had already been part of the answer to that prayer. They had lived before the official in a way that was consistent with his positive view of them. The picture we have of these young men in the book of Daniel is of competent, confident, winsome young men. They were *easy* to like.

The fact that Daniel approached the official privately reflects his wisdom. The Hebrews didn't begin with picketing the kitchen or holding a hunger strike. By going privately to the official Daniel gave him an opportunity to respond in a rational, clear-headed way, not pushing him into a corner where he might be forced to make a public "example" of them. Daniel also thought through in advance the difficulties that the official and the guard would likely face if they agreed to his request (Dan 1:11-14). He suggested a plausible, "empirical" solution: a ten-day trial period, where the Hebrews would follow their own diet, and let the results determine the outcome. It was a reasonable strategy that allowed the official to save face. It was also a strategy that depended on God to be at work, to confirm the credibility of what he had commanded. And it worked. At the end of the ten days the Hebrews were visibly healthier than the other students, and so were permitted to continue their own diet (Dan 1:15-16).

Do you see the blending of faith (trusting God and living accordingly) with reason (the rationality of wisdom) here? Daniel and his friends didn't close their eyes and "jump." They opened their eyes to reality as God had revealed it. They weighed the issues involved, thought through how to engage wisely those in authority over them, trusted God and proposed a wise but faithful course of action. They rationally lived by faith rather than by sight, and God richly blessed them and brought them further favor. And a big part of their success lay in the fact that they had already established credibility by living faithfully where God had put them.

FOLLOWING JESUS IN THE UNIVERSITY

If you seek to follow Jesus faithfully in the university, especially if you seek to do so as an insider who out-thinks and out-lives others in order to honor him, you will inevitably face similar situations. You will face social pressure to compromise your convictions, and you'll need to exercise wisdom to know when and how to take a stand. I can't tell you in advance which are the points of tension you'll face or how best to handle them. We are unique individuals with different gifts and personalities, and God places us in contexts with other unique individuals—in different circumstances, with different opportunities and challenges. No computer program or easy five-step method can tell us what to do in every situation. How we handle these situations requires good judgment. Wisdom.

But the example of Daniel and his friends is a great model to learn from. Once again I urge you to make sure you are in community with others who follow Jesus. Think and pray together, especially as these situations arise. Hold each other accountable to live credible lives among your fellow students and your professors and employers. As we've seen repeatedly in the example of Jesus, saturate your behavior with grace and truth (Jn 1:14). That's part of wisdom, as Paul suggests to the Colossians: "Be wise in the way you act toward outsiders; make the most of every opportunity. Let your conversation be always full of grace, seasoned with salt, so that you may know how to answer everyone" (Col 4:5-6).

And keep the big picture in mind. Remember that despite appearances (sight) at times, what God does call you to do in such situations makes sense. It is actually for your good. Sometimes there is a significant price to pay for being faithful to Jesus. It can mean being ostracized or looked down on by friends and peers, or even losing a job or taking a lower grade. In those cases it's a great comfort to realize that Jesus alone, walking closely with him, *is* our ultimate good. Sometimes we come to see that only when the other goods seem to be stripped away.

BACK TO TRUTH

In chapter three we saw that the Hebrew term *ĕmet* means "truth," both in the propositional sense of correspondence between a statement and reality, and in the personal sense of being faithful, dependable or authentic. When it comes to living well, not just thinking well, it's important to remember that truth is more than propositional.

Jesus stressed this. Those who are "on the side of truth," he said, listen to him (Jn 18:37). "But whoever lives by the truth [lit., *does* the truth] comes into the light" (Jn 3:21). In Ephesians 4:15, Paul describes the role of truth in building up the community of Jesus, the body of Christ. "Instead, speaking the truth in love, we will grow to become in every respect the mature body of him who is the head, that is, Christ." Although it sounds like propositional truth is in view, it's more than that. The original Greek text reads, literally, "*truthing* in love." Paul apparently made up a word here: he took the Greek noun meaning "truth" (*alētheia*) and converted it into a verb (a participle, *alētheuontes*) —from "truth" to "truthing." This makes perfect sense, in light of the fuller, biblical understanding of truth we have seen. "Truthing" includes "speaking the truth" to each other, but it also means *being* true, living lives that are faithful to God and each other. Lives that are authentic, not phony or two-faced. The propositional aspect of truth and the personal aspect go together. They are two sides of an integrated whole.

So also with thinking well and living well. Being true is a matter of character. It's what we have in mind, I think, when we talk about living with *integrity*—a term that comes from the Latin *integer*, meaning "whole."[12] People with integrity are not one thing among one group of friends and something entirely different among another group. You know where they're coming from. What you see is what you get. They are whole. They are true. When we live truly, as followers of Jesus, expressing his character, we make the gospel plausible—we help people to *see* that it is true.

LIVING THE GOOD LIFE

You and I will not say no to things that are attractive to us without saying yes to something bigger and better. Saying no only makes sense in light of a more compelling yes. Following the way of wisdom, the way of Jesus, is saying yes to life—the good life.

Recall Paul's picture of this process in Romans 12:2: "Do not be conformed to the pattern of this age, but be transformed by the renewing of your mind, so that you may discern and come to understand and accept by testing and experience what is the will of God—that which is good and pleasing and perfect" (author's translation).

In the final phrase, where Paul describes God's will as that which is "good, pleasing and perfect," is a further connection to the vision we've been exploring. The original Greek of each term includes a definite article: *the* good, *the* pleasing and *the* perfect. Particularly with the last term, *teleios*, which is related to *telos*, or "end," the picture here is of God's will as what we're really after. It's our telos. Paul is not merely saying that God's will is good. It is, in fact, *the* good we desire above all. God's will is the good life. Knowing God and walking closely with him is our true flourishing. But the passage also indicates that seeing God's will this way involves a perspective that grows over time. We only come fully to discern God's will as the good life through a process of testing and experience—as we say yes to God's will for our life, as our mind is being renewed, as we are engaged in the process of thinking well. Loving God with our minds and living accordingly, we come to see reality differently, truly. We become sane.

13

LESSONS FROM LE CHAMBON

A MORAL EXAMPLE

But if you falter in a time of trouble,
how small is your strength!
Rescue those being led away to death;
hold back those staggering toward slaughter.
If you say, "But we knew nothing about this,"
does not he who weighs the heart perceive it?
Does not he who guards your life know it?
Will he not repay everyone according to what they have done?

PROVERBS 24:10-12

There always comes a time in history when the person who dares
to say that two plus two equals four is punished with death.
And the issue is not what reward or what punishment will be the
outcome of that reasoning. The issue is simply whether or not
two plus two equals four.

ALBERT CAMUS, *The Plague*

In chapter two I told you of Oswieçim, a small village in southern Poland where the Nazis built their notorious concentration camp Auschwitz. Most of the victims of Auschwitz were killed simply because they were Jewish. All were killed because someone deemed their lives "unworthy of life"—*lebensunwertes Leben*.

Ideas have consequences: what you believe will determine how you behave and ultimately who you become. This is true for individuals, for families, for institutions and for cultures. The tale of Oswięçim illustrates that fundamental truth.

In this final chapter I want to pull together some of the central ideas we've examined and illustrate them by telling another story, the tale of another tiny village in Europe during the same time. But it's a very different story. While the Nazis were slaughtering innocent people in Auschwitz, something very different was happening in Le Chambon-sur-Lignon, in the mountains of France. For scholars of ethics, what occurred in the village of Le Chambon during World War II has made it nearly as famous as Auschwitz.

GOODNESS, TRUTH AND BEAUTY

Near the beginning of his documentary film *Weapons of the Spirit*, producer Pierre Sauvage makes this statement: "On March 25, 1944, a Jewish baby had the good fortune to see the light of day in a place on earth uniquely committed to its survival."[1]

The statement is autobiographical: the child is Sauvage himself. The place was Le Chambon.

In 1969, Jewish moral philosopher Phillip Hallie published an extensive study of the gruesome subject of cruelty.[2] Giving such attention to human depravity drove Hallie to despair. But a later experience brought him back to hope.

> Then one gray April afternoon I found a brief article on the French Village of Le Chambon-sur-Lignon. I shall not analyze here the tears of amazement and gladness and release from despair—in short, of joy— that I shed when I first read that story . . . at last I had discovered an embodiment of goodness in opposition to cruelty. I had discovered in the flesh and blood of history, in people with definite names in a definite place at a definite time in the nightmare of history, what [no one] could deny was goodness.[3]

What was so striking about Le Chambon? During World War II, Hallie explains,

> The French Protestant village of Le Chambon . . . with a population of about 3,500, saved the lives of about 6,000 people, most of them Jewish

children whose parents had been murdered in the killing camps of central Europe. Under a national government which was not only collaborating with the Nazi conquerors of France but frequently trying to outdo the Germans in anti-Semitism in order to please their conquerors, and later under the day-to-day threat of destruction by the German Armed SS, they started to save children in the winter of 1940, the winter after the fall of France, and they continued to do so until the war in France was over. They sheltered the refugees in their own homes and in various houses they established especially for them; and they took many of them across the terrible mountains to neutral Geneva, Switzerland, in the teeth of French and German police and military power. The people of Le Chambon are poor, and the Huguenot faith to which they belong is a diminishing faith in Catholic and atheist France; but their spiritual power, their capacity to act in unison against the victimizers who surrounded them, was immense, and more than a match for the military power of those victimizers.[4]

Discovering actual goodness again, in the Christian people of Le Chambon,[5] changed Hallie's life. It inspired him and gave him hope. Hallie went on to write a book about the village, called *Lest Innocent Blood Be Shed.*

The title comes from Deuteronomy 19, where God instructs his people to set up cities in the Promised Land, called "cities of refuge" (see also Num 35). They

> "Lest innocent blood be shed in your land that the LORD your God is giving you for an inheritance, and so the guilt of bloodshed be upon you."
>
> DEUTERONOMY 19:10 ESV

were places where people under threat of death could be safe from those who sought to take their lives. Refugees stayed in these cities until they were able to face a fair trial and justice could be served. Such protected places were necessary, God instructed, "lest innocent blood be shed." During a time of horrific bloodshed of the innocent, Le Chambon became just such a place.

WHAT EXPLAINS LE CHAMBON?

This obscure village has captured the imagination—and conscience—of contemporary scholars of ethics. It's considered the twentieth century's supreme example of *altruism*, or self-sacrificial love and care for others. But what explains Le Chambon? "Why," asks Pierre Sauvage, "when the world cared so little, did a few people care so much? And how is it, that in a time of unparalleled violence, the weapons of the spirit here were triumphant?" Seeking answers, Sauvage, now a Hollywood filmmaker, returned to Le Chambon with a film crew and asked the surviving villagers who had rescued him and other Jews why they did it. Hallie and other scholars have also traveled to Le Chambon to do the same.

The rescuers' answers are fascinating. The picture quickly emerges of simple people who see themselves as doing nothing extraordinary. We, of course, see it very differently. From our perspective, the Chambonnais were like the men of Issachar described in 1 Chronicles 12:32, who uniquely, in a desperate season, "understood the times and knew what Israel should do."

How is it that the people of Le Chambon could so understand their times, know what to do and do it? It's helpful for us who desire to live faithfully and sanely in the university to take notes on their experience. I certainly don't want to trivialize what the Chambonnais went through by equating it with typical college life. The challenges they faced were obviously on a very different level. But there is some common ground in the experiences of all who seek to follow Jesus where the perspectives of those around them may be alien or opposed to a biblical vision of life, and where the cultural momentum may push strongly in the opposite direction. Such challenges, whether great or small, require similar responses.

> "If you are faithful in little things, you will be faithful in large ones."
> LUKE 16:10 NLT

Consider three characteristics of the moral life of the people of Le Chambon that were crucial in enabling them to be and do what they were and did. All are features of a life of sanity that have emerged earlier in this book, but they take on a special resonance when we see them embodied in the lives of these people.

COMMUNITY

First, the people of Le Chambon lived and acted in *community*. The vast majority of those living in Europe during World War II did nothing to help the Jewish people escape the Holocaust. Some were Nazis or Nazi collaborators; most were just passive bystanders who looked on or looked away as injustice and genocide took place. There were pockets of individuals and groups who risked their lives to rescue Jews. But Le Chambon was unique in that the whole village united to put their homes and lives on the line together. They acted *as* a community. This is reflected in numerous ways in their efforts to save the Jews. To be effective, theirs had to be a massive, coordinated effort, one that required an interlocking network of people working together. But the communal, collaborative nature of what they did went beyond what was necessary to pull off their objective. They literally did what they did as a community: their individual roles blended together into one. Hallie writes:

> It is hard to summarize briefly what the Chambonnais did, and above all how they did it. The morning after a new refugee family came to town they would find on their front door a wreath with *"Bienvenue"* "Welcome!" painted on a piece of cardboard attached to the wreath. Nobody knew who brought the wreath; in effect, the whole town had brought it.[6]

Le Chambon was a community, and it acted as a community—a real community.

Expanding our souls. No doubt much of this had to do with the fact that Le Chambon was a small town, "out in the sticks." In a small town people know you, they know your parents, they know your cousins, they know your neighbors. They *are* your neighbors! In a small town what you do and who you are matters to everyone. That's not always comfortable. In its bad form—or when you want to be anonymous—it can be frustrating and constricting.

But the limitations a small community puts on life are often the very things that free us to be all we can be. They are protections and constraints that can help keep us sane. Communities provide webs of relationships, with multiple intersecting bonds that hold us up and keep us standing where we need to be and when we need to be, and keep us from falling when we are weak. Communities are made of relationships that give us models, hold us accountable, encourage us, comfort us and provide us opportunities for ministry. They give us a chance to make a difference in the world. They make us grow up, and they make us real. They keep us sane.

In community our souls are forced to expand, to grow, to learn, to reach out. That process is often uncomfortable, but it's liberating. Proverbs 27:17 teaches, "As iron sharpens iron, / so one person sharpens another." The only relationships that can truly keep us accountable are those that are hard to avoid—as small-town-type relationships are. Community doesn't stifle us. It's *not* being in community. Being alone, isolated and anonymous shrinks our soul. It makes us crazy.

> "The man who lives in a small community lives in a much larger world. . . . The reason is obvious. In a large community we can choose our companions. In a small community our companions are chosen for us."
>
> G. K. CHESTERTON[7]

I suspect that many of the courageous people in Le Chambon would not have done what they did were it not for the rest of the community doing it and expecting them to do it. Being part of a community helps us not to do the wrong things we might do if we were on our own, and it helps us do the right things we probably wouldn't do otherwise.

Made for community. Some years ago an old friend phoned to let me know that "Tim," a man I had mentored when he was a student, had recently left his wife for another woman—a tragic, all-too-common phenomenon. My friend asked if I would call Tim and try to bring him to his senses. (I tried, but Tim didn't return my calls.) I asked whether Tim, now living in another part of the country, had been in close community with other believers. My friend's answer, as I expected, was no. I pointed out the lesson I had been learning in my own life and had become increasingly convinced of in watching the lives of others: *The single most significant factor in whether we follow Jesus for the long haul is being connected in webs of relationships of encouragement and accountability with other believers.* She agreed, but went on to say, "It shouldn't be that way, but it is." We *should* be able to make it on our own, in other words, but many of us are just too weak or sinful to do so.

After we hung up, I pondered her view—a common one, and understandable. No doubt I had articulated it myself, and with great conviction. But it now struck me how wrong and dangerous it is, from a biblical perspective. It's *not* the case that we should be able to make it on our own, that relationships are necessary only if we are too weak or too sinful to pull it off. The fact is, we never were meant to make it on our own. God made us to live in community, to need it in order to flourish. Our fallen condition heightens our need, but it doesn't create it. "It is not good for the man to be alone," God said at the creation of humankind. "I will make a helper suitable for him" (Gen 2:18). Needing to live within webs of relationships and accountability is built in to who we are at the most basic level by God himself.

Community in the university. College students are typically uprooted from cities or isolated suburbs and put into the tighter social settings of classrooms, dormitories, Greek houses and apartments. This makes social life easier and more natural in college than almost any other time. In fact, college has some of the features of a small town. I encourage you to take advantage of this fact by cultivating the friendships that are there to be found. The same features also pose problems for following Jesus in the university, however. The tight environment intensifies social pressures to conform to the dominant beliefs, values and practices. We've seen that living as a minority community in such a context challenges our intellectual, spiritual and moral sanity. So it's crucial that we take life within our minority community seriously.

My conviction is stronger today than ever that the single most important factor in determining whether we will follow Jesus in the future is our community now—those we hang out with, those who become

> "Friendship is what brings the greatest pleasures, so much so that without friends even the most delightful things become tedious."
>
> THOMAS AQUINAS[8]

our closest friends. Not only are friendships a great source of joy, they make us who we are. To a significant extent we choose our character when we choose our friends. Proverbs stresses the importance of good friendships.

> A friend loves at all times,
>   and a brother is born for a time of adversity. (Prov 17:17)

> One who has unreliable friends soon comes to ruin,
>   but there is a friend who sticks closer than a brother. (Prov 18:24)

> Wounds from a friend can be trusted,
>   but an enemy multiplies kisses. (Prov 27:6)

> Perfume and incense bring joy to the heart,
>   and the pleasantness of a friend
>   springs from their heartfelt advice. (Prov 27:9)

Very often the friends we make in college and in the few years after that become our best, lifelong friends (not to mention our spouse). I have several friends from those years with whom I have walked ever since, though we've typically lived in very different locations. One, Greg, is the first friend with whom I dreamed together about engaging the marketplace of ideas of the university with a biblical worldview. At first neither of us knew anyone doing such a thing, and we had little idea what it would look like or what it would require. But we read and brainstormed and dreamed and prayed together about following that path. And we both followed that path. We moved to different parts of the world, attended different graduate universities and now teach in different places. But we keep in frequent contact with each other, pray regularly for each other, share ideas and figure out how to get together at least once every year. Today we are both following Jesus, teaching philosophy in universities, I in a Christian institution, he in a secular one. I can't express to you how much it has meant to me to be following that path together with my friend. I doubt that I would have done it alone.

I challenge you to take advantage of this crucial time in your life to cultivate friendships like that. Ask God to bring into your life one or more close friends, men and women who are the kind of people you want to become, and covenant together to pray, study, think, serve, encourage, rebuke and walk with Jesus—together.

CONVICTIONS

A second lesson we can learn from the people of Le Chambon is the importance of *convictions*, of our defining beliefs. Community is crucial, but not just any community will do. Most communities in Europe in World War II did nothing to help Jews. Even a community that is unified around a shared vision and values, as was Le Chambon, is not enough, because it is possible to unify around a wrong vision and wrong values. There were, no doubt, strong Nazi communities.

The community of Le Chambon was unified around a very specific set of convictions, a particular story that defined their lives and community—convictions about the nature of the world, about human beings and how they are to be treated, and about what kind of life we as human beings should live on this planet. The Chambonnais shared a common story about what's worth living for and what's worth dying for.

That is, they shared a *worldview*—although they would not have recognized the term. It was, in fact, a deeply Christian worldview. The people of Le Chambon were not scholars or highly educated. They were simple people, mostly farmers carving out a living from the French hills. But they took what they believed very seriously; it shaped who they were and everything they did

This becomes obvious as they respond to questions about why they did what they did.[9] One woman replied,

> It happened so naturally, we can't understand the fuss. It happened quite simply. I helped simply because they needed to be helped. What happened had a lot to do with people still believing in something. The Bible says to feed the hungry, to visit the sick. It's a normal thing to do.

Another woman explained,

> Your faith is in vain if works don't follow. Eat and drink all you need. But if you don't give to your brother, you're a wretched soul. The neigh-

bor to love as yourself is down the street. Remember the priest who saw the man fallen among thieves yet passed by on the other side. And the Jews, truly, had fallen among thieves.

These people knew their Bible! Their natural, unprepared responses to these questions drip with a rich, biblical understanding of life. Listen to the centrality of biblical categories in this exchange:

> The farm-woman opened the door to the refugee and invited her into the kitchen where it was warm. Standing in the middle of the floor the refugee, in heavily accented French, asked for eggs for her children. . . . The farm-woman looked into the eyes of the shawled refugee and asked, "Are you Jewish?" The woman started to tremble, but she could not lie, even though that question was usually the beginning of the end of life for Jews in Hitler's Fortress Europe. She answered, "Yes."
>
> The woman ran from the kitchen to the staircase nearby, and while the refugee trembled with terror in the kitchen, she called up the stairs, "Husband, children, come down, come down! We have in our house at this very moment a representative of the Chosen people!"[10]

The people of Le Chambon did what they did *because* of what they believed, because of their convictions.

Ideas have consequences. Not just any set of convictions produces a Le Chambon. Other convictions, different beliefs about the world and about human beings and the purpose of human life, will produce something very different. Like the Holocaust. Unfortunately, some of the same sorts of convictions that produced the Holocaust remain influential, particularly in the idea centers of American culture.

In fact, some of the same ideas were also influential among American intellectuals in the years leading up to World War II. Consider the famous American jurist Oliver Wendell Holmes Jr., who served as a U.S. Supreme Court Justice from 1902 to 1932. Along with many American and British intellectuals of the time, Holmes supported *eugenics*, an effort, based on the newly influential ideas of Darwinism, to "encourage" the evolutionary process by intervening to weed out "undesirable" humans and improve the genetic stock of the future. One popular expression of this at the time was the forced sterilization of the mentally handicapped. In an infamous Supreme Court decision,

> "The ways in which the [German] state, and many members of the medical profession, systematically betrayed the trust of those who consigned their relatives to their care are unfortunately only part of the story [of the original killing of "undesirables" in German medical facilities]. The gradual hardening of a particular moral climate . . . and the slow seepage of a post-Christian and illiberal ideology into the thoughts and actions of the generality are equally striking. Why did many plain people abandon concern for the 'weak', in favour of a vulgar Social Darwinist ideology which entailed a reversion to the laws of the farmyard or jungle? . . . What factors explain why some people were so susceptible to this ideology, and what explains those who rejected it?"
>
> MICHAEL BURLEIGH[11]

Holmes defended American laws that allowed this widely practiced injustice, arguing that "three generations of imbeciles are enough."[12] If you think this sounds like Nazi Germany, you're right. Tragically, Nazi ideologues borrowed much of their eugenicist vision from American thinkers and laws.

Just as the actions of the people of Le Chambon were based on their biblical convictions about human beings and how they should be treated, so were the ideas and proposals of Holmes and others based on a very different understanding of human beings and how they should be treated. "I see no reason," wrote Holmes, "for attributing to man a difference significant in kind from that which belongs to a baboon or a grain of sand."[13]

Unfortunately, similar ideas continue to be influential, particularly in universities. Philosopher Peter Singer, who serves as professor of bioethics and director of the Center for Human Values at Princeton University, self-consciously seeks to work out the consequences of rejecting a biblical understanding of humans as created in the image of God. He writes:

I have argued that the life of a fetus is of no greater value than the life of a nonhuman animal at a similar level of rationality, self-consciousness, awareness, capacity to feel, etc., and that since no fetus is a person no fetus has the same claim to life as a person. Now it must be admitted that these arguments apply to the newborn baby as much as to the fetus. . . . If the fetus does not have the same claim to life as a person, it appears that the newborn baby does not either, and the life of a newborn baby is of less value than the life of a pig, a dog, or a chimpanzee.[14]

We've seen the consequences of similar ideas.

It matters what we believe. It matters which ideas and values we live out in our lives. It also matters what ideas and values those around us believe and live out. It therefore is crucial for us to think out and articulate *true* ideas and values to a culture that deeply needs them. We need to know what we believe and why we believe it, and we need to be able to articulate it, defend it and, above all, live it. There is no more important place for this to occur than in the university, where the most influential ideas are still a matter of debate. Do you see how crucial for you, as a follower of Jesus, to love him with your mind *in* the university? Take ideas seriously, think well about them, to the best of your ability, and seek to engage them and those who hold them—as always, with "grace and truth" (Jn 1:14).

CHARACTER

Even community and convictions are not enough, however. Knowing the truth does not guarantee that we will live it out. Community helps greatly here, but if the individuals in the community are unwilling or unable to live by the truth, the community itself will go the other direction. Being "willing and able" is ultimately a matter of *character*—our final lesson from the people of Le Chambon.

> Sow a thought, reap an action;
> Sow an action, reap a habit;
> Sow a habit, reap a character;
> Sow a character, reap a destiny.
> ATTRIBUTED TO WILLIAM JAMES[15]

Interviews with rescuers consistently indicate that they found it "natural" to do the right thing. Without hesitation or fanfare, they just did what needed to be done. According to one rescuer, "It all happened very simply. We didn't ask ourselves why we were doing it. It was the human thing to do, or something like that. That's all I can say." Pierre Sauvage observes, "They genuinely don't feel that they were heroes, . . . they think they simply did what was natural, what came naturally to them."

Of course, "what came naturally" to the people of Le Chambon did not come naturally to most in Europe at that time, and it does not come naturally to most today. It required character. For example, it required the virtue of compassion—disposing them to care about the threatened people and what they were suffering, to "feel with" them and to want to meet their needs. It required the trait of courage—enabling them to act from that compassion in face of danger and pressure. And it required patience and perseverance—empowering them to keep up their practices of courageous and compassionate action over time, in face of continued, wearying opposition and danger.

Le Chambon was a community of character. Its people were shaped by their biblical understanding of the world. But that understanding did not remain at the level of "mere" conviction. Their worldview was incarnated (in-fleshed) in their character and behavior. They acted on it repeatedly, and it became part of the fabric of their lives. Character emerges in the choices and decisions we make. As we choose and act as we do, and as we engage in the practices we do, we become habituated to see, think and live in a certain way. It becomes "natural" for us to live that way, because that's who we *are*, who we have *become*.

Making a difference. For our ancestors in Le Chambon, character converged with community and conviction to change history. In my Bible, I've written "Le Chambon" into the margin next to Proverbs 10:7, which says: "The memory of the righteous will be a blessing, / but the name of the wicked will rot" (NIV 1984). Phillip Hallie and many others in the academic world are blessed and challenged today as they discover what the community of Le Chambon did sixty-plus years ago. The behavior of these poor French farmers continues to make the Christian worldview plausible. It doesn't make the worldview true, of course; it already is that. But their incarnating it in character and action helps us to *see* that it's true. The Chambonnais make it believable.

Jesus pointed to this kind of impact at the conclusion of his charge to be salt and light—a minority community of character, in the world but not of it. "In the same way, let your light shine before others, that they may see your good deeds and glorify your Father in heaven" (Mt 5:16). This fits the very structure and mission of God's people, as God established these in the very beginning:

> The LORD had said to Abram, "Go from your country, your people and your father's household to the land I will show you.
>
> "I will make you into a great nation,
>   and I will bless you;
> I will make your name great,
>   and you will be a blessing.
> I will bless those who bless you,
>   and whoever curses you I will curse;
> and all peoples on earth
>   will be blessed through you." (Gen 12:1-3)

Blessed to be a blessing—it's a pattern that flows throughout Scripture, both testaments. In biblical language, to bless is to show favor to someone, to do good to them, to seek their flourishing and well-being—their *shalom* (see Num 6:24-26). God blesses his people, he causes them to flourish, *so that* they will extend *shalom* to

> "But seek the welfare [*shalom*] of the city where I have sent you into exile."
>
> JEREMIAH 29:7 ESV

others in his name as channels or instruments of his blessing. When we do that we reflect, in a special way, who God is, and it points ultimately to him. That's why, when people "see your good deeds" they are drawn to "glorify your Father in heaven."

Character, for followers of Jesus, goes beyond personal integrity. We are called, as his representatives, to reflect *God's* character to the world (see Ex 19:4-6; Lev 11:44-45; 1 Pet 1:15), and we do this most distinctively as we do what he does: bless others. This is especially true, as the people of Le Chambon understood, when we bless those in pressing need: the poor (Prov 14:31), hungry (Ps 146:7), orphans (Jas 1:27), immigrants (Lev 19:33-34), prisoners (Heb 13:3), oppressed (Ps 146:7), sick or disabled (Mt 25:36), aged (1 Tim 5:9), brokenhearted (Ps 34:18), and in threat of death (Prov 24:10-12), just to pick a few examples. As we meet pressing human needs we express the heart of God and we make the gospel plausible. When the believers in Le Chambon responded to such needs, they were following the pattern of the earliest days of the Christian church.

The early church. The world in which the early Christians lived was one of wanton violence and repression. Life was cheap in Greece and Rome, especially that of non-Greek and non-Roman refugees, women, children and those who were handicapped. Abortion was common. So was infanticide, the killing of unwanted infants—those whose lives were deemed not worthy of life. Unwanted infants were usually females and the handicapped. The term used was *exposure:* the unwanted infant would be cast outside the city, exposing him or her to the elements of weather and wild animals. Also common was extreme bloodletting viewed as entertainment. This included public, fight-to-the-death gladiatorial contests and watching refugees and prisoners torn apart by wild animals.

"The difference between Christians and the rest of mankind is not a matter of nationality, or language, or customs. Christians do not live apart in separate cities of their own, speak any special dialect, nor practice any eccentric way of life. . . . They pass their lives in whatever township—Greek or foreign—each man's lot has determined; and conform to ordinary local usage in their clothing, diet, and other habits. . . . [T]hough they are residents at home in their own countries, their behaviour there is more like that of transients; they take their full part as citizens, but they also submit to anything and everything as if they were aliens. For them, any foreign country is a motherland, and any motherland is a foreign country. Like other men, they marry and beget children, though they do not expose their infants [infanticide]. Any Christian is free to share his neighbor's table, but never his marriage-bed. . . . They obey the prescribed laws, but in their own private lives they transcend the laws. They show love to all men—and all men persecute them."

EPISTLE TO DIOGNETUS, c. A.D. 180[16]

Christians (and Jews) were known for being radically distinct from their culture in each of these respects. According to sociologist Rodney Stark, "Christianity brought a new conception of humanity to a world saturated with capricious cruelty and the vicarious love of death."[17] Followers of Jesus were known for refusing to frequent the blood spectacles in the arenas, rejecting all trivialization and taking of innocent human life.[18] They rejected abortion and infanticide, and would rescue and raise infants left to die by exposure. These values set followers of Jesus radically apart from their culture. Tertullian observed that "This work of love [helping the poor, feeding the hungry, caring for orphans, etc.] is what marks us in the eyes of many. 'Look,' they say, 'how they love one another.'"[19] An emperor who opposed the church, Julian (331-363), alarmed by the growing influence of Christianity in the Roman Empire, instituted pagan charities to compete with those of the Christians, who had invented the first charities for the poor and hospitals for the sick. He noted the Christians' "benevolence toward strangers and care for the graves of the dead," and complained that "the impious Galileans [Christians] support not only their own poor, but ours as well."[20]

LIVING THE TRUTH

The early Christians and the believers in Le Chambon saw pressing human needs as the point where truth gets its hands and feet. At the conclusion of a book that is largely about ideas, about knowing truth and thinking well about it, I want to stress the importance of living the truth. Even in the university we should learn from our ancestors in the faith not to forget God's special heart for those in need. Ideas have consequences, and the most important ideas, like those in Oswięcim, Le Chambon and the university today, bear directly on the lives of people. We need, as I have stressed, to be able to engage those ideas at that level, to the best of our ability. But we also need to engage them at the deeply personal level, by spending ourselves in consistent, loving service to those who hurt.

In the past few years my family has experienced physical suffering significantly beyond what we had known before. Earlier (chap. 10) I described my own journey of chronic illness. Also during this period, my dear sister, Judi, suffered with cancer and died. Now, as I put the final touches on this manuscript, my precious wife, Debbie, faces her own battle with cancer. Frankly, prior to this season of my life I didn't think much about suffering. Now I think about it a lot. I've become far more aware of the needs around me, which I now see are often deep and difficult. I'm learning by testing and experience (Rom 12:2) that "the LORD is close to the brokenhearted" (Ps 34:18). I'm coming to see how pressing human needs are where truth gets its hands and feet. I earlier indicated some of the blessings I've experienced through these struggles. The one I'll mention now is experiencing truth's hands and feet as God's people have reached out to meet our family in our pain. As important as ideas are to me as a philosopher and academic, what I need at times like this is to *see* (and touch and hear) God's goodness, truth and beauty. And our family has, especially through God's people. It means a lot. Giving it hands and feet makes the truth plausible.

So as you mind your faith in college, I urge you to invest some of your time there to bless others in need, and to do so in community with others. There are innumerable possibilities; I don't want to tell you what they are, because I don't want to limit your imagination.[21] God will bring to mind needs that I could never think of. (Gary, one of my graduate students, drove weekly to a nursing home to dance with the elderly lady residents. You can bet they were blessed!) The needs are varied and great: from loneliness among the elderly to hunger on the streets to human trafficking. It's easy to be overwhelmed by them, to become "weary in doing good." But, as Paul promises, "we will reap a harvest if we do not give up. Therefore, as we have opportunity, let us do good to all people, especially to those who belong to the family of believers" (Gal 6:9-10).

CONCLUSION

One of the most influential atheistic existentialist writers of the twentieth century was the French thinker Albert Camus. He was also a bitter critic of Nazi totalitarianism. In an interesting twist of history, due to health problems Camus spent time during World War II convalescing in a small village in France: Le Chambon. Being there apparently had an impact on Camus, which is reflected in the book he began to write there, *The Plague*.[22] Not many years after the war he was tragically killed in an accident. In the last two years of his life, according to a minister friend of his, Camus was dissatisfied with existentialism and became very interested in the gospel. He may have come to embrace it.[23] We don't know what role, if any, the people of Le Chambon played in his spiritual change of heart. But when we see the "rest of the story" in heaven, I won't be surprised to discover that seeing their goodness was significant in making the gospel plausible for Camus.

In any case, *The Plague* contains the words that form the preface to *Weapons of the Spirit*:

> There always comes a time in history when the person who dares to say that two plus two equals four is punished with death. And the issue is not what reward or what punishment will be the outcome of that reasoning. The issue is simply whether or not two plus two equals four.[24]

The central question, according to Camus, is whether, when truth is challenged, we will care enough for it—even in its most trivial and obvious form—that we are willing to pay the ultimate price to know it and to live it.

Such a time in history came in World War II, with truth that was far from trivial—concerning human life and how it should be treated. The people of Le Chambon, like the men of Issachar, understood the times: they knew what God's people needed to do, and they did it. They were a community, shaped by biblical convictions, equipped in character to be faithful when it was most difficult but most needed.

My prayer for you, as you seek to follow Jesus in the university, is that you will follow their example of thinking, believing and living well in the time and context in which God has placed you.

APPENDIX

MORE RESOURCES

Listed here are a few initial resources to help you go further in each of the areas discussed in *Mind Your Faith*. Greatly expanded and updated lists and links can be found at MindYourFaithBook.com.

COLLEGE

Practical Help in Going to College
Malone, Michael S. *The Everything College Survival Book: From Social Life to Study Skills—All You Need to Know to Fit Right In!* 2nd ed. Avon, Mass.: Adams Media, 2005.

Navati Guides, Inc. *Navigating Your Freshman Year: How to Make the Leap to College Life—and Land on Your Feet.* Students Helping Students®. New York: Prentice-Hall, 2005.

Tyler, Suzette. *Been There, Should've Done That: 995 Tips for Making the Most of College.* 3rd ed. Lansing, Mich.: Front Porch Press, 2008.

Christian Help in Going to College
Collegeprep.org

ThinkChristianly.org

Budziszewski, J. *How to Stay Christian in College.* Colorado Springs: NavPress, 2004.

Chediak, Alex. *Thriving at College: Make Great Friends, Keep Your Faith, and Get Ready for the Real World.* Carol Stream, Ill.: Tyndale House, 2011.

Melleby, Derek. *Make College Count: A Faithful Guide to Life + Learning.* Grand Rapids: Baker Books, 2011.

Morrow, Jonathan. *Welcome to College: A Christ-Follower's Guide to the Journey.* Grand Rapids: Kregel, 2008.

Christian Campus Ministries—Fellowship, Growth, Outreach
Campus Crusade for Christ (http://campuscrusadeforchrist.com)

Everystudent.com (www.everystudent.com)

Chi Alpha Campus Ministries (www.chialpha.com)
InterVarsity Christian Fellowship (www.intervarsity.org)
The Navigators (www.navigators.org/us/ministries/college)
Reformed University Fellowship (www.ruf.org)
The Veritas Forum (www.veritas.org)

Christian Study Centers
Centers for Christian Study International (http://studycenters.org)
Consortium of Christian Study Centers (http://studycentersonline.org)
L'Abri Fellowship International (www.labri.org)

Studies About Spiritual Lives of College Students
Cherry, Conrad, Betty A. DeBerg and Amanda Porterfield. *Religion on Campus: What Religion Really Means to Today's Undergraduates*. Chapel Hill: University of North Carolina Press, 2001.
Garber, Steven. *The Fabric of Faithfulness: Weaving Together Belief and Behavior During the University Years*. Expanded ed. Downers Grove, Ill.: InterVarsity Press, 2007.
Social Science Research Council. "Essay Forum on the Religious Engagements of American Undergraduates." *The Religious Engagements of American Undergraduates*. http://religion.ssrc.org/reforum.

Moral and Safety Challenges at Universities
Eberstadt, Mary. "Bacchanalia Unbound: The Toxic Forces of Sex, Alcohol, and Drugs in College Life." *First Things*, November 2010, www.firstthings.com/article/2010/10/bacchanalia-unbound.
U.S. Department of Education, Higher Education Center for Alcohol, Drug Abuse, and Violence Prevention: List of Publications (alcohol, drugs, rape, violence on campus, etc.), www.higheredcenter.org/services/publications/full-list.

Studies About University Education
Marsden, George M. *The Soul of the American University: From Protestant Establishment to Established Nonbelief*. Oxford: Oxford University Press, 1994.
Poe, Harry Lee. *Christianity in the Academy: Teaching at the Intersection of Faith and Learning*. Grand Rapids: Baker Academic, 2004.
Willimon, William H., and Thomas H. Naylor. *The Abandoned Generation: Rethinking Higher Education*. Grand Rapids: Eerdmans, 1995.

MIND

The Importance of Thinking and Ideas
Berman, Morris. *The Twilight of American Culture*. New York: W. W. Norton, 2006.

Carr, Nicholas. *The Shallows: What the Internet Is Doing to Our Brains.* New York: W. W. Norton, 2010.

Postman, Neil. *Amusing Ourselves to Death: Public Discourse in the Age of Show Business.* New York: Penguin, 2005.

Weaver, Richard. *Ideas Have Consequences.* Chicago: University of Chicago Press, 1948.

Christian Perspectives on Thinking and the Intellectual Life

Blamires, Harry. *The Christian Mind: How Should a Christian Think?* Ann Arbor: Servant Books, 1963.

Green, Bradley G. *The Gospel and the Mind.* Wheaton, Ill.: Crossway, 2010.

Moreland, J. P. *Love Your God with All Your Mind: The Role of Reason in the Life of the Soul.* Colorado Springs: NavPress, 1997. (This book includes an extensive list of further resources.)

Noll, Mark. *Jesus Christ and the Life of the Mind.* Grand Rapids: Eerdmans, 2011.

Sertillanges, A. G. *The Intellectual Life: Its Spirit, Conditions, Methods,* translated by Mary Ryan. Washington, D.C.: Catholic University of America Press, 1987.

Sire, James. *Habits of the Mind: Intellectual Life as a Christian Calling.* Downers Grove, Ill.: InterVarsity Press, 2000.

Truth, Belief and Knowledge

Holmes, Arthur F. *All Truth Is God's Truth.* Downers Grove, Ill.: InterVarsity Press, 1977.

Lynch, Michael P. *True to Life: Why Truth Matters.* Cambridge, Mass.: MIT Press, 2004.

Newbigin, Lesslie. *Truth to Tell: The Gospel as Public Truth.* Grand Rapids: Eerdmans, 1991.

Willard, Dallas. *Knowing Christ Today: Why We Can Trust Spiritual Knowledge.* San Francisco: HarperCollins, 2009.

Thinking Contextually

Downs, Tim. *Finding Common Ground.* Chicago: Moody Press, 1999.

Henderson, David W. *Culture Shift: Communicating God's Truth to Our Changing World.* Grand Rapids: Baker Books, 1998.

Kinnaman, David, and Gabe Lyons. *unChristian: What a New Generation Really Thinks About Christianity . . . and Why It Matters.* Grand Rapids: Baker, 2007.

Moreland, J. P., and Tim Muehlhoff. *The God Conversation: Using Stories and Illustrations to Explain Your Faith.* Downers Grove, Ill.: InterVarsity Press, 2007.

See also Evangelism, Faith

Thinking Logically

Asking Good Questions

Koukl, Gregory. *Tactics: A Game Plan for Discussing Your Christian Convictions.* Grand Rapids: Zondervan, 2009.

Kreeft, Peter. *Socrates Meets Jesus: History's Great Questioner Confronts the Claims of Christ*. Downers Grove, Ill.: InterVarsity Press, 1987.

Newman, Randy. *Questioning Evangelism: Engaging People's Hearts the Way Jesus Did*. Grand Rapids: Kregel, 2004.

Giving Good Reasons (Logic, Argument)

Kreeft, Peter. *Socratic Logic*. South Bend, Ind.: St Augustine's Press, 2008.

Weston, Anthony. *A Rulebook for Arguments*. 2nd ed. Indianapolis: Hackett, 1992.

Thinking Worldviewishly

General

Axis (http://axisworldview.org)

Conversantlife.com (www.conversantlife.com)

Kingdom Triangle (J. P. Moreland) (www.kingdomtriangle.com)

Probe Ministries (www.probe.org)

Summit Ministries (www.summit.org)

ThinkChristianly.org (www.thinkchristianly.org)

Worldview Academy (www.worldview.org)

Bertrand, J. Mark. *Rethinking Worldview: Learning to Think, Live, and Speak in This World*. Wheaton, Ill.: Crossway, 2007.

Moreland, J. P. *Kingdom Triangle: Recover the Christian Mind, Renovate the Soul, Restore the Spirit's Power*. Grand Rapids: Zondervan, 2007.

Sire, James W. *The Universe Next Door: A Basic Worldview Catalog*. 5th ed. Downers Grove, Ill.: IVP Academic, 2009.

Wilkens, Steve, and Mark L. Sanford. *Hidden Worldviews: Eight Cultural Stories That Shape Our Lives*. Downers Grove, Ill.: IVP Academic, 2009.

Developing a Christian Worldview

Dockery, David S., and Gregory Alan Thornbury, eds. *Shaping a Christian Worldview: The Foundations of Christian Higher Education*. Nashville: Broadman and Holman, 2002.

Plantinga, Cornelius. *Engaging God's World: A Christian Vision of Faith, Learning, and Living*. Grand Rapids: Eerdmans, 2002.

Ryken, Philip Graham. *What Is the Christian Worldview?* Basics of the Reformed Faith. Phillipsburg, N.J.: P & R, 2006.

Humanities

Barge, Laura. *Exploring Worldviews in Literature: From William Wordsworth to Edward Albee*. Abilene, Tex.: Abilene Christian University Press, 2009.

Geivett, R. Douglas, and James S. Spiegel, eds. *Faith, Film and Philosophy: Big Ideas on the Big Screen*. Downers Grove, Ill.: InterVarsity Press, 2007.

Science

Lennox, John C. *God's Undertaker: Has Science Buried God?* Oxford: Lion, 2009.

Rescher, Nicholas. *The Limits of Science*. Revised ed. Pittsburgh: University of Pittsburgh Press, 1999.

Thaxton, Charles B., and Nancy R. Pearcey. *The Soul of Science: Christian Faith and Natural Philosophy*, edited by Marvin Olasky. Turning Point Christian Worldview Series. Wheaton, Ill.: Crossway, 1994.

History of Christian Thought

Ferguson, Everett. *Backgrounds of Early Christianity*. 3rd ed. Grand Rapids: Eerdmans, 2003.

Lane, Tony. *Exploring Christian Thought*. Nashville: Thomas Nelson, 1996.

Reynolds, John Mark. *When Athens Met Jerusalem: An Introduction to Classical and Christian Thought*. Downers Grove, Ill.: IVP Academic, 2009.

Biblical Studies and Theology

Horton, Michael. *The Christian Faith: A Systematic Theology for Pilgrims on the Way*. Grand Rapids: Zondervan, 2011.

Plummer, Robert L. *40 Questions About Interpreting the Bible,* edited by Benjamin L. Merkle. 40 Questions Series. Grand Rapids: Kregel, 2010.

Sailhamer, John H. *How We Got Our Bible*. Zondervan Quick Reference Library. Grand Rapids: Zondervan, 1998.

Philosophy

DeWeese, Garrett J., and J. P. Moreland. *Philosophy Made Slightly Less Difficult: A Beginner's Guide to Life's Big Questions*. Downers Grove, Ill.: InterVarsity Press, 2005.

Faith and Philosophy, journal of Society of Christian Philosophers, www.faithand philosophy.com.

Ganssle, Gregory E. *Thinking About God: First Steps in Philosophy*. Downers Grove, Ill.: InterVarsity Press, 2004.

Moreland, J. P., and William Lane Craig. *Philosophical Foundations for a Christian Worldview*. Downers Grove, Ill.: InterVarsity Press, 2003.

Philosophia Christi, journal of Evangelical Philosophical Society, www.epsociety .org/philchristi.

FAITH

Nature of Faith, Faith and Rationality

Clark, Kelly James. *Return to Reason: A Critique of Enlightenment Evidentialism and a Defense of Reason and Belief in God*. Grand Rapids: Eerdmans, 1990.

Craig, William Lane. *Reasonable Faith: Christian Truth and Apologetics*. 3rd ed. Wheaton, Ill.: Crossway, 2008.

Helm, Paul. *Faith with Reason*. Oxford: Clarendon, 2000.

John Paul II. *Fides et Ratio: On the Relationship Between Faith and Reason*. Boston: Pauline Books and Media, 1998.

Doubt

Clark, Kelly James. *When Faith Is Not Enough*. Grand Rapids: Eerdmans, 1997.

Craig, William Lane. *No Easy Answers: Finding Hope in Doubt, Failure, and Unanswered Prayer*. Chicago: Moody Press, 1990.

Guinness, Os. *God in the Dark: The Assurance of Faith Beyond a Shadow of Doubt*. Wheaton, Ill.: Crossway, 1996.

Apologetics

General

Apologetics.com (http://apologetics.com)

Biola University Christian Apologetics (lectures, degree programs) (www.biola.edu/academics/sas/apologetics)

Everystudent.com (www.everystudent.com)

J. P. Moreland website (www.jpmoreland.com)

Leadership University (www.leaderu.com)

Lee Strobel (www.leestrobel.com)

Probe Ministries (www.probe.org)

Ravi Zacharias International (www.rzim.org)

Reasonable Faith with William Lane Craig (www.reasonablefaith.org)

Reasons To Believe (www.reasons.org)

Stand to Reason with Greg Koukl (www.str.org)

    STR Place (youth oriented) (www.strplace.org)

ThinkChristianly.org (www.thinkchristianly.org/)

Cabal, Ted, ed. *The Apologetics Study Bible*. Nashville: Holman Bible Publishers, 2007.

Copan, Paul. *When God Goes to Starbucks: A Guide to Everyday Apologetics*. Grand Rapids: Baker Books, 2008.

Craig, William Lane. *Reasonable Faith: Christian Truth and Apologetics*. 3rd ed. Wheaton, Ill.: Crossway, 2008.

Keller, Timothy. *The Reason for God: Belief in an Age of Skepticism*. New York: Dutton, 2008.

Strobel, Lee. *The Case for Faith: A Journalist Investigates the Toughest Objections to Christianity*. Grand Rapids: Zondervan, 2000.

Biblical Reliability

Blomberg, Craig. *The Historical Reliability of the Gospels*. 2nd ed. Downers Grove, Ill.: IVP Academic, 2007.

Strobel, Lee. *The Case for Christ: A Journalist's Personal Investigation of the Evidence for Jesus*. Grand Rapids: Zondervan, 1998.

Evil

Carson, D. A. *How Long, O Lord? Reflections on Suffering and Evil.* Grand Rapids: Baker, 1990.

Dembski, William A. *The End of Christianity: Finding a Good God in an Evil World.* Nashville: B & H Academic, 2009.

Kreeft, Peter. *Making Sense out of Suffering.* Ann Arbor, Mich.: Servant, 1986.

Historical Evidence

Strobel, Lee. *The Case for Christ: A Journalist's Personal Investigation of the Evidence for Jesus.* Grand Rapids: Zondervan, 1998.

Wilkins, Michael J., and J. P. Moreland, eds. *Jesus Under Fire: Modern Scholarship Reinvents the Historical Jesus.* Grand Rapids: Zondervan, 1995.

Jesus

Bauckham, Richard. *Jesus and the Eyewitnesses: The Gospels as Eyewitness Testimony.* Grand Rapids: Eerdmans, 2006.

Strobel, Lee. *The Case for Christ: A Journalist's Personal Investigation of the Evidence for Jesus.* Grand Rapids: Zondervan, 1998.

Wilkins, Michael J., and J. P. Moreland, eds. *Jesus Under Fire: Modern Scholarship Reinvents the Historical Jesus.* Grand Rapids: Zondervan, 1995.

Wright, N. T. *The Challenge of Jesus: Rediscovering Who Jesus Was and Is.* Downers Grove, Ill.: InterVarsity Press, 1999.

Moral Objections to Christianity

Copan, Paul. *Is God a Moral Monster? Making Sense of the Old Testament God.* Grand Rapids: Baker, 2011.

Sampson, Philip J. *Six Modern Myths About Christianity and Western Civilization.* Downers Grove, Ill.: InterVarsity Press, 2001.

Schmidt, Alvin J. *How Christianity Changed the World.* Grand Rapids: Zondervan, 2004.

Wright, Bradley R. E. *Christians Are Hate-Filled Hypocrites . . . and Other Lies You've Been Told.* Minneapolis: Bethany House, 2010.

New Atheism

Berlinski, David. *The Devil's Delusion: Atheism and Its Scientific Pretensions.* New York: Basic Books, 2009.

Ganssle, Gregory E. *A Reasonable God: Engaging the New Face of Atheism.* Waco, Tex.: Baylor University Press, 2009.

Hart, David Bentley. *Atheist Delusions: The Christian Revolution and Its Fashionable Enemies.* New Haven, Conn.: Yale University Press, 2009.

Other Religions

Clendenin, Daniel B. *Many Gods, Many Lords: Christianity Encounters World Religions.* Grand Rapids: Baker, 1995.

Netland, Harold A. *Dissonant Voices: Religious Pluralism and the Question of Truth.* Grand Rapids: Eerdmans, 1991.

Science
Berlinski, David. *The Devil's Delusion: Atheism and Its Scientific Pretensions.* New York: Basic Books, 2009.
Lennox, John C. *God's Undertaker: Has Science Buried God?* Oxford: Lion, 2009.
Ross, Hugh. *The Fingerprint of God: Recent Scientific Discoveries Reveal the Unmistakable Identity of the Creator.* Orange, Calif.: Promise Publishing, 1991.

Evangelism
Choung, James. *True Story: A Christianity Worth Believing In.* Downers Grove, Ill.: InterVarsity Press, 2008.
Downs, Tim. *Finding Common Ground.* Chicago: Moody Press, 1999.
Newman, Randy. *Questioning Evangelism: Engaging People's Hearts the Way Jesus Did.* Grand Rapids: Kregel, 2004.
See also Thinking Contextually, Mind

CHARACTER

Ethics and Character—Moral and Spiritual Formation

General
Garber, Steven. *The Fabric of Faithfulness: Weaving Together Belief and Behavior During the University Years.* Expanded ed. Downers Grove, Ill.: InterVarsity Press, 2007.
Lunde, Jonathan. *Following Jesus, the Servant King: A Biblical Theology of Covenantal Discipleship.* Grand Rapids: Zondervan, 2010.
Willard, Dallas. *The Divine Conspiracy: Rediscovering Our Hidden Life in God.* San Francisco: HarperCollins, 1998.
———. *Knowing Christ Today: Why We Can Trust Spiritual Knowledge.* San Francisco: HarperCollins, 2009.

Christian Ethics
Charry, Ellen T. *God and the Art of Happiness.* Grand Rapids: Eerdmans, 2010.
Hays, Richard B. *The Moral Vision of the New Testament.* San Francisco: HarperCollins, 1996.
Plantinga, Cornelius, Jr. *Not the Way It's Supposed to Be: A Breviary of Sin.* Grand Rapids: Eerdmans, 1995.

Virtue and Vice
Edwards, Jonathan. *The Nature of True Virtue.* Ann Arbor: University of Michigan Press, 1966.
Wilson, Jonathan R. *Gospel Virtues: Practicing Faith, Hope, and Love in Uncertain Times.* Downers Grove, Ill.: InterVarsity Press, 1998.

Moral Issues

Budziszewski, J. *How to Stay Christian in College.* Colorado Springs: NavPress, 2004.

Meilaender, Gilbert. *Bioethics: A Primer for Christians.* 2nd ed. Grand Rapids: Eerdmanns, 2005.

Morrow, Jonathan. *Welcome to College: A Christ-Follower's Guide to the Journey.* Grand Rapids: Kregel, 2008.

Navigators, The. *The Grad's Guide to Choosing Well: Wisdom for Life on Your Own.* Colorado Springs: NavPress, 2010.

Rae, Scott B. *Moral Choices: An Introduction to Ethics.* 3rd ed. Grand Rapids: Zondervan, 2009.

Ministries of Blessing (Justice, Hunger, Trafficking, etc.)

Christian Alliance for Orphans (www.christianalliancefororphans.org)

Compassion International (www.compassion.com)

Crossroads (www.crossroadslink.org)

Food for Orphans (www.foodfororphans.org)

For Hearts and Souls (www.forheartsandsouls.org)

Freedom Summit (http://freedom-summit.org)

GAIN Global Aid Network (www.gainusa.org)

Here's Life Inner City (www.hlic.org)

Hope for Orphans (www.hopefororphans.org)

International Justice Mission (www.ijm.org)

Not For Sale Campaign (www.notforsalecampaign.org)

One (http://one.org/us)

Second Mile (www.2ndmile.org)

Sword and Spirit (www.swordandspirit.com)

The Gospel in Action (http://extendingthekingdom.org)

To Write Love On Her Arms (www.twloha.com)

World Relief (http://worldrelief.org)

World Vision (www.worldvision.org)

Haugen, Gary A. *Good News About Injustice: A Witness of Courage in a Hurting World.* 10th Anniv. ed. Downers Grove, Ill.: InterVarsity Press, 2009.

Keller, Timothy. *Generous Justice: How God's Grace Makes Us Just.* New York: Dutton, 2010.

Swanson, Eric, and Sam Williams. *To Transform a City: Whole Church, Whole Gospel, Whole City.* Grand Rapids: Zondervan, 2010.

NOTES

Chapter 1: Sanity in the University

[1]See David Wilson, "College Graduates to Make Global Economy More Productive," *Bloomberg*, May 18, 2010, www.bloomberg.com/news/2010-05-18/college-graduates-to-make-global-economy-more-productive-chart-of-the-day.html; "The College Completion Agenda," *College Board Advocacy and Policy Center*, http://com pletionagenda.collegeboard.org/reports.

[2]Steve Henderson, "A Question of Price Versus Cost," *Christianity Today*, February-March 2006, p. 86. Some studies are more optimistic. See Social Science Research Council, "Essay Forum on the Religious Engagements of American Undergraduates," *The Religious Engagements of American Undergraduates*, http://religion.ssrc.org/reforum. See also Conrad Cherry, Betty A. DeBerg and Amanda Porterfield, *Religion on Campus: What Religion Really Means to Today's Undergraduates* (Chapel Hill: University of North Carolina Press, 2001).

[3]A professor in one secular university where I worked informed the class at the beginning of the semester that there are "at least" five genders (masculine heterosexual, masculine homosexual, transgender, etc.), and that "you need to try out" the different genders in order to choose the one(s) for you. And, by the way, "we're having a party on Friday night where you can try them out."

[4]I believe the oft-repeated phrase, "ideas have consequences," was coined by Richard Weaver in *Ideas Have Consequences* (Chicago: University of Chicago Press, 1948).

[5]It is also true, of course, that some universities, particularly traditional religious colleges, can be biased in the other direction. My focus here is on secular universities. I should comment briefly, however, on how the marketplace of ideas should operate in a confessionally religious university. First, there is a legitimate difference here between secular and religious institutions. The latter, unlike the former, are organized specifically around a particular point of view, which they are chartered to privilege in their teaching and research. Their own marketplace of ideas should not be expected to be "free" in a way that restricts them from doing so. In fact, the freedom of such institutions to pursue and develop the full implications of their more particular perspectives is crucial to the richness anad diversity of broader marketplace of ideas. Still, confessional institutions should be careful to expose their students to the most important ideas and thinkers from a variety of alternative perspectives, and they should represent them fairly. Their own marketplace should be "free" in allowing such ideas to stand or fall on their own merits.

[6]For fuller diagnoses of how the American university has become "secularized," see the appendix.

[7]Expanded and updated lists and links may be found at MindYourFaithBook.com.

[8]Steven Garber, *The Fabric of Faithfulness: Weaving Together Belief and Behavior During the University Years* (Downers Grove, Ill.: InterVarsity Press, 2007), p. 47.

[9]Ibid.

[10]Ibid., pp. 51-52.

[11]For several years I have included much of this material in the Foundations of Christian Thought courses I teach at Biola University, a Christian university. My students have confirmed repeatedly how important it is for those attending a Christian university to engage these ideas and develop these skills.

[12]See Anthony Kenny, *A Brief History of Western Philosophy* (Oxford: Blackwell, 1998), p. 132.

[13]The first two "secular" colleges were the University of Pennsylvania and the University of Virginia. See David S. Dockery, "Integrating Faith and Learning in Higher Education," The Research Institute of the Ethics and Religious Liberty Commission, September 20, 2000, www.uu.edu/dockery/092000-erlc.htm.

Chapter 2: Loving God with Your Mind

[1]Karl Binding and Alfred Hoche, *Die Freigabe Der Vernichtung Lebensunwerten Lebens* (Authorization for the Destruction of Life Unworthy of Life) (Leipzig: F. Meiner, 1920). Both were distinguished professors, Binding in law and Hoche in psychiatry.

[2]Nor did the idea of lives that are unworthy of life end at Auschwitz. We return to its role in today's world in chap. 13.

[3]An estimated 1.5 million children in all were put to death by the Nazis. See Fredric Wertham, *The German Euthanasia Program* (Cincinnati: Hayes, 1978), p. 10.

[4]At least 275,000 psychiatric patients alone were killed (ibid., pp. 29-31). See also Fredric Wertham, *A Sign for Cain* (New York: Macmillan, 1966); Henry Friedlander, *The Origins of Nazi Genocide: From Euthanasia to the Final Solution* (Chapel Hill: University of North Carolina Press, 1995); and Robert Jay Lifton, *The Nazi Doctors: Medical Killing and the Psychology of Genocide* (New York: Basic Books, 1986). In addition, the forced sterilization of an estimated 400,000 began in 1933. See Susan Bachrach, "In the Name of Public Health—Nazi Racial Hygiene," *New England Journal of Medicine* 351, no. 5 (2004): 417-20, www.ushmm.org/museum/exhibit/online/deadlymedicine/related/naziracialhygiene.pdf.

[5]R. C. Sproul, "Burning Hearts Are Not Nourished by Empty Heads," *Christianity Today*, September 3, 1982, p. 100.

[6]Douglas Groothuis, *On Jesus* (Belmont, Calif.: Wadsworth, 2003), p. 33.

[7]See "Appendix: Summary of Maimonides' List of the Laws in the Torah," in John H. Sailhamer, *The Pentateuch as Narrative: A Biblical-Theological Commentary* (Grand Rapids: Zondervan, 1992).

[8]Gregory of Nyssa, *On the Making of Man* 8.5, in *Mark*, ed. Thomas C. Oden and Christopher A. Hall, Ancient Christian Commentary on Scripture (Downers Grove, Ill.: InterVarsity Press, 1998), p. 173.

[9]Paul Little, *Know Why You Believe* (Downers Grove, Ill.: InterVarsity Press, 1988), p. 145.

[10]See, e.g., William Dyrness, *Themes in Old Testament Theology* (Exeter, U.K.: Paternoster, 1979), pp. 89-91.

[11]Dallas Willard, *The Divine Conspiracy: Rediscovering Our Hidden Life in God* (San Francisco: HarperCollins, 1998), p. 352.

[12]H. Wheeler Robinson, "Hebrew Psychology," *The People in the Book*, ed. Arthur S. Peake (Oxford: Clarendon, 1925), p. 362.

[13]Augustine, *Letter to Consentius* (Letter 120), Patrologia Latina 33:0453. Unless otherwise indicated, English translations of citations originally written in Latin are my own.

[14]Ambrose, *Duties of the Clergy* 1.50.262, in *Exodus, Leviticus, Numbers, Deuteronomy*, ed. Joseph T. Lienhard, Ancient Christian Commentary on Scripture (Downers Grove, Ill.: InterVarsity Press, 2001), p. 284.

[15]See Os Guinness, *The Call: Finding and Fulfilling the Central Purpose of Your Life* (Nashville: W Publishing, 2003).

[16]C. S. Lewis, "Learning in War-Time," in *The Weight of Glory and Other Addresses*, ed. Walter Hooper (New York: Simon & Schuster, 1996), p. 58.

Chapter 3: The Truth About Truth

[1]Isaac Watts, *Logic: Or The Right Use of Reason in the Inquiry After Truth with a Variety of Rules to Guard Against Error in the Affairs of Religion and Human Life, as well as in the Sciences* (Morgan, Penn.: Soli Deo Gloria, 1996), p. 1. This edition is a reprint taken from the 1847 edition published by William Milner.

[2]Ibid., p. 2.

[3]Ibid.

[4]Augustine, *City of God* 8.1, Patrologia Latina 41:0225.

[5]Watts, *Logic*, p. 2.

[6]Blaise Pascal, *Pensées* 739, trans. and ed. A. J. Krailsheimer (London: Penguin, 1995), p. 229.

[7]Francis Bacon, "Of Truth" (1625), in *The Essays: or Counsels, Civil and Moral: and The Wisdom of the Ancients* (Boston: Little, Brown, 1877), p. 4.

[8]This is how deductive logical validity is defined. An argument is deductively valid when its conclusion follows necessarily from its premises: if the premises are true, the conclusion must be true.

[9]These distinctions are reflected in English grammar: sentences expressing propositions are stated in the indicative or fact-stating grammatical mood, as opposed to other grammatical moods such as imperative, subjunctive and optative—moods that express commands, wishes or hopes.

[10]Of course, these may also be stated in propositions that are not indexed to time. The proposition *George W. Bush is the forty-third president of the United States* is still true.

[11]Aristotle, *Metaphysics* 4.7, 1011b25-26, in *The Complete Works of Aristotle: The Revised Oxford Translation*, trans. W. D. Ross, ed. Jonathan Barnes (Princeton, N.J.: Princeton University Press, 1995).

[12]"Douglas Adams' Interview with American Atheists," *American Atheist* 37, no. 1 (2002), www.nichirenbuddhist.org/Religion/Atheists/DouglasAdams/Interview-American-Atheists.html. See also Douglas Adams, *The Salmon of Doubt: Hitchhiking the Galaxy One Last Time* (New York: Ballantine, 2002).

[13]C. S. Lewis, "Man or Rabbit?" in *God in the Dock: Essays on Theology and Ethics*, ed. Walter Hooper (Grand Rapids: Eerdmans, 1970), pp. 108-9.

[14]For further development of what follows, see Douglas Groothuis, *Truth Decay: Defending Christianity Against the Challenges of Postmodernism* (Downers Grove, Ill.: InterVarsity Press, 2000), chap. 3.

[15]The cited passages are rendered differently by different translations. In the passage from Psalm 85, for example, the KJV and NASB versions translate *'ĕmet* as "truth," while most other versions translate it "faithfulness." •

[16]The nonpropositional aspect of truth applies not only to persons, of course. As noted, we speak, in related senses, of "true north," to "true up" a line, etc. For our purposes, however, we will limit ourselves to truth as it is related to the two central cases of propositions and persons.

[17]Augustine, *De Ordine* 2.20.52, Patrologia Latina 32:1019-1020.

[18]Note that similar problems face even a more modest skeptical proposition, like "Propositional truth is unimportant." If this proposition is true, then it is unimportant. But if it's unimportant, why assert it? And why should anyone take the trouble to believe it?

[19]Watts, *Logic*, p. 2.

Chapter 4: The Truth About Belief and Knowledge

[1]A different sense of subjective truth was emphasized by nineteenth-century Christian philosopher Søren Kierkegaard (see sidebar in chap. 8) in relation to Christian faith. He wrote in

his *Journal:* "The thing is to understand myself, to see what God really wishes me to do; the thing is to find a truth which is true *for me*, to find the idea *for which I can live and die*. What would be the use of discovering so-called objective truth, . . . what good would it do me to be able to explain the meaning of Christianity if it had no deeper significance *for me and for my life;*—what good would it do me if truth stood before me, cold and naked, not caring whether I recognized her or not, and producing in me a shudder of fear rather than a trusting devotion?" (Cited in Tony Lane, *Exploring Christian Thought* [Nashville: Thomas Nelson, 1996], p. 213.) Kierkegaard is reacting here to the "dead orthodoxy" of Lutheranism in Denmark at the time, where people viewed faith as merely agreeing to a set of propositions that required no personal engagement on the part of the believer. As I understand him, Kierkegaard did not reject objective truth as such.

[2]It may be that Bill here equates *belief* with *faith*, and assumes, further, that faith means irrationally accepting something without evidence. This is a widely held but mistaken understanding of faith, as I will argue in part two. Even in this interpretation, (H) is deeply problematic. Here, however, we'll understand Bill's claim according to the standard philosophical account of "belief."

[3]I'm using *reasonable* and *rational* synonymously.

[4]Aristotle, *Nicomachean Ethics* 1094b24-25.

[5]Philosophy students will be aware of how much more there is to say here, for example, about Gettier-type problems. Two helpful resources here, in order of difficulty, are Garrett J. De-Weese and J. P. Moreland, *Philosophy Made Slightly Less Difficult: A Beginner's Guide to Life's Big Questions* (Downers Grove, Ill.: InterVarsity Press, 2005), chap 3; and J. P. Moreland and William Lane Craig, *Philosophical Foundations for a Christian Worldview* (Downers Grove, Ill.: InterVarsity Press, 2003), chaps. 3, 5, 6.

[6]Which is certainly false: since Bill is not omniscient, he cannot reasonably claim to have *only* rationally justified true beliefs.

[7]See, e.g., Alvin Plantinga, *Warrant and Proper Function* (Oxford: Oxford University Press, 1993).

[8]Dallas Willard, *Knowing Christ Today: Why We Can Trust Spiritual Knowledge* (San Francisco: HarperCollins, 2009), p. 39.

[9]Ibid., p. 7.

Chapter 5: Thinking Contextually

[1]For a brief definition of *worldview,* see sidebar on p. 20.

[2]Tertullian, *Prescription of Heretics* 7, cited in Tony Lane, *Exploring Christian Thought* (Nashville: Thomas Nelson, 1996), p. 19.

[3]Gordon R. Lewis, "Mission to the Athenians, Part I: The Men of Athens and Paul's Approach," *Seminary Series*, p. 2.

[4]From Don Everts and Doug Schaupp, *I Once Was Lost: What Postmodern Skeptics Taught Us About Their Path to Jesus* (Downers Grove, Ill.: InterVarsity Press, 2008), p. 56.

[5]Gordon R. Lewis, "Mission to the Athenians, Part II: The Gods of Athens and Paul's God," *Seminary Series*, p. 2.

[6]See John Mark Reynolds, *When Athens Met Jerusalem: An Introduction to Classical and Christian Thought* (Downers Grove, Ill.: IVP Academic, 2009), esp. chap. 10.

[7]John Calvin, *Institutes of the Christian Religion* 1.3.1, trans. Henry Beveridge (Peabody, Mass.: Hendrickson, 2008).

[8]Lewis, "Mission to the Athenians, Part II," p. 8.

Chapter 6: Thinking Logically

[1]Dallas Willard, "Jesus the Logician," *Christian Scholar's Review* 28, no. 4 (1999): p. 610.

[2]Ibid., p. 606, his emphasis.

[3]Some English translations render it "spiritual." Although *logikos* can refer to what is spiritual (in contrast to physical), its more natural meaning, especially in this context, is "reasonable." See Douglas J. Moo, *The Epistle to the Romans* (Grand Rapids: Eerdmans, 1996), pp. 752-54.

[4]John Wesley, "An Address to the Clergy," in *Selections from the Writings of the Rev. John Wesley, M.A.*, comp. Herbert Welch (New York: Methodist Book Concern, 1918), p. 265, emphasis added.

[5]For an engaging introduction to Socratic questioning, try philosopher Peter Kreeft's fictional Socratic dialogues: *The Unaborted Socrates: A Dramatic Debate on the Issues Surrounding Abortion* (Downers Grove, Ill.: InterVarsity Press, 1983), and *Socrates Meets Jesus: History's Great Questioner Confronts the Claims of Christ* (Downers Grove, Ill.: InterVarsity Press, 1987).

[6]Don Everts and Doug Schaupp, *I Once Was Lost: What Postmodern Skeptics Taught Us About Their Path to Jesus* (Downers Grove, Ill.: InterVarsity Press, 2008), p. 54.

[7]Blaise Pascal, *Pensées* 10, trans. W. F. Trotter (Mineola, N.Y.: Dover, 2003), p. 4.

[8]Robert L. Alden, *Proverbs: A Commentary on an Ancient Book of Timeless Advice* (Grand Rapids: Baker, 1983), p. 20.

[9]I first learned these questions from the late Dan Davis, my colleague with Christian Research Associates in Denver. I have developed them further, and in some different ways, but I owe the basic framework to Dan. Many thanks also to Tom Trento for helping my early thinking here, as in many other areas.

[10]Bart Kosko, "The Problem With Faith-Based Funding Is Faith Itself," *Los Angeles Times*, February 19, 2001, p. B11.

[11]Weaker forms of scientism can be evaluated along similar lines, with adjustments for their various qualifications. All forms of scientism share the same basic logic and general difficulties.

[12]For more on scientism and its problems see Garrett J. DeWeese and J. P. Moreland, *Philosophy Made Slightly Less Difficult: A Beginner's Guide to Life's Big Questions* (Downers Grove, Ill.: InterVarsity Press, 2005), pp. 134-38.

[13]Nicholas Rescher, *The Limits of Science* (Berkeley: University of California Press, 1984), p. 247.

[14]Of course, *clues* of an afterlife may be available within the natural order, evidence that is best explained on that hypothesis. According to some scholars, some records of after-death or near-death experiences constitute evidence that the subjects' lives have persisted after physical death, outside of their physical bodies. See J. P. Moreland, *The God Question: An Invitation to a Life of Meaning* (Eugene, Ore.: Harvest House, 2009), chap. 11.

[15]Francis A. Schaeffer, *The Francis A. Schaeffer Trilogy: The God Who Is There (1968), Escape from Reason (1968), He Is There and He Is Not Silent (1972)* (Wheaton, Ill.: Crossway, 1990), pp. 129-42. Schaeffer discusses this kind of reasoning in *The God Who Is There*, the first book in this trilogy.

[16]Logic in the strict sense is particularly concerned with the final aspect, concerning the structure of reasoning. For further resources related to logic, see J. P. Moreland and William Lane Craig, *Philosophical Foundations for a Christian Worldview* (Downers Grove, Ill.: InterVarsity Press, 2003), chap. 2. For a more historical approach, see Peter Kreeft, *Socratic Logic* (South Bend, Ind.: St. Augustine's Press, 2008).

[17]For our purposes, I will limit the discussion to deductive arguments. Another kind of argument, *inductive*, draws generalizations (*All swans are white*) from particular instances (white swan 1, white swan 2, etc.). The conclusions of inductive arguments are probable rather than necessary.

¹⁸In more technical logical notation, not only the variables (P, Q) but also the logical operators
(If . . . then, therefore) are expressed in symbols. A common way to express the logical form of
this argument is: P⊛Q, P, ∴ Q.

¹⁹Willard, "Jesus the Logician," p. 606.

Chapter 7: Thinking Worldviewishly

¹Jean Paul Sartre, *The Words: The Autobiography of Jean-Paul Sartre*, trans. Bernard Frechtman
(New York: Random House, 1964), p. 253.

²See, e.g., Psalms 22; 31; 69—all cited by Jesus on the cross.

³Ayn Rand, *Romantic Manifesto* (New York: Signet, 1971), p. 19.

⁴Thanks to Greg Ganssle for this example.

⁵A note of caution: the term *worldview*, especially for some evangelical Christians, can be a kind
of slogan, often emptied of meaning (attached to any and every idea) or exploited (identified
with a narrow political agenda). Unfortunately, many contemporary worldview discussions in
popular books and seminars fall into these traps. I recommend James Sire's *Universe Next Door*
(Downers Grove, Ill.: IVP Academic, 2009) as the best thorough introduction available. Another caution: worldviews are not just sets of beliefs or structures of propositions. A worldview,
as Sire says, is "a fundamental orientation of the heart"—in the full, biblical sense of *heart:* the
center of one's personality, including one's thinking, feeling, choices, attitudes and loyalties.
How we look at the world shapes and is shaped by all of these aspects. Our focus here is on
beliefs, but keep these other aspects in mind. For critiques of a narrowly propositional and intellectual approach to worldviews, see J. Mark Bertrand, *Rethinking Worldview: Learning to
Think, Live, and Speak in this World* (Wheaton, Ill.: Crossway, 2007); and James K. A. Smith,
Desiring the Kingdom: Worship, Worldview, and Cultural Formation (Grand Rapids: Baker Academic, 2009).

⁶Sire, *Universe Next Door*, p. 20.

⁷An allusion to Douglas Adams's humorous take on the "big questions": *Life, the Universe and
Everything* (New York: Del Rey/Random House, 2005).

⁸This represents a philosophical approach to worldviews. For an approach that features linguistic and cultural analysis of worldviews, see Paul G. Hiebert, *Transforming Worldviews: An
Anthropological Understanding of How People Change* (Grand Rapids: Baker, 2008).

⁹Charles Taylor, *A Secular Age* (Cambridge, Mass.: Harvard University Press, 2007), p. 13.

¹⁰Bruno Bettelheim, *The Uses of Enchantment: The Meaning and Importance of Fairy Tales* (New
York: Alfred A. Knopf, 1977), p. 45.

¹¹Sire identifies eight in *Universe Next Door* (pp. 22-23).

¹²Dallas Willard, *Knowing Christ Today: Why We Can Trust Spiritual Knowledge* (San Francisco:
HarperCollins, 2009), p. 43.

¹³As in the quotation from T. S. Eliot at the beginning of this chapter. See T. S. Eliot, "The
Aims of Education," in *To Criticize the Critic, and Other Writings* (New York: Farrar, Straus &
Giroux, 1965), p. 74.

¹⁴Bertrand Russell, "A Free Man's Worship," in *Bertrand Russell: "Why I Am Not a Christian" and
Other Essays on Religion and Related Subjects*, ed. Paul Edwards (New York: Simon & Schuster,
1957), pp. 104-16.

¹⁵Sire distinguishes nine worldviews: Christian theism, deism, naturalism, nihilism, existentialism, Eastern pantheistic monism, the New Age, postmodernism, and Islamic theism.
Wilkens and Sanford provide a somewhat different list of nine: individualism, consumerism,
nationalism, moral relativism, scientific naturalism, the New Age, postmodern tribalism, sal-

vation by therapy and the Christian story. See Steve Wilkens and Mark L. Sanford, *Hidden Worldviews: Eight Cultural Stories That Shape Our Lives* (Downers Grove, Ill.: IVP Academic, 2009).

[16]In chap. 4 I described "Jerusalem" as, more specifically, "biblical theism." Our interest here is more general.

[17]Much of what follows, including some of the worldview diagrams, is drawn from material I first learned from Tom Trento and Gordon Lewis. I have also learned much in these matters from Doug Groothuis.

[18]Some contemporary thinkers deny the traditional view that Christian theism requires holding the mind or soul to be immaterial. See Kevin J. Corcoran, ed., *Soul, Body, and Survival: Essays on the Metaphysics of Human Persons* (Ithaca, N.Y.: Cornell University Press, 2001); and Nancey Murphy, *Bodies and Souls, or Spirited Bodies* (Cambridge: Cambridge University Press, 2006).

[19]Carl Sagan, *Cosmos* (New York: Random House, 1980), p. 1.

[20]For more detailed analysis (and critique), see Sire, *Universe Next Door*, chap. 9; and Douglas Groothuis, *Truth Decay: Defending Christianity Against the Challenges of Postmodernism* (Downers Grove, Ill.: InterVarsity Press, 2000). More positive takes on postmodernism may be found in Philip D. Kenneson, "There's No Such Thing as Objective Truth, and It's a Good Thing," in *Christian Apologetics in the Postmodern World*, ed. Timothy Phillips and Dennis Okholm (Downers Grove, Ill.: InterVarsity Press, 1995), pp. 155-70, and in the writings of Christian philosophers Merold Westphal and James K. A. Smith.

[21]Jean-François Lyotard, *The Postmodern Condition: A Report on Knowledge*, trans. Geoff Bennington and Brian Massumi (Minneapolis: University of Minnesota Press, 1984), p. xxiv.

[22]There is also a specifically theistic form of existentialism, however, found especially in the thought of Søren Kierkegaard. See Sire, *Universe Next Door*, pp. 131-43.

[23]Mortimer J. Adler and William Gorman, eds., *The Great Ideas: A Syntopicon of the Great Books of the Western World* (Chicago: University of Chicago Press, 1952), 1:543.

[24]For examples of moral agreement between cultures and religions, see the appendix in C. S. Lewis, *The Abolition of Man: How Education Develops Man's Sense of Morality* (San Francisco: HarperSanFrancisco, 2001).

[25]John Calvin, *Calvin's Commentaries: The Second Epistle of Paul the Apostle to the Corinthians and the Epistles to Timothy, Titus and Philemon*, ed. David W. Torrance and Thomas F. Torrance (Grand Rapids: Eerdmans, 1964), pp. 363-64.

[26]Willard, *Knowing Christ Today*, p. 29.

Chapter 8: The Nature of Faith

[1]Sam Harris, *The End of Faith: Religion, Terror, and the Future of Reason* (New York: W. W. Norton, 2005).

[2]In the history of philosophy, for example, *rationalism* is often used in an unrelated way, in contrast to *empiricism*. They represent two different approaches to the sources of knowledge. *Fideism* has also been used to describe a range of faith-oriented positions, not all of which correspond to the view here.

[3]See also chap. 4, n. 1.

[4]An excellent guide to Kierkegaard's thought is C. Stephen Evans, *Kierkegaard: An Introduction* (Cambridge: Cambridge University Press, 2009).

[5]Christopher Hitchens, among others, attributes this to Tertullian. See Christopher Hitchens, *God Is Not Great: How Religion Poisons Everything* (New York: Twelve, 2007), p. 71.

[6]On the idea of believing absurdities, see my chapter, "*Aut Deus Aut Malus Homo*: A Defense of

C. S. Lewis's 'Shocking Alternative,'" in *C. S. Lewis as Philosopher: Truth, Goodness and Beauty*, ed. David J. Baggett, Gary R. Habermas and Jerry L. Walls (Downers Grove, Ill.: InterVarsity Press, 2008), pp. 68-84.

[7]See Tertullian's *De Carne Christi* 5.4.

[8]"[Tertullian's] great treatise *On the Soul . . .* can stand its own with any philosophical work of antiquity" (Gerald Bray, "Tertullian," in *Shapers of Christian Orthodoxy: Engaging with Early and Medieval Theologians*, ed. Bradley G. Green [Downers Grove, Ill.: IVP Academic, 2010], p. 67).

[9]Ibid., p. 65. To Tertullian's query ("What has Athens to do with Jerusalem?") John Mark Reynolds responds, "A great deal as it turned out, since Tertullian's own writings echoed Greek philosophy on nearly every page" (John Mark Reynolds, *When Athens Met Jerusalem: An Introduction to Classical and Christian Thought* [Downers Grove, Ill.: IVP Academic, 2009], p. 17).

[10]Tertullian, *De Poenitenia* 1.2, Patrologia Latina 1:1227. See also Tertullian, *Apology* 21; Bray, "Tertullian," p. 72.

[11]What follows loosely reflects considerations raised by Kierkegaard and others. It is not meant to provide an account of any particular thinker's writings.

[12]Many other New Testament examples of appealing to reasons and evidence could be given. Notice, for example, Luke's description of why and how he wrote his Gospel account of Jesus (Lk 1:1-4), and Peter's proclamation of Jesus' resurrection in Jerusalem, just forty days after it happened, to an audience that had witnessed his death and knew that his tomb was empty (Acts 2:22). In both cases, there is an appeal to eyewitness evidence to confirm the truth of what is being presented.

[13]See, e.g., Linda Trinkaus Zagzebski, *Virtues of the Mind: An Inquiry into the Nature of Virtue and the Ethical Foundations of Knowledge* (Cambridge: Cambridge University Press, 1996).

[14]The simple or naive person in Proverbs usually refers to a young person whose character or heart has not yet been formed. It also can refer to someone who is older but has refused to commit him- or herself to what is right, remaining willfully open and gullible toward evil, when he or she should know better.

[15]See also Prov 14:15.

[16]See, for example, C. S. Lewis's treatment of faith and belief in *Mere Christianity*, bk. 3, chaps. 11-12.

[17]Twain attributes this to *Pudd'nhead Wilson's New Calendar* in his *Following the Equator: A Journey Around the World , Vol. 1.* See Mark Twain, *The Works of Mark Twain (the Authorized Uniform Edition): Following the Equator: A Journey Around the World, Vol. 1* (Holicong, Penn.: Wildside Press, 1899), p. 114.

[18]I spell out all four elements of faith in our discussion here in order to develop an understanding of faith that makes explicit how all the different aspects we have seen are connected. I suggest that in your conversations, however, you follow the simpler strategy.

[19]Thomas Fuller, *Gnomologia, Adagies and Proverbs, Wise Sayings and Witty Sayings, Ancient and Modern, Foreign and British, Collected by Thomas Fuller, M.D.* (London: B. Barker, A. Bettesworth and C. Hitch, 1732), p. 71.

[20]John Henry Newman, "Saving Knowledge," in *Parochial and Plain Sermons* (San Francisco: Ignatius, 1997), p. 329.

Chapter 9: The Necessity of Faith

[1]My references to new atheists are limited to these three figures and to their views in the following books: Richard Dawkins, *The God Delusion* (New York: Houghton Mifflin, 2006);

Christopher Hitchens, *God Is Not Great: How Religion Poisons Everything* (New York: Twelve, 2007); and Sam Harris, *The End of Faith: Religion, Terror, and the Future of Reason* (New York: W. W. Norton, 2004). For a balanced philosophical analysis and response to these writers, see Gregory E. Ganssle, *A Reasonable God: Engaging the New Face of Atheism* (Waco, Tex.: Baylor University Press, 2009). A biting historical analysis of new atheist claims is given by David Bentley Hart, *Atheist Delusions: The Christian Revolution and its Fashionable Enemies* (New Haven, Conn.: Yale University Press, 2009). Terry Eagleton critiques Dawkins and Hitchens in his *Reason, Faith, and Revolution: Reflections on the God Debate* (New Haven, Conn.: Yale University Press, 2009). A recent, magisterial critique of secularism by a prominent philosopher, Charles Taylor, is *A Secular Age* (Cambridge, Mass.: Harvard University Press, 2007).

[2]Richard Dawkins, *The Selfish Gene,* new ed. (Oxford: Oxford University Press, 1989), p. 303.

[3]Ibid., p. 198.

[4]Richard Dawkins, "On Debating Religion," *The Nullifidian*, December 1994. In addition, "Faith is an evil precisely because it requires no justification and brooks no argument" (*God Delusion*, p. 308), and the citation on the first page of this chapter ("Is Science a Religion?" *Humanist*, January-February 1997, www.thehumanist.org/humanist/articles/dawkins.html).

[5]Sam Harris's analysis in *The End of Faith* initially promises to be a counterexample to this (as one would hope, given the centrality of faith and reason in his argument—as reflected in his title), but this is not realized. In chapter two, "The Nature of Belief," Harris gives a careful analysis of belief, along the lines of my account in part one. When he turns specifically to religious faith, however, precision and objectivity are replaced by mere, unargued, definitional assertion: "The truth is that religious faith is simply *unjustified* belief in matters of ultimate concern" (p. 65, his emphasis). Nothing in his subsequent antitheistic arguments justifies this claim.

[6]Neither faith nor reason is examined by Hitchens in *God Is Not Great*. Dawkins addresses faith briefly in *The God Delusion* (in the tendentious manner already noted). But neither *reason* nor *rationality* merit inclusion in the index. By contrast, agnostic Oxford philosopher Sir Anthony Kenny provides careful and thorough treatments of both faith and reason in *What Is Faith? Essays in the Philosophy of Religion* (Oxford: Oxford University Press, 1992). Kenny is not a rationalist, in our terms, because he does not reject the reasonableness of faith as such. He acknowledges that faith is universal, unavoidable and often fully reasonable.

[7]As acknowledged in note 5, Harris explicitly affirms belief.

[8]As physicist Paul Davies (not a Christian) notes: "Just because the sun has risen every day of your life, there is no guarantee that it will rise tomorrow. The belief that it will—that there are indeed dependable regularities of nature—is an act of faith, but one which is indispensable to the progress of science." Paul Davies, *The Mind of God: The Scientific Basis for a Rational World* (New York: Simon & Schuster, 1992), p. 81.

[9]Francis Fukuyama, *Trust: The Social Virtues and the Creation of Prosperity* (New York: Simon & Schuster, 1995), p. 7.

[10]See Immanuel Kant, *Grounding for the Metaphysics of Morals*, 2nd ed., trans. James W. Ellington (Indianapolis: Hackett, 1981), 2.422-23 (p. 31), and "On a Supposed Right to Lie Because of Philanthropic Concerns," in ibid., pp. 63-67.

[11]See Robert M. Adams, "The Virtue of Faith," in *The Virtue of Faith and Other Essays in Philosophical Theology* (Oxford: Oxford University Press, 1987), pp. 9-24.

[12]The latest edition is Frederic M. Wheelock, *Wheelock's Latin*, 6th ed., rev. Richard A. LaFleur (San Francisco: HarperCollins, 2005).

[13]See Anselm, *Proslogion* 1, in *Anselm of Canterbury: The Major Works*, ed. Brian Davies and

G. R. Evans (Oxford: Oxford University Press, 1998), p. 87; Augustine, *On Free Choice of the Will*, trans. Thomas Williams (Indianapolis: Hackett, 1993), 2.2.

[14]If they did attempt to personally replicate all previous experiments and discoveries, of course they would need to trust the reliability of their memory beliefs about their own experiments. And those experiments would involve trusting their perceptual capacities, the uniformity of nature, etc.

[15]To his credit, Harris acknowledges this: "We believe most of what we believe about the world because others have told us. Reliance upon the authority of experts and upon the testimony of ordinary people is the stuff of which worldviews are made. In fact, the more educated we become, the more our beliefs come to us second hand. A person who believes only those propositions for which he can provide full sensory or theoretical justification will know almost nothing about the world; that is, if he is not swiftly killed by his own ignorance. How do you know that falling from a great height is hazardous to your health? Unless you have witnessed someone die in this way, you have adopted this belief on the authority of others. This is not a problem. Life is too short, and the world too complex, for any of us to go it alone in epistemological terms" (*End of Faith*, pp. 73-74). But see note 18 of this chapter.

[16]C. S. Lewis, *Mere Christianity* (San Francisco: HarperCollins, 2000), p. 62.

[17]Robert Audi, *Epistemology: A Contemporary Introduction to the Theory of Knowledge* (London: Routledge, 1998), pp. 143-44.

[18]We saw above (note 15) that Harris acknowledges that trust is permissible and even necessary for reason. Harris is not a strong or hard rationalist about *all* faith. Therefore, my in-principle critique of rationalism is insufficient to refute his position. It fails on other grounds. Although Harris does not reject all faith, he rejects all *religious* faith, which he describes as "simply *unjustified* belief in matters of ultimate concern" (*End of Faith*, p. 65). Again, however, this description essentially operates as a *definition* of religious faith, for Harris—as an assertion he does not justify but simply assumes to be the case. It functions as a starting point or premise, rather than an argued conclusion, of his argument that all religious faith is irrational, intolerant, violent and should not be tolerated. But this begs the relevant part of the question.

[19]Kenny, *What Is Faith?* p. 32.

[20]G. A. Studdert Kennedy, *The Hardest Part* (London: Hodder & Stoughton, 1919), pp. 83-84.

Chapter 10: Challenges to Faith

[1]See the appendix and MindYourFaithBook.com.

[2]Blaise Pascal, *Pensées* 423, ed. and trans. A. J. Krailsheimer (London: Penguin, 1995), p. 127.

[3]This story comes from Os Guinness, *The Devil's Gauntlet: The Church and the Challenge of Society* (Downers Grove, Ill.: InterVarsity Press, 1989), p. 4.

[4]You can think through for yourself how the wheelbarrow of "tolerance" plays this sort of role as well.

[5]See Dennis Hollinger, "The Church as Apologetic: A Sociology of Knowledge Perspective," in *Christian Apologetics in the Postmodern World*, ed. Timothy R. Phillips and Dennis L. Okholm (Downers Grove, Ill.: InterVarsity Press, 1995), pp. 182-93.

[6]Os Guinness, *In Two Minds: The Dilemma of Doubt and How to Resolve It* (Downers Grove, Ill.: InterVarsity Press, 1976), p. 47.

[7]G. K. Chesterton, *The Autobiography of G. K. Chesterton* (San Francisco: Ignatius, 2006), p. 217.

[8]Less radical forms of skepticism about religious matters face a similar problem. They're often based on questionable assumptions like scientism, which also need to be called into doubt.

[9]Timothy Keller, *The Reason for God: Belief in an Age of Skepticism* (New York: Dutton, 2008), pp. xvi-xvii.

[10]My condition has improved in the more than a year since I wrote this section. As I now edit it, I am able to read some new books, including some editions of the Bible, without mask or gloves.

[11]This may be found in a slightly different translation in Carl R. Proffer, ed., *The Unpublished Dostoevsky: Diaries and Notebooks (1860-81)*, trans. Arline Boyer and David Lapeza (Ann Arbor, Mich.: Ardis, 1976), 3:175.

[12]I owe this wise counsel to my friend Rick Howe.

[13]Language slightly modified from sermon delivered May 13, 1877. Published in Charles Haddon Spurgeon, *The Metropolitan Tabernacle Pulpit: Sermons Preached and Revised by C. H. Spurgeon During the Year 1877* (London: Passmore & Alabaster, 1878), 23:294.

[14]See C. S. Lewis, *Mere Christianity* (San Francisco: HarperCollins, 2000), chap. 11.

[15]Ibid., p. 139.

[16]Augustine, *Tractates (Lectures) on the Gospel of John* 3.20, Patrologia Latina 35:1404.

[17]George Orwell, quoted in George Packer, "The Independent of London: Review of *Why Orwell Matters* by Christopher Hitchens," *New York Times*, September 29, 2002, http://query.nytimes.com/gst/fullpage.html?res=980DEFDE1030F93AA1575AC0A9649C8B63&pagewanted=1.

Chapter 11: The Credibility of Faith

[1]See C. S. Lewis, *Surprised by Joy: The Shape of My Early Life* (Orlando: Harcourt Brace, 1955).

[2]See J. R. R. Tolkien, "On Fairy Stories," in *The Tolkien Reader* (New York: Ballantine, 1966), pp. 60, 74.

[3]Antony Flew, "The Presumption of Atheism," in *The Presumption of Atheism and Other Philosophical Essays on God, Freedom, and Immortality* (London: Elek, 1976), p. 22.

[4]See the interview with Flew in *C. S. Lewis as Philosopher: Truth, Goodness and Beauty*, ed. David J. Baggett, Gary R. Habermas and Jerry Walls (Downers Grove, Ill., InterVarsity Press, 2008), chap. 2.

[5]William J. Abraham, "Soft Rationalism," in *Philosophy of Religion: Selected Readings*, 2nd ed., ed. Michael Peterson et al. (New York: Oxford University Press, 2001), p. 99.

[6]My approach here is influenced by the work of philosopher and theologian Gordon R. Lewis. See his *Testing Christianity's Truth Claims: Approaches to Christian Apologetics* (Chicago: Moody Press, 1976).

[7]I draw this analogy from C. Stephen Evans, *Why Believe? Reason and Mystery as Pointers to God* (Grand Rapids: Eerdmans, 1996).

[8]See, e.g., James W. Sire, *The Universe Next Door: A Basic Worldview Catalog*, 5th ed. (Downers Grove, Ill.: InterVarsity Press, 2009), chap. 11; and Kenneth Richard Samples, *A World of Difference: Putting Christian Truth-Claims to the Worldview Test* (Grand Rapids: Baker, 2007), chap. 2.

[9]Aristotle, *Metaphysics* 4.3, 1005b19–20, *The Complete Works of Aristotle: The Revised Oxford Translation*, trans. W. D. Ross and ed. Jonathan Barnes (Princeton, N.J.: Princeton University Press, 1995).

[10]Roger Scruton, *Modern Philosophy: An Introduction and Survey* (New York: Penguin, 1994), p. 6.

[11]C. S. Lewis puts this memorably: "Do what they will, then, we remain conscious of a desire which no natural happiness will satisfy. But is there any reason to suppose that reality offers

any satisfaction to it? 'Nor does the being hungry prove that we have bread.' But I think it may be urged that this misses the point. A man's physical hunger does not prove that man will get any bread; he may die of starvation on a raft in the Atlantic. But surely a man's hunger does prove that he comes of a race which repairs its body by eating and inhabits a world where eatable substances exist. In the same way, though I do not believe (I wish I did) that my desire for Paradise proves that I shall enjoy it, I think it a pretty good indication that such a thing exists and that some men will. A man may love a woman and not win her; but it would be very odd if the phenomenon called 'falling in love' occurred in a sexless world" ("The Weight of Glory," in *The Weight of Glory and Other Addresses*, ed. Walter Hooper [New York: Simon & Schuster, 1996], pp. 32-33).

[12]Jean Paul Sartre, "Conversations With Jean-Paul Sartre," in Simone De Beauvoir, *Adieu: A Farewell to Sartre*, trans. Patrick O'Brian (New York: Pantheon, 1984), p. 438.

Chapter 12: College Life and the Good Life

[1]Statistics summarized from "Alcohol and Other Drugs on Campus—The Scope of the Problem," *Higher Education Center*, www.higheredcenter.org/services/publications/alcohol-and-other-drugs-campus-scope-problem, and "Sexual Violence and Alcohol and Other Drug Use on Campus," *Higher Education Center*, www.higheredcenter.org/services/publications/sexual-violence-and-alcohol-and-other-drug-use-campus.

[2]Dietrich Bonhoeffer, *Letters and Papers from Prison*, trans. Reginald H. Fuller, ed. Eberhard Bethge, Bonhoeffer's Works (New York: Simon & Schuster, 1997), 8:495.

[3]Cornelius Plantinga Jr., *Not the Way It's Supposed to Be: A Breviary of Sin* (Grand Rapids: Eerdmans, 1995), p. 10.

[4]Dallas Willard, *The Divine Conspiracy: Rediscovering Our Hidden Life in God* (San Francisco: HarperCollins, 1998), pp. 97-98.

[5]According to one scholar, "To anyone with an open mind, one huge fact stands out in the history of morality: for the ancients, Christians and pagans alike, the question of happiness was primary. As they saw it, morality in its totality was simply the answer to this question. The thing was obvious; it never occurred to them to talk about it" (Servais Pinckaers, *The Sources of Christian Ethics*, trans. Mary Thomas Noble [Washington, D.C.: Catholic University of America Press, 1995], p. 18).

[6]This approach is called "eudaimonistic" ethics, because of its relation to *eudaimonia*. For a further description of this approach from the perspective of Christian ethics and how it characterized C. S. Lewis's thought, see David Horner, "The Pursuit of Happiness: C. S. Lewis' Eudaimonistic Understanding of Ethics," in *Pursuit of Truth: A Journal of Christian Scholarship*, April 21, 2009, www.cslewis.org/journal/?p=169.

[7]C. S. Lewis, "The Weight of Glory," in *The Weight of Glory and Other Addresses*, ed. Walter Hooper (New York: Simon & Schuster, 1996), p. 26.

[8]Augustine, *Confessions* 1.1, trans. Henry Chadwick (Oxford: Oxford University Press, 1991), p. 3.

[9]Although it came to be called Deuteronomy for other reasons, "repetition of the law" is an apt description of the book.

[10]See also Deuteronomy 4:1; 6:23, 18, 24; 7:11-16; 8:1; 11:8-9, 26-32; 12:25, 28; 15:18; 16:20; 19:13; 30:6-10.

[11]C. S. Lewis, speaking of Owen Barfield and other friends, in "Hamlet: The Prince or the Poem?" in *They Asked for a Paper: Papers and Addresses* (London: Geoffrey Bles, 1962), p. 63.

[12]In mathematics, integers are whole numbers greater than zero.

Chapter 13: Lessons from Le Chambon

[1]*Weapons of the Spirit*, written, produced and directed by Pierre Sauvage, Chambon Foundation and Greenvalley Productions, 1989.

[2]Phillip Hallie, *The Paradox of Cruelty* (Middletown, Conn.: Wesleyan University Press, 1969).

[3]Philip Hallie, *Lest Innocent Blood Be Shed* (New York: Harper & Row, 1979), p. 93.

[4]Ibid., pp. 93-94.

[5]The Huguenots were members of the Protestant Reformed (Calvinist) Church of France. They were persecuted terribly for their faith from the sixteenth through the eighteenth centuries.

[6]Hallie, *Lest Innocent*, p. 96.

[7]G. K. Chesterton, "On Certain Modern Writers and the Institution of the Family," in *Heretics* (Nashville: Sam Torode Book Arts, 2010), p. 77.

[8]Thomas Aquinas, *De regno ad regem Cypri* 1.11. *Corpus Thomisticum, S. Thomae De Aquino Opera Omnia, Opuscula*, Taurin 1954, ed. Roberto Busa, www.corpusthomis ticum.org/iopera .html.

[9]All uncited quotations are from the film interviews of *Weapons of the Spirit*.

[10]Hallie, *Lest Innocent Blood Be Shed*, pp. 97-98.

[11]Michael Burleigh, *Death and Deliverance: "Euthanasia" in Germany 1900-1945* (Cambridge: Cambridge University Press, 1994), p. 4.

[12]*Buck v. Bell*, 274 U.S. 200 (1927), at 207, Holmes writing for the majority.

[13]Oliver Wendell Holmes Jr., letter to Sir Frederick Pollock, August 30, 1929, in *Holmes-Pollock Letters: The Correspondence of Mr. Justice Holmes and Sir Frederick Pollock, 1874-1932*, ed. Mark DeWolfe Howe (Cambridge, Mass.: Belknap, 1961), p. 252.

[14]Peter Singer, *Practical Ethics* (New York: Cambridge University Press, 1979), pp. 122-23.

[15]This aphorism is widely attributed to James, but also to others (including Ralph Waldo Emerson, Charles Reade, Samuel Smiles and William Makepeace Thackeray). It is probably impossible to establish its origin with certainty. Liesl Olson attributes it to James, but notes (note 1): "James wrote this aphorism in his own copy of the Briefer Course, the shortened version of Principles of Psychology, across the top of the first recto page of the chapter on habit. . . . It is attributed to the English novelist Charles Reade (1814-84) by F. A. Russell, but it bears out James's belief in the productive power of habit as well as his notion of how every young, educated man should proceed in life." Liesl M. Olson, "Gertrude Stein, William James and Habit in the Shadow of War," *Twentieth Century Literature* (Fall 2003), http://findarticles.com/p/ articles/mi_m0403/is_3_49/ai_n6130107/pg_16/?tag=content;col1.

[16]*Epistle to Diognetus* 5, in *Early Christian Writings*, trans. Maxwell Staniforth, rev. Andrew Louth (London: Penguin, 1987), pp. 144-45.

[17]Rodney Stark, *The Rise of Christianity: How the Obscure, Marginal Jesus Movement Became the Dominant Religious Force in the Western World in a Few Centuries* (San Francisco: HarperSanFrancisco, 1996), p. 214.

[18]See Tertullian, *De Spectaculis*.

[19]Tertullian, *Apology* 39, Patrologia Latina 1:0471.

[20]Julian, "Epistle 22, to Arsacius, High Priest of Galatia," in *The Works of the Emperor Julian: With an English Translation by Wilmer Cave Wright*, trans. and ed. Wilmer Cave Wright (Cambridge, Mass.: Harvard University Press, 1923), 3:68-70.

[21]See MindYourFaithBook.com for links to students who are involved in significant ministries of blessing.

²²See Patrick Henry, "Albert Camus, Panelier, and *La Peste*," *Literary Imagination* 5, no. 3 (2003): 383-404, doi: http://litimag.oxfordjournals.org/content/5/3/383.full.pdf+html. See also Jeanette Rosenfeld, *"Love Your Neighbor as Yourself"*: *Nonviolent Resistance in Le Chambon* (New York: Elie Wiesel Foundation for Humanity), pp. 7, 11, www.eliewieselfoundation.org/CM_Images/UploadedImages/WinnersEssays/Jeanette_Rosenfeld.pdf.

²³See Howard Mumma, *Albert Camus and the Minister* (Brewster, Mass.: Paraclete, 2000), cited in James W. Sire, *The Universe Next Door: A Basic Worldview Catalog*, 5th ed. (Downers Grove, Ill.: IVP Academic, 2009), p. 130.

²⁴A slightly different translation is found in Albert Camus, *The Plague*, trans. Stuart Gilbert (New York: Vintage, 1975), p. 132.

Index